The Betrayal of the American Right

The Ludwig von Mises Institute dedicates this volume to all of its generous donors and wishes to thank these Patrons, in particular:

The Lowndes Foundation,
Douglas E. French and Deanna Forbush,
Frederick L. Maier, Mr. and Mrs. Leland L. Young

Ross K. Anderson, John Hamilton Bolstad, Mr. and Mrs. J. Robert Bost,
Mr. and Mrs. Roger H. Box, Martin Brusse, Timothy J. Caldwell,
Carl S. Creager, Kerry E. Cutter, Peter C. Earle, Reza Ektefaie,
Ramallo Pallast Wakefield & Partner, Mr. and Mrs. Willard Fischer,
Keith M. Harnish, John F. Kane, Roland R. Manarin,
Mr. and Mrs. William W. Massey, Jr., Dr. and Mrs. Donald W. Miller, Jr.,
James M. Rodney, Sheldon Rose, Walter M. Simons,
Norman K. Singleton, *top dog*™, Sol West III, Peter J. White,
Mr. and Mrs. Walter Woodul III

Lloyd Alaback, Anonymous, Regis Alain Barbier, Helio Beltrao,
Dr. Karl Blasius, Roman J. Bowser, Dr. John Brätland, John E. Burgess,
Aubrey T. Carruth, R. Leahman Davidson, Mr. and Mrs. Jeremy S. Davis,
Paul Dietrich, Dr. and Mrs. George G. Eddy, Dr. Larry J. Eshelman,
Jason H. Fane, Lundy Fetterman Family Foundation,
Greene View Foundation, Charles C. Groff, James E. Hall,
Curtis and LaRae Hamilton, Dr. Frederic Herman, Robert S. James,
Martin Jungbluth, Robert N. Kennedy, Richard J. Kossman, M.D.,
Carlton W. Laird, William M. Laub, Sr., Arthur L. Loeb, Björn Lundahl,
Jack E. Magoulakis, Dr. Douglas R. Mailly, Joseph Edward Paul Melville,
Anders Mikkelsen, Robert A. Moore, James O'Neill, Vincent J. O'Neill,
Professor and Mrs. Stanley E. Porter, Mr. and Mrs. Wilfried A. Puscher,
Robert M. Renner, Mr. and Mrs. Joseph P. Schirrick, Conrad Schneiker,
Mr. Jeff Schwartz and Dr. Jeanne Schwartz, Andrew Sirkis,
Henri Etel Skinner, Andrew J. Slain, Jim and Mary Smith,
William V. Stephens, Mr. and Mrs. David S. Swain, Jr.,
Kenneth S. Templeton, Mr. and Mrs. Reginald Thatcher,
Lawrence Van Someren, Sr., Mr. and Mrs. Quinten E. Ward,
David Westrate, Brian J. Wilton

The Betrayal of the American Right

Murray N. Rothbard

Edited with an Introduction by
Thomas E. Woods, Jr.

Ludwig von Mises Institute
Auburn, Alabama

THE MISES INSTITUTE, founded in 1982, is an education and research center for the study of Austrian economics. In support of the school of thought represented by Ludwig von Mises, Murray N. Rothbard, Henry Hazlitt, and F.A. Hayek, we publish books and journals, sponsor student and professional conferences, and provide online education. Mises.org is a vast resource of free material for anyone in the world interested in these ideas. We advocate a radical shift in the intellectual climate, away from statism and toward a private property order.

For more information, see mises.org, write us at contact@mises.org, or phone us at 1.800.OF.MISES.

Published 2007 by the Mises Institute
Reprinted 2024 by the Mises Institute

Mises Institute
518 West Magnolia Ave.
Auburn, Ala. 36832
contact@mises.org
mises.org

ISBN: 978-1-61016-774-1

To the memory of
Howard Homan Buffett,
Frank Chodorov,
and the Old Right

Contents

Introduction

It is a cliché of publishing to observe, when a book appears before the public years after it was first written, that it is more relevant now than ever. But it is difficult to think of how else *The Betrayal of the American Right* can be described. Murray N. Rothbard chronicles the emergence of an American right wing that gave lip service to free-market principles and "limited government," but whose first priority, for which it was willing to sacrifice anything else, was military interventionism around the world. That sounds familiar, to be sure, but as Rothbard shows, it is neither recent nor anomalous. It goes back to the very beginnings of the organized conservative movement in the 1950s.

Since this book is likely to reach beyond Rothbard's traditional audience, an initial word about the author is in order. Murray N. Rothbard was a scholar and polymath of such extraordinary productivity as almost to defy belief. His *Man, Economy, and State*, a 1,000-page treatise on economic principles, was one of the great contributions to the so-called Austrian School of economics. *For a New Liberty* became the standard libertarian manifesto. In *The Ethics of Liberty* Rothbard set out the philosophical implications of the idea of self-ownership. He told the story of colonial America in his four-volume *Conceived in Liberty*. His *America's Great Depression*, now in a fifth edition, used the explanatory power of the Austrian theory of the business cycle to show that monetary interventionism, rather than "capitalism," was to blame for that catastrophe. He also wrote a great many groundbreaking articles. To name just two: "Toward a Reconstruction of Utility and Welfare Economics" laid out a distinctly Austrian approach to the contentious area of welfare economics, and "Law, Property Rights, and Air

Pollution" may be the best brief Austrian contribution to the study of law and economics. In addition to his 25 books and three thousand articles, which spanned several disciplines, Rothbard also taught economics, edited two academic journals and several popular periodicals, wrote movie reviews, and carried on a mountain of correspondence with a diverse array of American intellectuals.

Even this overview of Rothbard's work cannot do justice to his legendary productivity. But we learn a great deal about Murray N. Rothbard from a simple fact: more Rothbard books have appeared since his death than most college professors publish in a lifetime. Two volumes of *An Austrian Perspective on the History of Economic Thought*, which Rothbard had been working on at the time of his death, were released in 1995. *The Logic of Action* (1997) consisted of a thousand pages of Rothbard's scholarly articles, now conveniently available for the general public. *A History of Money and Banking in the United States* (2002) brought together much of Rothbard's important work in monetary history, much of which had previously been available only in scholarly journals or as chapters in books long out of print. It may as well have been a brand new Rothbard book.

It wasn't only Rothbard's scholarly work that was assembled into handsome volumes and made available for general consumption; his popular writing began to appear in new collections as well. *Making Economic Sense* (1995) collected a hundred of Rothbard's shorter economic articles in a book that can instruct and entertain beginner and specialist alike. A 20,000-word article Rothbard had written for a small-circulation investment newsletter became the 1995 Center for Libertarian Studies monograph *Wall Street, Banks, and American Foreign Policy*. *The Irrepressible Rothbard* (2000) assembled some of Rothbard's contributions to the *Rothbard-Rockwell Report* of the 1990s, where we encounter the master at his funniest and, at times, his most scathing.

The present book, however, consists of material being made available to the public for the very first time. The manuscript was written in the 1970s, as Rothbard points out in the Preface, and went through periodic edits and additions over the years as publication opportunities arose. Each time, though, unforeseen circumstances interfered with the book's release, and so it is finally appearing only now, under the Mises Institute's imprint.

To be sure, Rothbard had written published articles on the Old Right: in the *Journal of Libertarian Studies*, *Continuum*, and the *Rothbard-Rockwell Report*, among other venues. But here he tells the full story, from the point of view of someone who was not only a witness to these events but also an important participant.

What was this Old Right, anyway? Rothbard describes it as a diverse band of opponents of the New Deal at home and interventionism abroad. More a loose coalition than a self-conscious "movement," the Old Right drew inspiration from the likes of H.L. Mencken and Albert Jay Nock, and featured such writers, thinkers, and journalists as Isabel Paterson, Rose Wilder Lane, John T. Flynn, Garet Garrett, Felix Morley, and the *Chicago Tribune*'s Colonel Robert McCormick. They did not describe or think of themselves as conservatives: they wanted to repeal and overthrow, not conserve.

A 1992 Rothbard retrospective on the Old Right drew out its principles:

> If we know what the Old Right was against, what were they *for*? In general terms, they were for a restoration of the liberty of the Old Republic, of a government strictly limited to the defense of the rights of private property. In the concrete, as in the case of any broad coalition, there were differences of opinion within this overall framework. But we can boil down those differences to this question: how much of existing government would you repeal? How far would you roll government back?
>
> The *minimum* demand which almost all Old Rightists agreed on, which virtually defined the Old Right, was total abolition of the New Deal, the whole kit and kaboodle of the welfare state, the Wagner Act, the Social Security Act, going off gold in 1933, and all the rest. Beyond that, there were charming disagreements. Some would stop at repealing the New Deal. Others would press on, to abolition of Woodrow Wilson's New Freedom, including the Federal Reserve System and especially that mighty instrument of tyranny, the income tax and the Internal Revenue Service. Still others,

> extremists such as myself, would not stop until we repealed the Federal Judiciary Act of 1789, and maybe even think the unthinkable and restore the good old Articles of Confederation.[1]

In addition to being a history of the Old Right, this book is the closest thing to an autobiography of this extraordinary man that readers can expect to see. It is not just a history of the Old Right, or of the anti-interventionist tradition in America. It is the story—at least in part—of Rothbard's own political and intellectual development: the books he read, the people he met, the friends he made, the organizations he joined, and so much more.

Rothbard's discussion of his intellectual evolution begins with his days as a young boy and carries through his time in Ludwig von Mises's New York seminar (from which so many important libertarian thinkers would emerge), his early writing career and his libertarian activism, all the way through his interaction with the New Left in the 1960s. We accompany Rothbard during the moment when he discovers he can no longer be a minimal-state libertarian, or minarchist, and we learn exactly what it was that led him into anarchism. He discusses his derivation (on the basis of the nonaggression principle) of peace and nonintervention as libertarian principles, his evolving political allegiances in the 1950s in light of his resolute noninterventionism, and his attraction to the forbidden subject of Cold War revisionism.

Still, we cannot overlook or underestimate the importance of this book as a work of history. Rothbard fills a crucial gap both in the history of American foreign policy as well as in the histories of American conservatism and libertarianism. In fact, we can go even further: *The Betrayal of the American Right* is an important missing chapter in the received story of America. Important if long-forgotten thinkers, writers, and activists spring to life once again in these pages. Any number of topics for research papers and even

---

[1]Murray N. Rothbard, "A Strategy for the Right," in *The Irrepressible Rothbard*, Llewellyn H. Rockwell, Jr., ed. (Burlingame, Calif.: Center for Libertarian Studies, 2000), p. 4.

full-length books might be gleaned from the issues Rothbard raises here.

It is safe to say that very few Americans, conservatives included—indeed, *especially* conservatives—know that some of the most consistent and outspoken opponents of Harry Truman's early Cold War measures were budget-conscious Republicans, ideologically averse to international crusades. Senator Robert A. Taft, for instance, was the most prominent if perhaps the least consistent of the Republican noninterventionists who greeted Harry Truman's early Cold War policies with skepticism. Taft was critical of the Truman Doctrine, the Marshall Plan, and NATO, each of which he viewed as either unnecessarily provocative or ruinously expensive. Taft, along with lesser-known figures from the House and Senate like George Bender, Howard Buffett, and Kenneth Wherry, constituted the political arm of the Old Right.

Contrary to the erroneous impression of left-liberalism as antiwar and peace-loving, voices of mainstream liberalism adopted the standard interventionist line against the "isolationist" heretic: Taft, wrote the prominent liberal columnist Richard Rovere, was an unsuitable presidential candidate in 1948 since the next president "should be an executive of the human race . . . who will boldly champion freedom before the world and for the world . . . [which] Taft simply could not do." Likewise, *The Nation* called Taft and his allies in Congress "super-appeasers" whose policies "should set the bells ringing in the Kremlin."[2]

Naturally, for his efforts Rothbard was himself red-baited from time to time by people on the Right. That his anti-Communist credentials were as bulletproof as one could ask for hardly seemed to matter: he opposed the global anti-Communist crusade, and that was what counted. Ironically, it was precisely Rothbard's *contempt* for Communism that persuaded him that an ongoing military campaign against it, one that would surely have terrible short- and long-term consequences for American society and government (not

---

[2]John Moser, "Principles Without Program: Senator Robert A. Taft and American Foreign Policy," *Ohio History* 108 (1999): 177–92.

to mention the mischief it could cause abroad), was actually unnecessary: Ludwig von Mises had already shown the insuperable obstacles that confronted truly socialist economies; and the Soviet Union's acquisition of a string of satellites each of which was an economic basket case in need of subsidy did not seem like an especially menacing imperial strategy.

Old Right members of Congress like Howard Buffett argued, to the cheers of Rothbard, that the cause of freedom in the world was to be advanced by the force of American example rather than by the force of arms, and that American interventionism would play into the hands of Soviet propaganda that portrayed the U.S. as a self-interested imperialist rather than a disinterested advocate for mankind. Here was the traditional libertarian position, drawn from the great statesmen of the nineteenth century, the era of classical liberalism. Thus Richard Cobden, the great British classical liberal, had once said:

> England, by calmly directing her undivided energies to the purifying of her own internal institutions, to the emancipation of her commerce . . . would, by thus serving as it were for the beacon of other nations, aid more effectually the cause of political progression all over the continent than she could possibly do by plunging herself into the strife of European wars.[3]

Likewise, Henry Clay, not himself a classical liberal, nevertheless summed up the practically unanimous opinion of mid-nineteenth-century America:

> By the policy to which we have adhered since the days of Washington . . . we have done more for the cause of liberty than arms could effect; we have shown to other nations the way to greatness and happiness. . . . Far better is it for ourselves, for Hungary, and the cause of liberty, that, adhering to our pacific system and avoiding the distant wars of Europe,

---

[3]Richard Cobden, "Commerce is the Great Panacea," in *The Political Writings of Richard Cobden*, F.W. Chesson, ed. (London: T. Fisher Unwin, 1903), vol. 1, p. 35.

> we should keep our lamp burning brightly on this western shore, as a light to all nations, than to hazard its utter extinction amid the ruins of fallen and falling republics in Europe.[4]

This was the principle in which Rothbard continued to believe.

What we laughingly call the "conservative movement" today has little incentive to remind people of the skeptics of interventionism to be found among conservative Republicans in the Truman years. In these pages Rothbard makes a compelling case that the Right's embrace of global interventionism was not inevitable, but was instead the result of contingent factors: the deaths of key representatives of the Old Right at particularly inauspicious moments, the organizational skill of the opposition, and internal difficulties within Old Right institutions.

But it isn't just modern conservatism that is at fault for the disappearance of the Old Right down the Orwellian memory hole. Libertarians, too, must in some cases share the blame. In the late 1970s, Rothbard was personally responsible for inserting the noninterventionist plank into the Libertarian Party platform—at a time when, to his amazement, foreign policy seemed to arouse relatively little interest among libertarians. The 2003 Iraq war was justified on the basis of propaganda worthy of the old *Pravda*; that people calling themselves libertarians—who, after all, are supposed to have an eye for government propaganda—swallowed the government's case whole suggests that the problem has not altogether disappeared. (One can only imagine what Mencken, one of Rothbard's heroes, would have had to say about that war, its architects, and an American population that continued to believe the discredited weapons of mass destruction [WMD] claims long after everyone, on all sides, had agreed the charges were false.)

---

[4]Ralph Raico, "American Foreign Policy—The Turning Point, 1898–1919," in *The Failure of America's Foreign Wars*, Richard M. Ebeling and Jacob G. Hornberger, eds. (Fairfax, Va.: Future of Freedom Foundation, 1996), pp. 55–56.

Rothbard's cooperation with the New Left in the 1960s has aroused much interest and some criticism. With the noninterventionist Right essentially routed and no institutional or publishing arm interested in noninterventionism and *laissez-faire*, Rothbard began to look elsewhere for allies in the fight against war, which he was coming to view as the most fundamental issue of all. ("I am getting more and more convinced that the war-peace question is *the key* to the whole libertarian business," Rothbard had noted privately in 1956.[5]) Mainstream liberalism was, naturally, out of the question, since it had long since adopted the main contours of Cold War interventionism; it was liberals, as we have seen, who condemned the conservative Taft for his skepticism of foreign intervention. At this moment of intellectual isolation, Rothbard looked with interest and sympathy upon the emergence of the New Left and the libertarian instincts he found there—particularly its interest in decentralization and free speech—that he hoped could be nurtured.

Rothbard came to appreciate the work of New Left historian William Appleman Williams, and befriended a number of his students (including Ronald Radosh, with whom Rothbard later edited *A New History of Leviathan*, an important collection of essays on the corporate state). In Williams himself Rothbard found not only congenial foreign-policy analysis, but also important hints of opposition to the central state in domestic affairs. "The core radical ideals and values of community, equality, democracy, and humaneness," Rothbard quoted Williams as saying,

> simply cannot in the future be realized and sustained—nor should they be sought—through more centralization and consolidation. These radical values can most nearly be realized through decentralization and through the creation of many truly human communities. If one feels the need to go ancestor-diving in the American past and spear a tradition

---

[5]John Payne, "Rothbard's Time on the Left," *Journal of Libertarian Studies* 19 (Winter, 2005): 9.

> that is relevant to our contemporary predicament, then the prize trophy is the Articles of Confederation.[6]

Although themselves isolated and perhaps discouraged, there are still some voices on the Left today that bring to mind what Rothbard sought to cultivate in the New Left. Kirkpatrick Sale's words from 2006 may as well be a postscript to those of William Appleman Williams on the Articles of Confederation:

> I am convinced, believe it or not, that secession—by state where the state is cohesive (the model is Vermont, where the secessionist movement is the Second Vermont Republic), or by region where that makes more sense (Southern California or Cascadia are the models here)—is the most fruitful objective for our political future. Peaceful, orderly, popular, democratic, and legal secession would enable a wide variety of governments, amenable to all shades of the anti-authoritarian spectrum, to be established within a modern political context. Such a wide variety, as I see it, that if you didn't like the place you were, you could always find a place you liked.[7]

For a time, Rothbard's optimism about the alliance was reciprocated. "In a strong sense, the Old Right and the New Left are morally and politically coordinate," wrote Carl Oglesby of Students for a Democratic Society (SDS) in 1967.[8] What went wrong—the collapse of SDS and Rothbard's break with the whole movement—is the subject of the final chapter of this book.

Here we encounter still another endearing aspect of *The Betrayal of the American Right*: Rothbard's willingness to acknowledge mistakes, or cases when things took unfortunate turns that he did not anticipate—rarities in the memoir genre. "Looking back

---

[6]Ibid., p. 14.

[7]Kirkpatrick Sale, roundtable contribution, *The American Conservative* (August 28, 2006): 28.

[8]Carl Oglesby and Richard Shaull, *Containment and Change* (New York: Macmillan, 1967), pp. 166–67.

over the experiment of alliance with the New Left," Rothbard recalled,

> it also became clear that the result had in many cases been disastrous for libertarians; for, isolated and scattered as these young libertarians were, the Clarks and the Milchmans and some of the Glaser-Kansas group were soon to *become* leftists in fact, and in particular to abandon the very devotion to individualism, private property rights, and the free-market economy that had brought them to libertarianism, and then to the New Left alliance, in the first place.[9]

He concluded that

> a cadre with no organization and with no continuing program of "internal education" and reinforcement is bound to defect and melt away in the course of working with far stronger allies.[10]

That cadre has long since been built, of course, thanks in large part to Rothbard's own labors.

In the Introduction, Rothbard speaks of a final chapter of the manuscript that brought the narrative up through the end of the Cold War and the intellectual and strategic realignments that that happy occasion made possible. That chapter, unfortunately, has not been found, and thus the story Rothbard tells here must to some degree remain incomplete. With the reappearance of a non-interventionist Right following the end of the Cold War, Rothbard's rhetoric at the time reflected an unmistakable sense of returning home. With old battle lines withering away, more opportunities than ever had begun to open up for cross-ideological cooperation among opponents of war. Questions that had not been asked in some intellectual quarters in decades—about the proper U.S. role in the world and the moral and material dangers

---

[9]See pages 223–24 in this volume.

[10]Ibid., p. 224.

of foreign intervention—were once again being heard, and some of the most withering attacks on U.S. foreign policy were coming from old-fashioned conservatives. "The Old Right is suddenly back!" a delighted Rothbard declared in 1992.

The fruits of this collaboration ultimately proved disappointing, though Rothbard forged some valuable and cherished friendships with a good many people who continue to admire and learn from him to this day. Today, formal alliances of this sort, while still strategically useful, seem much less important than they were even 15 years ago. When there is only a handful of publications and platforms sympathetic to libertarian ideas, there is a natural desire to want to forge an express alliance between libertarians and those outlets. But in the age of the Internet, when the number of outlets in which one can publish (and reach a great many people) is so high, and in which each person can have his own website and blog, libertarians can have very loud voices without erecting any formal alliance with some other group.

In a way, it may be fortuitous that *The Betrayal of the American Right* is appearing only now rather than 20 years ago. The folly of the Iraq war and the propaganda campaign that launched it are making even people heretofore settled in their views stop and think. Listening to Bush administration propaganda, they can't help but wonder if that is what they themselves sounded like during the Cold War. And even if they do not share Rothbard's analysis of the Cold War, plenty of people today, anticipating with dread the endless U.S. wars that the future appears to portend, may be willing to consider at least one important argument against Cold War interventionism: it nurtured a military-industrial complex, born in World War II, that is evidently incapable of ever being dismantled. Milton Friedman's dictum that there is nothing so permanent as a "temporary" government program has found no more striking vindication than in the American "defense" sector, which always seems to find a rationale for higher spending and more intervention.

In short, more people than ever are skeptical of the official government version of just about anything, and are open to revisiting old questions. As usual, Rothbard is prepared to ask those questions, and to follow the answers wherever they lead him.

Thomas E. Woods, Jr.
Auburn, Alabama
May 2007

Preface to the 1991 Revision

The manuscript of the greater part of this book, *The Betrayal of the American Right*, was written in 1971 and revised in 1973. Little of this original manuscript has been changed here. In a profound sense, it is more timely today than when it was first written. The book was a cry in the wilderness against what I saw as the betrayal of what I here call the "Old Right." Or, to allay confusion about various "olds" and "news," we call it the Original Right. The Old Right arose during the 1930s as a reaction against the Great Leap Forward (or Backward) into collectivism that characterized the New Deal. That Old Right continued and flourished through the 1940s and down to about the mid-1950s. The Old Right was staunchly opposed to Big Government and the New Deal at home and abroad: that is, to both facets of the welfare-warfare state. It combated U.S. intervention in foreign affairs and foreign wars as fervently as it opposed intervention at home.

At the present time, many conservatives have come to realize that the old feisty, antigovernment spirit of conservatives has been abraded and somehow been transformed into its statist opposite. It is tempting, and, so far as it goes, certainly correct, to put the blame on the Right's embrace in the 1970s of Truman-Humphrey Cold War liberals calling themselves "neoconservatives," and to allow these ex-Trotskyites and ex-Mensheviks not only into the tent but also to take over the show. But the thesis of the book is that those who wonder what happened to the good old cause must not stop with the neocons: that the rot started long before, with the founding in 1955 of *National Review* and its rapid rise to dominance of the conservative movement. It was *National Review* that, consciously and cleverly, transformed the content of the Old Right into something very like its opposite, while preserving the old forms and rituals, such as lip service to the free market and to the

Constitution of the United States. It was, as the great Garet Garrett said about the New Deal in the American polity, a "revolution within the form." As this book points out, the Right happened to be vulnerable to takeover at this time, its old leaders recently dead or retired. While younger, or yuppie, conservatives may puzzle at this statement, the good old days of the Old Right in politics were not the Goldwater campaign but the campaign of Robert A. Taft.

This book discusses the Old Right, details the *National Review* takeover, and treats the odyssey of myself and like-minded libertarians out of our formerly honored position as the "extreme" wing of the Old Right, breaking with *National Review* conservatism, and anxious to find a home for libertarian ideas and activities. The book was written after the end of our alliance with the New Left, which had begun promisingly in the early and mid-1960s but had ended in the mad if short-lived orgy of violence and destruction at the end of the decade. The manuscript ends with the beginning of the emergence of the libertarian movement as a separate, self-conscious ideological and even political entity in the United States, aiming to be a separate or Third Force in America drawing from the congenial elements of both Left and Right.

The final section, chapter 14, written at the present time, fills in the history of the libertarian movement and of the right in the last two decades, and explains how brand new circumstances, notably the astounding death of the Cold War, combined with the collapse of the conservative movement and changes among libertarians, present new challenges and fruitful alliances for libertarians.[1]

The inspiration for this manuscript came from Bob Kephart, then publisher of the *Libertarian Review*, who planned to publish books under the imprint of the Libertarian Review Press. This press did publish a collection of my essays around that time.[2] Ramparts Press put a blurb for the publication of this book into its 1971 catalog, but they wanted extensive changes which I refused to

---

[1]Such a chapter has not been found in Rothbard's papers.—Ed.

[2]Murray N. Rothbard, *Egalitarianism as a Revolt Against Nature and Other Essays* (Washington, D.C.: Libertarian Review Press, 1974).

make.[3] I had tried, ever since the early 1960s, to get my story of the betrayal of the Old Right into print, but there were no periodicals open to this message. Particularly incensed at the Goldwater campaign of 1964, the first campaign dominated by the *National Review* Right, I could only air my views, very briefly, in the only extant libertarian periodical, the Los Angeles newsletter *The Innovator*; searching for an outlet for a longer piece, I could find only the obscure peace-Catholic quarterly *Continuum*.[4]

After that, my political views were largely aired in my own periodicals: *Left and Right*, 1965–1968, edited by Leonard Liggio and myself, a vehicle for alliance with the New Left; the weekly and then monthly *Libertarian Forum*, 1969–1984, an expression of a self-conscious libertarian movement; and, for more scholarly articles, the *Journal of Libertarian Studies*, founded in 1977 as a publishing arm of the Center for Libertarian Studies and still continuing. Part of the analysis in the present manuscript appeared as my "The Foreign Policy of the Old Right."[5]

At about the same time the *Betrayal* was written, there also appeared a master's essay along similar lines by the young libertarian historian Joseph R. Stromberg.[6] Of the scholarly work done since, one of the most valuable on the Old Right is the study of

---

[3]I had published my view of the Old Right and its fall in *Ramparts*, then the leading New Left periodical. Murray N. Rothbard, "Confessions of a Right-Wing Liberal," *Ramparts* 6, no. 11 (June 15, 1968): 48–52.

[4]Murray N. Rothbard, "The Transformation of the American Right," *Continuum* 2 (Summer, 1964): 22–31.

[5]*Journal of Libertarian Studies* 2 (Winter, 1978): 85–96. The original version of this article was a paper delivered at a session on the Right at the 1972 annual meeting of the Organization of American Historians, a session organized by the brilliant Marxist historian Eugene D. Genovese.

[6]Joseph R. Stromberg, "The Cold War and the Transformation of the American Right: The Decline of Right-Wing Liberalism" (M.A. essay, Florida Atlantic University, 1971).

Frank Chodorov by Charles Hamilton.[7] Also particularly valuable is Justus Doenecke's study of the response of World War II isolationists to the emergence of the Cold War, down to 1954, and Felix Morley's autobiography, particularly the last two chapters on his experience with *Human Events*.[8,9]

Since the 1970s, *The Betrayal of the American Right* has remained dormant, although copies, some barely legible, have been circulating in *samizdat* among young libertarian scholars.

Finally, the dramatic collapse of Communism and the Cold War in 1989, and the subsequent rethinking among both conservatives and libertarians, has recently aroused interest in the *Betrayal*. Study into the Old Right by Tom Fleming, editor of *Chronicles*, led me to dig out the manuscript, and the enthusiastic suggestion of Justin Raimondo, editor of the *Libertarian Republican*, inspired me to update the *Betrayal* and led directly to the present publication. As always, I am deeply grateful to Burt Blumert and to Lew Rockwell for their enthusiasm and help over the years, and with this publication.

Murray N. Rothbard
Las Vegas, 1991

---

[7]Charles H. Hamilton, "Introduction," in *Fugitive Writings: Selected Writings of Frank Chodorov*, Hamilton, ed. (Indianapolis, Ind.: Liberty Press, 1980), pp. 11–30.

[8]Justus D. Doenecke, *Not to the Swift: The Old Isolationists in the Cold War Era* (Lewisburg, Penn.: Bucknell University Press, 1979). Also see Ronald Radosh, *Prophets on the Right: Profiles of Conservative Critics of American Globalism* (New York: Simon and Schuster, 1975).

[9]An especially valuable study done before the writing of the *Betrayal* is a doctoral dissertation on the 1950s libertarian movement by Eckard Vance Toy, Jr., even though it is almost exclusively based on the fortunately extensive papers and correspondence of Seattle industrialist James W. Clise. Toy is particularly good on the Foundation for Economic Education (FEE) and Spiritual Mobilization, although he neglects the William Volker Fund and does not concern himself with foreign policy. Eckard Vance Toy, Jr., "Ideology and Conflict in American Ultra-Conservatism, 1945–1960" (Ph.D. diss., University of Oregon, 1965).

1
Two Rights, Old and New

In the spring of 1970, a new political term—"the hard hats"—burst upon the American consciousness. As the hard-hatted construction workers barreled their way around the Wall Street area, beating up college kids and peace demonstrators, earning the admiration of the right wing and a citation from President Nixon, one of the banners they raised summed up in a single phrase how remarkably the right wing has changed over the past two decades. For the banner said simply: "God Bless the Establishment." In that single phrase, so typical of the current right wing, the hard-hats were expressing the age-old political philosophy of Conservatism, that philosophy which formed the central core of the originally labeled "Conservatism" of early nineteenth-century Europe. In fact, it is the philosophy that has marked genuinely conservative thought, regardless of label, since the ancient days of Oriental despotism: an all-encompassing reverence for "Throne-and-Altar," for whatever divinely sanctioned State apparatus happened to be in existence. In one form or another, "God Bless the Establishment" has always been the cry on behalf of State power.

But how many Americans realize that, not so long ago, the American right wing was almost the exact opposite of what we know today? In fact, how many know that the term "Establishment" itself, now used almost solely as a term of opprobrium by the Left, was first applied to America not by C. Wright Mills or other Left sociologists, but by *National Review* theoretician Frank S. Meyer, in the early days of that central organ of the American Right? In the mid-1950s, Meyer took a term which had previously been used only—and rather affectionately—to describe the ruling institutions of Great Britain, and applied the term with proper acidity to the American scene. Broader and more subtle than "ruling class," more permanent and institutionalized than a "power elite," "the Establishment" quickly became a household word. But the ironic and crucial point is that Meyer's and *National Review*'s use of the term in those days was bitterly critical: the spirit of the right wing, then and particularly earlier, was far more "God Damn" than "God Bless" the establishment.[1] The difference between the two right wings, "Old" and "New," and how one was transformed into the other, is the central theme of this book.

The Old Right, which constituted the American right wing from approximately the mid-1930s to the mid-1950s, was, if nothing else, an Opposition movement. Hostility to the Establishment was its hallmark, its very lifeblood. In fact, when in the 1950s the monthly newsletter *RIGHT* attempted to convey to its readers news of the right wing, it was of course forced to define the movement it would be writing about—and it found that it could define the right wing only in negative terms: in its total opposition to what it conceived to be the ruling trends of American life. In brief, the Old Right was born and had its being as the opposition movement to the New Deal, and to everything, foreign and domestic, that the New Deal encompassed: at first, to burgeoning New Deal statism at home, and then, later in the '30s, to the drive for American global intervention abroad. Since the essence of the Old Right was a reaction against runaway Big Government at home and overseas, this meant that the Old Right was necessarily, even if not always consciously, libertarian rather than statist, "radical" rather than traditional conservative apologists for the existing order.

---

[1]By the 1964 campaign, the irreverent Rightist Noel E. Parmentel, Jr., was writing, in his "Folk Songs for Conservatives":

Won't you come home, Bill Buckley,
Won't you come home
From the Establishment?

2

Origins of the Old Right I: Early Individualism

Individualism, and its economic corollary, *laissez-faire* liberalism, has not always taken on a conservative hue, has not always functioned, as it often does today, as an apologist for the status quo. On the contrary, the Revolution of modern times was originally, and continued for a long time to be, *laissez-faire* individualist. Its purpose was to free the individual person from the restrictions and the shackles, the encrusted caste privileges and exploitative wars, of the feudal and mercantilist orders, of the Tory *ancien régime*. Tom Paine, Thomas Jefferson, the militants in the American Revolution, the Jacksonian movement, Emerson and Thoreau, William Lloyd Garrison and the radical abolitionists—all were basically *laissez-faire* individualists who carried on the age-old battle for liberty and against all forms of State privilege. And so were the French revolutionaries—not only the Girondins, but even the much-abused Jacobins, who were obliged to defend the Revolution against the massed crowned heads of Europe. All were roughly in the same camp. The individualist heritage, indeed, goes back to the first modern radicals of the seventeenth century—to the Levellers in England, and to Roger Williams and Anne Hutchinson in the American colonies.

The conventional historical wisdom asserts that while the radical movements in America were indeed *laissez-faire* individualist before the Civil War, that afterwards, the *laissez-fairists* became conservatives, and the radical mantle then fell to groups more familiar to the modern Left: the Socialists and Populists. But this is a distortion of the truth. For it was elderly New England Brahmins, *laissez-faire* merchants and industrialists like Edward Atkinson, who had financed John Brown's raid at Harper's Ferry, who were the ones to leap in and oppose the U.S. imperialism of the Spanish-American War with all their might. No opposition to that war was more thoroughgoing than that of the *laissez-faire* economist and sociologist William Graham Sumner or than that of Atkinson who, as head of the Anti-Imperialist League, mailed antiwar pamphlets to American troops then engaged in conquering the Philippines. Atkinson's pamphlets urged our troops to mutiny, and were consequently seized by the U.S. postal authorities.

In taking this stand, Atkinson, Sumner and their colleagues were not being "sports"; they were following an antiwar, anti-imperialist tradition as old as classical liberalism itself. This was the tradition of Price, Priestley, and the late eighteenth-century British radicals that earned them repeated imprisonment by the British war machine; and of Richard Cobden, John Bright, and the *laissez-faire* Manchester School of the mid-nineteenth century. Cobden, in particular, had fearlessly denounced every war and every imperial maneuver of the British regime. We are now so used to thinking of opposition to imperialism as Marxian that this kind of movement seems almost inconceivable to us today.[1]

By the advent of World War I, however, the death of the older *laissez-faire* generation threw the leadership of the opposition to America's imperial wars into the hands of the Socialist Party. But other, more individualist-minded men joined in the opposition, many of whom would later form the core of the isolationist Old Right of the late 1930s. Thus, the hardcore antiwar leaders included the individualist Senator Robert LaFollette of Wisconsin and such *laissez-faire* liberals as Senators William E. Borah (Republican) of Idaho and James A. Reed (Democrat) of Missouri. It also included Charles A. Lindbergh, Sr., father of the Lone Eagle, who was a congressman from Minnesota.

---

[1]Thus, see William H. Dawson, *Richard Cobden and Foreign Policy* (London: George Allen and Unwin, 1926).

Almost all of America's intellectuals rushed to enlist in the war fervor of World War I. A leading exception was the formidable *laissez-faire* individualist Oswald Garrison Villard, editor of the *Nation*, grandson of William Lloyd Garrison and former member of the Anti-Imperialist League. Two other prominent exceptions were friends and associates of Villard who were later to serve as leaders of libertarian thought in America: Francis Neilson and especially Albert Jay Nock. Neilson was the last of the *laissez-faire* English Liberals, who had emigrated to the U.S.; Nock served under Villard during the war, and it was his *Nation* editorial denouncing the pro-government activities of Samuel Gompers that got that issue of the magazine banned by the U.S. Post Office. And it was Neilson who wrote the first revisionist book on the origins of World War I, *How Diplomats Make War* (1915). The first revisionist book by an American, in fact, was Nock's *Myth of a Guilty Nation* (1922), which had been serialized in *LaFollette's Magazine*.

The world war constituted a tremendous trauma for all the individuals and groups opposed to the conflict. The total mobilization, the savage repression of opponents, the carnage and the U.S. global intervention on an unprecedented scale—all of these polarized a large number of diverse people. The shock and the sheer overriding fact of the war inevitably drew together the diverse antiwar groups into a loose, informal and oppositional united front—a front in a new kind of fundamental opposition to the American system and to much of American society. The rapid transformation of the brilliant young intellectual Randolph Bourne from an optimistic pragmatist into a radically pessimistic anarchist was typical, though in a more intense form, of this newly created opposition. Crying, "War is the health of the State," Bourne declared:

> Country is a concept of peace, of balance, of living and letting live. But State is essentially a concept of power. . . . And we have the misfortune of being born not only into a country but into a State. . . .

> The State is the country acting as a political unit, it is the group acting as a repository of force. . . . International politics is a "power politics" because it is a relation of States and that is what States infallibly and calamitously are, huge aggregations of human and industrial force that may be hurled against each other in war. When a country acts as a whole in relation to another country, or in imposing laws on its own inhabitants, or in coercing or punishing individuals or minorities, it is acting as a State. The history of America as a country is quite different from that of America as a State. In one case it is the drama of the pioneering conquest of the land, of the growth of wealth and the ways in which it was used . . . and the carrying out of spiritual ideals. . . . But as a State, its history is that of playing part in the world, making war, obstructing international trade . . . punishing those citizens whom society agrees are offensive, and collecting money to pay for it all.[2]

If the opposition was polarized and forced together by the war, this polarization did not cease with the war's end. For one thing, the war and its corollary repression and militarism were shocks that started the opposition thinking deeply and critically about the American system per se; for another, the international system established by the war was frozen into the status quo of the postwar era. For it was obvious that the Versailles Treaty meant that British and French imperialism had carved up and humiliated Germany, and then intended to use the League of Nations as a permanent world guarantor of the newly imposed status quo. Versailles and the League meant that America could not forget the war; and the ranks of the Opposition were now joined by a host of disillusioned Wilsonians who saw the reality of the world that President Wilson had made.

The wartime and postwar opposition joined together in a coalition including Socialists and all manner of progressives and individualists. Since they and the coalition were now clearly anti-militarist and anti-"patriotic," since they were increasingly radical

---

[2]Randolph Bourne, *Untimely Papers* (New York: B.W. Huebach, 1919), pp. 229–30.

in their antistatism, the individualists were universally labeled as "leftists"; in fact, as the Socialist Party split and faded badly in the postwar era, the Opposition was given an increasingly individualistic cast during the 1920s. Part of this opposition was also cultural: a revolt against hidebound Victorian mores and literature. Part of this cultural revolt was embodied in the well-known expatriates of the "Lost Generation" of young American writers, writers expressing their intense disillusion with the wartime "idealism" and the reality that militarism and the war had revealed about America. Another phase of this revolt was embodied in the new social freedom of the jazz and flapper eras, and the flowering of individual expression, among increasing numbers of young men and women.

3

Origins of the Old Right II: The Tory Anarchism of Mencken and Nock

Leading the cultural struggle in America was H.L. Mencken, undoubtedly the single most influential intellectual of the 1920s; a notable individualist and libertarian, Mencken sailed into battle with characteristic verve and wit, denouncing the stodgy culture and the "Babbittry" of businessmen, and calling for unrestricted freedom of the individual. For Mencken, too, it was the trauma of World War I, and its domestic and foreign evils, that mobilized and intensified his concern for politics—a concern aggravated by the despotism of Prohibition, surely the greatest single act of tyranny ever imposed in America.

Nowadays, when Prohibition is considered a "right-wing" movement, it is forgotten that every reform movement of the nineteenth century—every moralistic group trying to bring the "uplift" to America by force of law—included Prohibition as one of its cherished programs. To Mencken, the battle against Prohibition was merely a fight against the most conspicuous of the tyrannical and statist "reforms" being proposed against the American public.

And so, Mencken's highly influential monthly *The American Mercury*, founded in 1924, opened its pages to writers of all parts of the Opposition—especially to attacks on American culture and mores, to assaults on censorship and the championing of civil liberties, and to revisionism on the war. Thus, the *Mercury* featured two prominent revisionists of World War I: Harry Elmer Barnes and Barnes's student, C. Hartley Grattan, whose delightful series in the magazine, "When Historians Cut Loose," acidly demolished the war propaganda of America's leading historians. Mencken's cultural scorn for the American "booboisie" was embodied in his famous "Americana" column, which simply reprinted news items on the idiocies of American life without editorial comment.

The enormous scope of Mencken's interests, coupled with his scintillating wit and style (Mencken was labeled by Joseph Wood Krutch as "the greatest prose stylist of the twentieth century"), served to obscure for his generation of youthful followers and admirers the remarkable consistency of his thought. When, decades after his former prominence, Mencken collected the best of his old writings in *A Mencken Chrestomathy* (1948), the book was reviewed in the *New Leader* by the eminent literary critic Samuel Putnam. Putnam reacted in considerable surprise; remembering Mencken from his youth as merely a glib cynic, Putnam found to his admiring astonishment that H.L.M. had always been a "Tory anarchist"—an apt summation for the intellectual leader of the 1920s.

But H.L. Mencken was not the only editor leading the new upsurge of individualistic opposition during the 1920s. From a similar though more moderate stance, the *Nation* of Mencken's friend Oswald Garrison Villard continued to serve as an outstanding voice for peace, revisionism on World War I, and opposition to the imperialist status quo imposed at Versailles. Villard, at the end of the war, acknowledged that the war had pushed him far to the left, not in the sense of adopting socialism, but in being thoroughly "against the present political order." Denounced by conservatives as pacifist, pro-German, and "Bolshevist," Villard found himself forced into a political and journalistic alliance with socialists and progressives who shared his hostility to the existing American and world order.[1]

---

[1]Villard to Hutchins Hapgood, May 19, 1919. Michael Wreszin, *Oswald Garrison Villard* (Bloomington: Indiana University Press, 1965), pp. 75 and 125–30.

From a still more radical and individualist perspective, Mencken's friend and fellow "Tory anarchist" Albert Jay Nock co-founded and coedited, along with Francis Neilson, the new weekly *Freeman* from 1920 to 1924. The *Freeman*, too, opened its pages to all left-oppositionists to the political order. With the *laissez-faire* individualist Nock as principal editor, the *Freeman* was a center of radical thought and expression among oppositionist intellectuals. Rebuffing the *Nation*'s welcome to the new *Freeman* as a fellow liberal weekly, Nock declared that he was not a liberal but a radical. "We can not help remembering," wrote Nock bitterly, "that this was a liberal's war, a liberal's peace, and that the present state of things is the consummation of a fairly long, fairly extensive, and extremely costly experiment with liberalism in political power."[2] To Nock, radicalism meant that the State was to be considered as an antisocial institution rather than as the typically liberal instrument of social reform. And Nock, like Mencken, gladly opened the pages of his journal to all manner of radical, anti-Establishment opinion, including Van Wyck Brooks, Bertrand Russell, Louis Untermeyer, Lewis Mumford, John Dos Passos, William C. Bullitt, and Charles A. Beard.

In particular, while an individualist and libertarian, Nock welcomed the Soviet revolution as a successful overthrow of a frozen and reactionary State apparatus. Above all, Nock, in opposing the postwar settlement, denounced the American and Allied intervention in the [Russian] Civil War. Nock and Neilson saw clearly that the American intervention was setting the stage for a continuing and permanent imposition of American might throughout the world. After the folding of the *Freeman* in 1924, Nock continued to be prominent as a distinguished essayist in the leading magazines, including his famous "Anarchist's Progress."[3]

---

[2]Albert Jay Nock, "Our Duty Towards Europe," *The Freeman* 7 (August 8, 1923): 508; quoted in Robert M. Crunden, *The Mind and Art of Albert Jay Nock* (Chicago: Henry Regnery, 1964), p. 77.

[3]Albert Jay Nock, *On Doing the Right Thing, and Other Essays* (New York: Harper and Row, 1928).

Most of this loose coalition of individualistic radicals was totally disillusioned with the political process, but to the extent that they distinguished between existing parties, the Republican Party was clearly the major enemy. Eternal Hamiltonian champions of Big Government and intimate government "partnership" with Big Business through tariffs, subsidies, and contracts, long-time brandishers of the Imperial big stick, the Republicans had capped their antilibertarian sins by being the party most dedicated to the tyranny of Prohibition, an evil that particularly enraged H.L. Mencken. Much of the opposition (e.g., Mencken, Villard) supported the short-lived LaFollette Progressive movement of 1924, and the Progressive Senator William E. Borah (R-Idaho) was an opposition hero in leading the fight against the war and the League of Nations, and in advocating recognition of Soviet Russia. But the nearest political home was the conservative Bourbon, non-Wilsonian or "Cleveland" wing of the Democratic Party, a wing that at least tended to be "wet," was opposed to war and foreign intervention, and favored free trade and strictly minimal government. Mencken, the most politically minded of the group, felt closest in politics to Governor Albert Ritchie, the states-rights Democrat from Maryland, and to Senator James Reed, Democrat of Missouri, a man staunchly "isolationist" and anti-intervention in foreign affairs and pro-*laissez-faire* at home.

It was this conservative wing of the Democratic Party, headed by Charles Michelson, Jouett Shouse, and John J. Raskob, which launched a determined attack on Herbert Hoover in the late 1920s for his adherence to Prohibition and to Big Government generally. It was this wing that would later give rise to the much-maligned Liberty League.

To Mencken and to Nock, in fact, Herbert Hoover—the prowar Wilsonian and interventionist, the Food Czar of the war, the champion of Big Government, of high tariffs and business cartels, the pious moralist and apologist for Prohibition—embodied everything they abhorred in American political life. They were clearly leaders of the individualist opposition to Hoover's conservative statism.

Since they were, in their very different styles, the leaders of libertarian thought in America during the 1920s, Mencken and Nock deserve a little closer scrutiny.

The essence of Mencken's remarkably consistent "Tory anarchism" was embodied in the discussion of government that he was later to select for his *Chrestomathy*:

> All government, in its essence, is a conspiracy against the superior man: its one permanent object is to oppress him and cripple him. If it be aristocratic in organization, then it seeks to protect the man who is superior only in law against the man who is superior in fact; if it be democratic, then it seeks to protect the man who is inferior in every way against both. One of its primary functions is to regiment men by force, to make them as much alike as possible . . . to search out and combat originality among them. All it can see in an original idea is potential change, and hence an invasion of its prerogatives. The most dangerous man, to any government, is the man who is able to think things out for himself, without regard to the prevailing superstitions and taboos. Almost inevitably he comes to the conclusion that the government he lives under is dishonest, insane and intolerable, and so, if he is romantic, he tries to change it. And even if he is not romantic personally [as Mencken clearly was not] he is very apt to spread discontent among those who are. . . .
>
> The ideal government of all reflective men, from Aristotle onward, is one which lets the individual alone—one which barely escapes being no government at all. This ideal, I believe, will be realized in the world twenty or thirty centuries after I have . . . taken up my public duties in Hell.[4]

Again, Mencken on the State as inherent exploitation:

> The average man, whatever his errors otherwise, at least sees clearly that government is something lying outside him and outside the generality of his fellow men—that it is a separate,

---

[4]From the *Smart Set*, December 1919. H.L. Mencken, *A Mencken Chrestomathy* (New York: Knopf, 1949), pp. 145–46. See also Murray N. Rothbard, "H.L. Mencken: The Joyous Libertarian," *New Individualist Review* 2, no. 2 (Summer, 1962): 15–27.

independent and often hostile power, only partly under his control and capable of doing him great harm. . . . Is it a fact of no significance that robbing the government is everywhere regarded as a crime of less magnitude than robbing an individual, or even a corporation? . . .

What lies behind all this, I believe, is a deep sense of the fundamental antagonism between the government and the people it governs. It is apprehended, not as a committee of citizens chosen to carry on the communal business of the whole population, but as a separate and autonomous corporation, mainly devoted to exploiting the population for the benefit of its own members. Robbing it is thus an act almost devoid of infamy. . . . When a private citizen is robbed a worthy man is deprived of the fruits of his industry and thrift; when the government is robbed the worst that happens is that certain rogues and loafers have less money to play with than they had before. The notion that they have earned that money is never entertained; to most sensible men it would seem ludicrous. They are simply rascals who, by accidents of law, have a somewhat dubious right to a share in the earnings of their fellow men. When that share is diminished by private enterprise the business is, on the whole, far more laudable than not.

The intelligent man, when he pays taxes, certainly does not believe that he is making a prudent and productive investment of his money; on the contrary, he feels that he is being mulcted in an excessive amount for services that, in the main, are downright inimical to him. . . . He sees in even the most essential of them an agency for making it easier for the exploiters constituting the government to rob him. In these exploiters themselves he has no confidence whatever. He sees them as purely predatory and useless. . . . They constitute a power that stands over him constantly, ever alert for new chances to squeeze him. If they could do so safely, they would strip him to his hide. If they leave him anything at all, it is simply prudentially, as a farmer leaves a hen some of her eggs.

This gang is well-nigh immune to punishment. . . . Since the first days of the Republic, less than a dozen of its members have been impeached, and only a few obscure understrappers have been put into prison. The number of men sitting at Atlanta and Leavenworth for revolting against the

> extortions of government is always ten times as great as the number of government officials condemned for oppressing the taxpayers to their own gain. Government, today, has grown too strong to be safe. There are no longer any citizens in the world; there are only subjects. They work day in and day out for their masters; they are bound to die for their masters at call. . . . On some bright tomorrow, a geological epoch or two hence, they will come to the end of their endurance.[5]

In letters to his friends, Mencken reiterated his emphasis on individual liberty. At one time he wrote that he believed in absolute human liberty "up to the limit of the unbearable, and even beyond." To his old friend Hamilton Owens he declared,

> I believe in only one thing and that thing is human liberty. If ever a man is to achieve anything like dignity, it can happen only if superior men are given absolute freedom to think what they want to think and say what they want to say . . . [and] the superior man can be sure of freedom only if it is given to all men.[6]

And in a privately written "Addendum on Aims," Mencken declared that

> I am an extreme libertarian, and believe in absolute free speech. . . . I am against jailing men for their opinions, or, for that matter, for anything else.[7]

Part of Mencken's antipathy to reform stemmed from his oft-reiterated belief that "all government is evil, and that trying to improve it is largely a waste of time." Mencken stressed this theme in the noble and moving peroration to his Credo, written for a "What I Believe" series in a leading magazine:

---

[5]From the *American Mercury*, February 1925. Mencken, *Chrestomathy*, pp. 146–48.

[6]Guy Forgue, ed., *Letters of H.L. Mencken* (New York: Knopf, 1961), pp. xiii, 189.

[7]Ibid.

> I believe that all government is evil, in that all government must necessarily make war upon liberty, and that the democratic form is as bad as any of the other forms. . . .
>
> I believe in complete freedom of thought and speech—alike for the humblest man and the mightiest, and in the utmost freedom of conduct that is consistent with living in organized society.
>
> I believe in the capacity of man to conquer his world, and to find out what it is made of, and how it is run.
>
> I believe in the reality of progress. I—
>
> But the whole thing, after all, may be put very simply. I believe that it is better to tell the truth than to lie. I believe that it is better to be free than to be a slave. And I believe that it is better to know than to be ignorant.[8]

Insofar as he was interested in economic matters, Mencken, as a corollary to his libertarian views, was a staunch believer in capitalism. He praised Sir Ernest Benn's paean to a free-market economy, and declared that to capitalism "we owe . . . almost everything that passes under the general name of civilization today." He agreed with Benn that "nothing government does is ever done as cheaply and efficiently as the same thing might be done by private enterprise."[9]

But, in keeping with his individualism and libertarianism, Mencken's devotion to capitalism was to the free market, and not to the monopoly statism that he saw ruling America in the 1920s. Hence he was as willing as any socialist to point the finger at the responsibility of Big Business for the growth of statism. Thus, in analyzing the 1924 presidential election, Mencken wrote:

---

[8]H.L. Mencken, "What I Believe," *The Forum* 84 (September 1930): 139.

[9]H.L. Mencken, "Babbitt as Philosopher" (review of Henry Ford, *Today and Tomorrow*, and Ernest J.P. Benn, *The Confessions of a Capitalist*), *The American Mercury* 9 (September 1926): 126–27. Also see Mencken, "Capitalism," *Baltimore Evening Sun*, January 14, 1935, reprinted in *Chrestomathy*, p. 294.

> Big Business, it appears, is in favor of him [Coolidge]. . . . The fact should be sufficient to make the judicious regard him somewhat suspiciously. For Big Business, in America . . . is frankly on the make, day in and day out. . . . Big Business was in favor of Prohibition, believing that a sober workman would make a better slave than one with a few drinks in him. It was in favor of all the gross robberies and extortions that went on during the war, and profited by all of them. It was in favor of all the crude throttling of free speech that was then undertaken in the name of patriotism, and is still in favor of it.[10]

As for John W. Davis, the Democratic candidate, Mencken noted that he was said to be a good lawyer—not, for Mencken, a favorable recommendation, since lawyers

> are responsible for nine-tenths of the useless and vicious laws that now clutter the statute-books, and for all the evils that go with the vain attempt to enforce them. Every Federal judge is a lawyer. So are most Congressmen. Every invasion of the plain rights of the citizen has a lawyer behind it. If all lawyers were hanged tomorrow . . . we'd all be freer and safer, and our taxes would be reduced by almost a half.

And what is more,

> Dr. Davis is a lawyer whose life has been devoted to protecting the great enterprises of Big Business. He used to work for J. Pierpont Morgan, and he has himself said that he is proud of the fact. Mr. Morgan is an international banker, engaged in squeezing nations that are hard up and in trouble. His operations are safeguarded for him by the manpower of the United States. He was one of the principal beneficiaries of the late war, and made millions out of it. The Government hospitals are now full of one-legged soldiers who gallantly protected his investments then, and the public schools are full of boys who will protect his investments tomorrow.[11]

---

[10]H.L. Mencken, "Breathing Space," *Baltimore Evening Sun*, August 4, 1924; reprinted in H.L. Mencken, *A Carnival of Buncombe* (Baltimore: Johns Hopkins Press, 1956), pp. 83–84.

[11]Ibid.

In fact, the following brief analysis of the postwar settlement combines Mencken's assessment of the determining influence of Big Business with the bitterness of all the individualists at the war and its aftermath:

> When he was in the Senate Dr. Harding was known as a Standard Oil Senator—and Standard Oil, as everyone knows, was strongly against our going into the League of Nations, chiefly because England would run the league and be in a position to keep Americans out of the new oil fields in the Near East. The Morgans and their pawnbroker allies, of course, were equally strong for going in, since getting Uncle Sam under the English hoof would materially protect their English and other foreign investments. Thus the issue joined, and on the Tuesday following the first Monday of November 1920, the Morgans, after six years of superb *Geschaft* under the Anglomaniacal Woodrow, got a bad beating.[12]

But as a result, Mencken went on, the Morgans decided to come to terms with the foe, and therefore, at the Lausanne Conference of 1922–23, "the English agreed to let the Standard Oil crowd in on the oil fields of the Levant," and J.P. Morgan visited Harding at the White House, after which "Dr. Harding began to hear a voice from the burning bush counseling him to disregard the prejudice of the voters who elected him and to edge the U.S. into a Grand International Court of Justice."[13]

While scarcely as well known as Mencken, Albert Nock more than any other person supplied twentieth-century libertarianism with a positive, systematic theory. In a series of essays in the 1923 *Freeman* on "The State," Nock built upon Herbert Spencer and the great German sociologist and follower of Henry George, Franz Oppenheimer, whose brilliant little classic, *The State*,[14] had

[12]H.L. Mencken, "Next Year's Struggle," *Baltimore Evening Sun*, June 11, 1923; reprinted in Mencken, *A Carnival of Buncombe*, pp. 56–57.

[13]Ibid.

[14]Albert Jay Nock, *Our Enemy, the State* (1922; New York: William Morrow, 1935), pp. 162ff.

just been reprinted. Oppenheimer had pointed out that man tries to acquire wealth in the easiest possible way, and that there were two mutually exclusive paths to obtain wealth. One was the peaceful path of producing something and voluntarily exchanging that product for the product of someone else; this path of production and voluntary exchange Oppenheimer called the "economic means." The other road to wealth was coercive expropriation: the seizure of the product of another by the use of violence. This Oppenheimer termed the "political means." And from his historical inquiry into the genesis of States Oppenheimer defined the State as the "organization of the political means." Hence, Nock concluded, the State itself was evil, and was always the highroad by which varying groups could seize State power and use it to become an exploiting, or ruling, class, at the expense of the remainder of the ruled or subject population. Nock therefore defined the State as that institution which "claims and exercises the monopoly of crime" over a territorial area; "it forbids private murder, but itself organizes murder on a colossal scale. It punishes private theft, but itself lays unscrupulous hands on anything it wants."[15]

In his *magnum opus*, *Our Enemy, the State*, Nock expanded on his theory and applied it to American history, in particular the formation of the American Constitution. In contrast to the traditional conservative worshippers of the Constitution, Nock applied Charles A. Beard's thesis to the history of America, seeing it as a succession of class rule by various groups of privileged businessmen, and the Constitution as a strong national government brought into being in order to create and extend such privilege. The Constitution, wrote Nock,

> enabled an ever-closer centralization of control over the political means. For instance . . . many an industrialist could see the great primary advantage of being able to extend his exploiting opportunities over a nationwide free-trade area walled in by a general tariff. . . . Any speculator in depreciated public securities would be strongly for a system that could offer him the use of the political means to bring back their

---

[15]Ibid.

> face value. Any shipowner or foreign trader would be quick to see that his bread was buttered on the side of a national State which, if properly approached, might lend him the use of the political means by way of a subsidy, or would be able to back up some profitable but dubious freebooting enterprise with "diplomatic representations" or with reprisals.

Nock concluded that those economic interests, in opposition to the mass of the nation's farmers, "planned and executed a *coup d'etat*, simply tossing the Articles of Confederation into the wastebasket."[16]

While the Nock-Oppenheimer class analysis superficially resembles that of Marx, and a Nockian would, like Lenin, look at all State action whatever in terms of "Who? Whom?" (Who is benefiting at the expense of Whom?), it is important to recognize the crucial differences. For while Nock and Marx would agree on the Oriental Despotic and feudal periods' ruling classes in privilege over the ruled, they would differ on the analysis of businessmen on the free market. For to Nock, antagonistic classes, the rulers and the ruled, can only be *created by* accession to State privilege; it is the use of the State instrument that brings these antagonistic classes into being. While Marx would agree on pre-capitalistic eras, he of course also concluded that businessmen and workers were in class antagonism to each other even in a free-market economy, with employers exploiting workers. To the Nockian, businessmen and workers are in harmony—as are everyone else—in the free market and free society, and it is only through State intervention that antagonistic classes are created.[17]

---

[16]Ibid.

[17]This idea of classes as being created by States was the pre-Marxian idea of classes; two of its earliest theorists were the French individualist and libertarian thinkers of the post-Napoleonic Restoration period, Charles Comte and Charles Dunoyer. For several years after the Restoration, Comte and Dunoyer were the mentors of Count Saint-Simon, who adopted their class analysis; the later Saint-Simonians then modified it to include businessmen as being class-exploiters of workers,

Thus, to Nock the two basic classes at any time are those running the State and those being run by it: as the Populist leader Sockless Jerry Simpson once put it, "the robbers and the robbed." Nock therefore coined the concepts "State power" and "social power." "Social power" was the power over nature exerted by free men in voluntary economic and social relationships; social power was the progress of civilization, its learning, its technology, its structure of capital investment. "State power" was the coercive and parasitic expropriation of social power for the benefit of the rulers: the use of the "political means" to wealth. The history of man, then, could be seen as an eternal race between social power and State power, with society creating and developing new wealth, later to be seized, controlled, and exploited by the State.

No more than Mencken was Nock happy about the role of big business in the twentieth century's onrush toward statism. We have already seen his caustic Beardian view toward the adoption of the Constitution. When the New Deal arrived, Nock could only snort in disdain at the mock wails about collectivism raised in various business circles:

> It is one of the few amusing things in our rather stodgy world that those who today are behaving most tremendously about collectivism and the Red menace are the very ones who have cajoled, bribed, flattered and bedeviled the State into taking each and every one of the successive steps that lead straight to collectivism. . . . Who hectored the State into the shipping business, and plumped for setting up the Shipping Board? Who pestered the State into setting up the Interstate Commerce Commission and the Federal Farm Board? Who got the State to go into the transportation business on our inland waterways? Who is always urging the State to "regulate" and

---

and the latter was adopted by Marx. I am indebted to Professor Leonard Liggio's researches on Comte and Dunoyer. As far as I know, the only discussion of them in English, and that inadequate, is Elie Halevy, *The Era of Tyrannies* (Garden City, N.Y.: Doubleday and Co., 1965), pp. 21–60. Gabriel Kolko's critique of Marx's theory of the State is done from a quite similar perspective. Gabriel Kolko, *The Triumph of Conservatism* (Glencoe, Ill.: The Free Press, 1963), pp. 287ff.

> "supervise" this, that, and the other routine process of financial, industrial, and commercial enterprise? Who took off his coat, rolled up his sleeves, and sweat blood hour after hour over helping the State construct the codes of the late-lamented National Recovery Act? None but the same Peter Schlemihl who is now half out of his mind about the approaching spectre of collectivism.[18]

Or, as Nock summed it up,

> The simple truth is that our businessmen do not want a government that will let business alone. They want a government they can use. Offer them one made on Spencer's model, and they would see the country blow up before they would accept it.[19]

---

[18] Albert Jay Nock, "Imposter-Terms," *Atlantic Monthly* (February 1936): 161–69.

[19] Nock to Ellen Winsor, August 22, 1938. F.W. Garrison, ed., *Letters from Albert Jay Nock* (Caldwell, Id.: Caxton Printers, 1949), p. 105.

4
The New Deal and the Emergence of the Old Right

During the 1920s, then, the emerging individualists and libertarians—the Menckens, the Nocks, the Villards, and their followers—were generally considered Men of the Left; like the Left generally, they bitterly opposed the emergence of Big Government in twentieth-century America, a government allied with Big Business in a network of special privilege, a government dictating the personal drinking habits of the citizenry and repressing civil liberties, a government that had enlisted as a junior partner to British imperialism to push around nations across the globe. The individualists were opposed to this burgeoning of State monopoly, opposed to imperialism and militarism and foreign wars, opposed to the Western-imposed Versailles Treaty and League of Nations, and they were generally allied with socialists and progressives in this opposition.

All this changed, and changed drastically, however, with the advent of the New Deal. For the individualists saw the New Deal quite clearly as merely the logical extension of Hooverism and World War I: as the imposition of a fascistic government upon the economy and society, with a Bigness far worse than Theodore Roosevelt ("Roosevelt I" in Mencken's label) or Wilson or Hoover had ever been able to achieve. The New Deal, with its burgeoning corporate state, run by Big Business and Big Unions as its junior partner, allied with corporate liberal intellectuals and using welfarist rhetoric, was perceived by these libertarians as fascism come to America. And so their astonishment and bitterness were great when they discovered that their former, and supposedly knowledgeable, allies, the socialists and progressives, instead of joining in with this insight, had rushed to embrace and even deify the New Deal, and to form its vanguard of intellectual apologists. This embrace by the Left was rapidly made unanimous when the Communist Party and its allies joined the parade with the advent of the Popular Front in 1935. And the younger generation of intellectuals, many of whom had been followers of Mencken and Villard, cast aside their individualism to join the "working class" and to take their part as Brain Trusters and planners of the seemingly new Utopia taking shape in America. The spirit of technocratic dictation over the American citizen was best expressed in the famous poem of Rex Tugwell, whose words were to be engraved in horror on all "right-wing" hearts throughout the country:

> I have gathered my tools and my charts,
> My plans are finished and practical.
> I shall roll up my sleeves—make America over.

Only the few *laissez-faire* liberals saw the direct filiation between Hoover's cartelist program and the fascistic cartelization imposed by the New Deal's NRA and AAA, and few realized that the origin of these programs was specifically such Big Business collectivist plans as the famous Swope Plan, spawned by Gerard Swope, head of General Electric in late 1931, and adopted by most big business groups in the following year. It was, in fact, when Hoover refused to go this far, denouncing the plan as "fascism" even though he had himself been tending in that direction for years, that Henry I. Harriman, head of the U.S. Chamber of Commerce, warned Hoover that Big Business would throw its weight to Roosevelt, who had agreed to enact the plan, and indeed was to carry out his agreement. Swope himself, Harriman, and their powerful mentor, the financier Bernard M. Baruch, were indeed heavily involved both in drafting and administering the NRA and AAA.[1]

---

[1]See Murray N. Rothbard, *America's Great Depression* (Princeton, N.J.: D. Van Nostrand Co., 1963), pp. 245–51.

The individualists and *laissez-faire* liberals were stunned and embittered, not just by the mass desertion of their former allies, but also by the abuse these allies now heaped upon them as "reactionaries" "fascists," and "Neanderthals." For decades Men of the Left, the individualists, without changing their position or perspectives one iota, now found themselves bitterly attacked by their erstwhile allies as benighted "extreme right-wingers." Thus, in December 1933, Nock wrote angrily to Canon Bernard Iddings Bell: "I see I am now rated as a Tory. So are you—ain't it? What an ignorant blatherskite FDR must be! We have been called many bad names, you and I, but that one takes the prize." Nock's biographer adds that "Nock thought it odd that an announced radical, anarchist, individualist, single-taxer and apostle of Spencer should be called conservative."[2]

From being the leading intellectual of his day, Mencken was rapidly discarded by his readership as reactionary and *passé*, unequipped to deal with the era of the Depression. Retiring from the *Mercury*, and thereby deprived of a national forum, Mencken could only see his creation fall into New Deal-liberal hands. Nock, once the toast of the monthlies and reviews, virtually dropped from sight. Villard succumbed to the lure of the New Deal, and at any rate he retired as editor of the *Nation* in 1933, leaving that journal too in solidly New Deal-liberal hands. Only isolated cases remained: thus John T. Flynn, a muckraking economic journalist, writing for *Harper's* and the *New Republic*, criticized the Big Business and monopolizing origins of such crucial New Deal measures as the RFC and the NRA.

Isolated and abused, treated by the New Dispensation as Men of the Right, the individualists had no alternative but to *become*, in effect, right-wingers, and to ally themselves with the conservatives, monopolists, Hooverites, etc., whom they had previously despised.

---

[2]Robert M. Crunden, *The Mind and Art of Albert Jay Nock* (Chicago: Henry Regnery, 1964), p. 172.

It was thus that the modern right wing, the "Old Right" in our terminology, came into being: in a coalition of fury and despair against the enormous acceleration of Big Government brought about by the New Deal. But the intriguing point is that, as the far larger and more respectable conservative groups took up the cudgels against the New Deal, the only rhetoric, the only ideas available for them to use were precisely the libertarian and individualist views which they had previously scorned or ignored. Hence the sudden if highly superficial accession of these conservative Republicans and Democrats to the libertarian ranks.

Thus, there were Herbert Hoover and the conservative Republicans, they who had done so much in the twenties and earlier to pave the way for New Deal corporatism, but who now balked strongly at going the whole way. Herbert Hoover himself suddenly jumped into the libertarian ranks with his anti-New Deal book of 1934, *Challenge to Liberty*, which moved the bemused and wondering Nock to exclaim: "Think of a book on such a subject, by such a man!" A prescient Nock wrote:

> Anyone who mentions liberty for the next two years will be supposed to be somehow beholden to the Republican party, just as anyone who mentioned it since 1917 was supposed to be a mouthpiece of the distillers and brewers.[3]

Such conservative Democrats as the former anti-Prohibitionists Jouett Shouse, John W. Davis, and Dupont's John J. Raskob formed the American Liberty League as an anti-New Deal organization, but this was only slightly less distasteful. While Nock wrote in his journal of his distrust at the dishonest origins of the League, he already showed willingness to consider an alliance:

> The thing may open the way occasionally for something . . . a little more intelligent and objective than the dreary run of propagandist outpouring. . . . I shall look into it . . . and if a proper chance is open, I shall lend a hand.[4]

---

[3]Albert Jay Nock, *Journal of Forgotten Days* (Hinsdale, Ill.: Henry Regnery, 1948), p. 33.

[4]Ibid., pp. 44–45.

In fact, the individualists were in a bind at this sudden accession of old enemies as allies. On the positive side, it meant a rapid acceleration of libertarian rhetoric on the part of numerous influential politicians. And, furthermore, there were no other conceivable political allies available. But, on the negative side, the acceptance of libertarian ideas by Hoover, the Liberty League, *et al.*, was clearly superficial and in the realm of general rhetoric only; given their true preferences, not one of them would have accepted the Spencerian *laissez-faire* model for America. This meant that libertarianism, as spread throughout the land, would remain on a superficial and rhetorical level, and, furthermore, would tar all libertarians, in the eyes of intellectuals, with the charge of duplicity and special pleading.

In any case, however, the individualists had no place to go but an alliance with the conservative opponents of the New Deal. And so H.L. Mencken, formerly the most hated single person in the Right Left of the 1920s, now wrote for the conservative *Liberty* magazine, and concentrated his energies on opposition to the New Deal and on agitation for the Landon ticket in the 1936 campaign. And when the young libertarian Paul Palmer assumed the editorship of the *American Mercury* in 1936, Mencken and Nock cheerfully signed on as regular columnists in opposition to the New Deal regime, with Nock as virtual coeditor. Fresh from the publication of *Our Enemy, the State*, Nock, in his first column for the new *Mercury*, very astutely pointed out that the New Deal was a continuation of the very two things that the entire Left had hated in the statism of the 1920s: Prohibition and government aid to business. It was like Prohibition because in both cases a determined minority of men "wished to do something to America for its own good," and "both relied on force to achieve their ends"; it was like the 1920s economically because

> Coolidge had done his best to use the government to help business, and Roosevelt was doing exactly the same thing. . . . In other words, most Americans wanted government to help only them; this was the "American tradition" of rugged individualism.[5]

---

[5]Crunden, *Mind and Art*, pp. 164–65.

But the attempt was hopeless; in the eyes of the bulk of the intellectuals and of the general public, Nock, Mencken, and the individualists were, simply, "conservatives," and "extreme rightists," and the label stuck. In one sense, the "conservative" label for Nock and Mencken was, and had been, correct, as it is for all individualists, in the sense that the individualist believes in human differences and therefore in inequalities. These are, to be sure, "natural" inequalities, which, in the Jeffersonian sense, would arise out of a free society as "natural aristocracies"; and these contrast sharply with the "artificial" inequalities that statist policies of caste and special privilege impose on society. But the individualist must always be antiegalitarian. Mencken had always been a frank and joyous "elitist" in this sense, and at least as strongly opposed to democratic egalitarian government as to all other forms of government. But Mencken emphasized that, as in the free market, "an aristocracy must constantly justify its existence. In other words, there must be no artificial conversion of its present strength into perpetual rights."[6] Nock came by this elitism gradually over the years, and it reached its full flowering by the late 1920s. Out of this developed position came Nock's brilliant and prophetic, though completely forgotten, *Theory of Education in the United States*,[7] which had grown out of 1931 lectures at the University of Virginia.

A champion of the older, classical education, Nock chided the typical conservative detractors of John Dewey's progressive educational innovations for missing the entire point. These conservatives attacked modern education for following Dewey's views in shifting from the classical education to a proliferating kitchen-midden of vocational and what would now be called "relevant" courses, courses in driver-education, basket-weaving, etc. Nock pointed out that the problem was not with vocational courses per se, but with the accelerating commitment in America to the concept of *mass* education. The classical education confined itself to a

---

[6]Robert R. LaMonte and H.L. Mencken, *Men versus the Man* (New York: Henry Holt and Co., 1910), p. 73.

[7]New York: Harcourt Brace, 1932.

small minority, an elite, of the youth population. And only a small minority, according to Nock, is really "educable," and thus suitable for this sort of curriculum. Spread the idea that *everyone* must have a higher education, however, bring the great mass of ineducable youth into the schools, and the schools *necessarily* have to turn to basket-weaving and driver-ed courses, to mere vocational training, instead of genuine education. Nock clearly believed, then, that the compulsory attendance laws, as well as the new great myth that everyone must graduate from high school and college, was wrecking the lives of most of the young, forcing them into jobs and occupations for which they were not suitable and which they disliked, and also wrecking the educational system in the process.

It is clear that, from an equally libertarian (though from a "right-wing" rather than a "left-wing" anarchist) perspective, Nock was anticipating a very similar position by Paul Goodman thirty and forty years later. While clothed in egalitarian rhetoric, Goodman's view equally condemns the current system, including compulsory attendance laws, for forcing a mass of kids into school when they should really be out working in purposeful and relevant jobs.

One of the most forceful aspects of the developing ideology of the Right was the focusing on the dangers of the growing tyranny of the Executive, and especially the President, at the expense of the withering of power everywhere else in society: in the Congress and in the judiciary, in the states, and among the citizenry. More and more power was being centered in the President and the Executive branch; the Congress was being reduced to a rubber stamp of Executive decrees, the states to servitors of federal largesse. Regulatory bureaus substituted their own arbitrary decrees, or "administrative law," for the normal, even-handed process of the courts. Again and again, the Liberty League and other Rightists hammered away at the enormous accession of Executive power. It was this apprehension that led to the storm, and the defeat of the administration, over the famous plan to "pack" the Supreme Court in 1937, a defeat engineered by frightened liberals who had previously gone along with all New Deal legislation.

Gabriel Kolko, in his brilliant *Triumph of Conservatism*, has pointed out the grave error in liberal and Old Left historiography of the alleged "reactionary" role of the Supreme Court in the late nineteenth and early twentieth centuries in striking down regulatory legislation. The Court has always been treated as a spokesman of Big Business interests trying to obstruct progressive measures; in truth, these judges were honest believers in *laissez-faire* who were trying to block statist measures engineered by Big Business interests. The same may one day be said of the "reactionary" Nine Old Men who struck down New Deal legislation in the 1930s.

One of the most sparkling and influential attacks on the New Deal was written in 1938 by the well-known writer and editor Garet Garrett. Garrett began his pamphlet "The Revolution Was" on a startlingly perceptive note: conservatives, he wrote, were mobilizing to try to prevent a statist revolution from being imposed by the New Deal; but this revolution had already occurred. As Garrett beautifully put it in his opening sentences:

> There are those who still think they are holding the pass against a revolution that may be coming up the road. But they are gazing in the wrong direction. The revolution is behind them. It went by in the Night of Depression, singing songs to freedom.[8]

The New Deal, Garrett charged, was a systematic "revolution within the form" of American laws and customs. The New Deal was not, as it superficially seemed to be, a contradictory and capricious mass of pragmatic error.

> In a revolutionary situation mistakes and failures are not what they seem. They are scaffolding. Error is not repealed. It is compounded by a longer law, by more decrees and regulations, by further extensions of the administrative hand. As deLawd said in *The Green Pastures*, that when you have passed a miracle you have to pass another one to take care of it, so it was with the New Deal. Every miracle it passed, whether it went right or wrong, had one result. Executive power over the social and economic life of the nation was increased.

---

[8]Garet Garrett, "The Revolution Was," in *The People's Pottage* (Caldwell, Id.: Printers, 1953), p. 15.

> Draw a curve to represent the rise of executive power and look there for mistakes. You will not find them. The curve is consistent.[9]

The New Deal and businessmen were using words in two very different senses, added Garrett, when each spoke of preserving the "American system of free private enterprise." To the businessmen these words "stand for a world that is in danger and may have to be defended." But to the New Deal they "stand for a conquered province," and the New Deal has the correct interpretation, for the "ultimate power of initiative" has passed from private enterprise to government. Led by a revolutionary elite of intellectuals, the New Deal centralized political and economic power in the Executive, and Garrett traced this process step by step. As a consequence, the "ultimate power of initiative" passed from private enterprise to government, which "became the great capitalist and enterpriser. Unconsciously business concedes the fact when it talks of a mixed economy, even accepts it as inevitable."[10]

---

[9]Ibid., pp. 16–17.
[10]Ibid., p. 72.

5

Isolationism and the Foreign New Deal

During World War I and the 1920s, "isolationism," that is, opposition to American wars and foreign intervention, was considered a Left phenomenon, and so even the *laissez-faire* isolationists and Revisionists were considered to be "leftists." Opposition to the postwar Versailles system in Europe was considered liberal or radical; "conservatives," on the other hand, were the proponents of American war and expansion and of the Versailles Treaty. In fact, Nesta Webster, the Englishwoman who served as the dean of twentieth century anti-Semitic historiography, melded opposition to the Allied war effort with socialism and communism as the prime evils of the age. Similarly, as late as the mid-1930s, to the rightist Mrs. Elizabeth Dilling pacifism was, per se, a "Red" evil. Not only were such lifelong pacifists as Kirby Page, Dorothy Detzer, and Norman Thomas considered to be "Reds"; but Mrs. Dilling similarly castigated General Smedley D. Butler, former head of the Marine Corps and considered a "fascist" by the Left, for daring to charge that Marine Corps interventions in Latin America had been a "Wall Street racket." Not only was the Nye Committee of the mid-thirties to investigate munitions makers and U.S. foreign policy in World War I, but also old progressives such as Senators Burton K. Wheeler and especially *laissez-fairist* William E. Borah were condemned as crucial parts of the pervasive Communistic "Red Network."[1]

---

[1]Elizabeth Dilling, *The Roosevelt Red Record and Its Background* (Chicago: Elizabeth Dilling, 1936).

And yet, in a few short years, the ranking of isolationism on the ideological spectrum was to undergo a sudden and dramatic shift. In the late 1930s, the Roosevelt administration moved rapidly toward war in Europe and the Far East. As it did so, and especially after war broke out in September 1939, the great bulk of the liberals and the Left "flip-flopped" drastically on behalf of war and foreign intervention. Gone without a trace was the old Left's insight into the evils of the Versailles Treaty, the Allied dismemberment of Germany, and the need for revision of the treaty. Gone was the old opposition to American militarism, and to American and British imperialism. Not only that; but to the liberals and Left the impending war against Germany and even Japan became a great moral crusade, a "people's war for democracy" and against "fascism"—outrivaling in the absurdity of their rhetoric the very Wilsonian apologia for World War I that these same liberals had repudiated for two decades. The President who was dragging the nation reluctantly into war was now lauded and almost deified by the Left, as were in retrospect all of the strong (i.e., dictatorial) Presidents throughout American history. For liberals and the Left the Pantheon of America now became, in almost endless litany, Jackson-Lincoln-Wilson-FDR.

Still worse was the attitude of these new interventionists toward those erstwhile friends and allies who continued to persist in their old beliefs; these latter were now castigated and denounced day in and day out, with extreme bitterness and venom, as "reactionaries," "fascists," "anti-Semites, and "followers of the Goebbels line."[2] Joining with great enthusiasm in this smear campaign was the Communist Party and its allies, from the "collective security" campaign of the Soviet Union in the late 1930s and again after the Nazi attack on Russia on June 22, 1941. Before and during the war the Communists were delighted to leap to their newfound role as American superpatriots, proclaiming that "Communism is twentieth-century Americanism," and that

[2]For the grisly record of the liberal flip-flop, see James J. Martin, *American Liberalism and World Politics*, 2 vols. (New York: Devin-Adair, 1964).

any campaign for social justice within America had to take a back seat to the sacred goal of victory in the war. The only exception for the Communists in this role was their "isolationist period"—which, again in subservience to the needs of the Soviet Union, lasted from the time of the Stalin-Hitler pact of August 1939 to the attack on Russia two years later.

The pressure upon the liberals and progressives who continued to oppose the coming war was unbelievably bitter and intense. Many personal tragedies resulted. Charles A. Beard, distinguished historian and most eminent of Revisionists, was castigated unmercifully by the liberals, many of them his former students and disciples. Dr. Harry Elmer Barnes, the liberal dean of World War I (and later World War II) revisionists, whose New York *World Telegram* column "The Liberal Viewpoint" had achieved the eminence of Walter Lippmann, was unceremoniously kicked out of his column in May 1940 by the pressure of pro-war advertisers.[3]

Typical of the treatment accorded to those who held fast to their principles was the purgation from the ranks of liberal journalism of John T. Flynn and Oswald Garrison Villard. In his regular column in the *Nation*, Villard had continued to oppose Roosevelt's "abominable militarism" and his drive to war. For his pains, Villard was forced out of the magazine that he had long served as a distinguished editor. In his "Valedictory" in the issue of June 22, 1940, Villard declared that "my retirement has been precipitated by the editors' abandonment of the *Nation*'s steadfast opposition to all preparations for war, for this in my judgment has been the chief glory of its great and honorable past." In a letter to the editor, Freda Kirchwey, Villard wondered how it was that

> Freda Kirchwey, a pacifist in the last war, keen to see through shams and hypocrisy, militant for the rights of minorities and

---

[3]Clyde R. Miller, "Harry Elmer Barnes' Experience in Journalism," in *Harry Elmer Barnes: Learned Crusader*, A. Goddard, ed. (Colorado Springs, Colo.: Ralph Myles, 1968), pp. 702–04.

> the downtrodden had now struck hands with all the forces of reaction against which the *Nation* had battled so strongly.

Kirchwey's editorial reply was characteristic: such writings as Villard's were frightening, and "a danger more present than Fascism," for Villard's policy was "exactly the policy for America that the Nazi propaganda in this country supports."[4]

John T. Flynn, in his turn, was booted out of his column "Other People's Money" in November 1940; the column had appeared continuously in the *New Republic* since May 1933. Again, the now pro-war editors could not tolerate Flynn's continuing attacks on war preparations and on the artificial boom induced by armament spending.

Neither did the old-time libertarian leaders fare much better. When the libertarian and isolationist Paul Palmer lost his editorship of the *American Mercury* in 1939, H.L. Mencken and Albert Jay Nock lost their monthly opportunity to lambaste the New Deal. His national outlet gone, Mencken retired from politics and into autobiography and his study of the American language. Apart from a few essays in the *Atlantic Monthly*, Nock could find an outlet only in the isolationist *Scribner's Commentator*, which folded after Pearl Harbor and left Nock with no opportunity whatever to be heard. In the meanwhile, Nock's personal disciples, who constituted the libertarian wing of the Henry George movement, were dealt a heavy blow when his outstanding disciple, Frank Chodorov, was fired as director of the Henry George School of New York for maintaining his opposition to American entry into the war.

But Nock had managed to get in a few blows before the changing of the guard at the *Mercury*. Nock had warned that the emerging war in Europe was the old story of competing imperialisms,

---

[4]Martin, *American Liberalism and World Politics*, pp. 1155–56; Michael Wreszin, *Oswald Garrison Villard* (Bloomington: Indiana University Press, 1965), pp. 259–63.

with the Liberals available, once again, to provide ideological cover with such Wilsonian slogans as "make the world safe for democracy." Nock commented scornfully that "make the world safe for U.S. investments, privileges, and markets" far better expressed the real intent of the coming intervention. Thus "after the sorry sight which American Liberals made of themselves twenty years ago," they were ready once again "to save us from the horrors of war and militarism [by] plunging us into war and militarism." Decrying the developing hysteria about the foreign Enemy, Nock pinpointed the true danger to liberty at home:

> No alien State policy will ever disturb us unless our Government puts us in the way of it. We are in no danger whatever from any government except our own, and the danger from that is very great; therefore our own Government is the one to be watched and kept on a short leash.[5]

The opponents of war were not only being shut out from liberal journals and organizations but from much of the mass media as well. As the Roosevelt administration moved inexorably toward war, much of the Establishment that had been repelled by the left-wing rhetoric of the New Deal eagerly made its peace with the government, and swiftly moved into positions of power. In Roosevelt's own famous phrase, "Dr. New Deal" had been replaced by "Dr. Win the War," and, as the armaments orders poured in, the conservative elements of Big Business were back in the fold: in particular, the Wall Street and Eastern Establishment, the bankers and industrialists, the Morgan interests, the Ivy League Entente, all happily returned to the good old days of World War I and the battle of the British Empire against Germany. The new reconciliation was typified by the return to a high government post of the prominent Wall Street lawyer Dean Acheson, now in the State Department, who had departed his post of Undersecretary of the Treasury in the early 1930s in high dudgeon at Roosevelt's

---

[5]Albert Jay Nock, "The Amazing Liberal Mind," *American Mercury* 44, no. 176 (August 1938): 467–72.

unsound monetary and fiscal schemes. Still more significant was FDR's appointment as Secretary of War in June 1940 of a man who virtually embodied the wealthy Eastern Establishment—Acheson's mentor, Henry Lewis Stimson: a conservative, pro-war and imperialist Republican Wall Street lawyer close to the Morgan interests who had been a devoted follower of Teddy Roosevelt, Secretary of War under Taft, and Secretary of State under Hoover. The fruit of the new policy was the famous "Willkie blitz" at the Republican national convention, in which the 1940 Republican nomination was virtually stolen from the antiwar favorites for the presidency, Senator Robert A. Taft and Thomas E. Dewey. A tremendous Wall Street pressure campaign, using all the devices of the Eastern-controlled media and blackmail of delegates by Wall Street bankers, swung the nomination to the unknown but safely pro-intervention big businessman, Wendell Willkie.

If the Eastern Big Business conservatives were solidly back in the Roosevelt camp on the agreed program of entering the war, why were interventionist forces successful in pinning the "extreme right-wing" label on the anti-interventionist or "isolationist" position? For two reasons. First, because the Old Left and the official organs of liberalism had been captured by the pro-war forces, who had successfully purged the liberal media of all those who continued to cling to their original principles of antiwar liberalism and leftism. The pro-war liberals were thereby able to serve as the intellectual apologists for the Roosevelt administration and the Eastern Establishment, spearheading the latter in vilifying the isolationists as "reactionaries," "Neanderthals," and tools of the Nazis. And second, not all of business had swung into line behind the war. Much of Midwestern capital, not tied to investments in Europe and Asia, was able to reflect the isolationist sentiments of the people of their region. Midwestern and small-town business were therefore the stronghold of isolationist sentiment, and the pre-war years saw a powerful struggle between the mighty Eastern and Wall Street interests tied to foreign investments and foreign markets, and Midwestern capital who had few such ties. It was no accident, for example, that the America First Committee, the leading antiwar organization, was founded by R. Douglas Stuart, then a student at Yale but a scion of the Chicago Quaker Oats fortune, or that leading supporters of the organization were General Robert E. Wood, head of Sears Roebuck of Chicago, and Colonel Robert R. McCormick, publisher of the *Chicago Tribune*. Or that the isolationist leader in the Senate, Robert A. Taft, came from the leading family of Cincinnati. But the Eastern propagandists were cunningly able to use this split to spread the image of their opposition as narrow, provincial, small-minded, reactionary Midwesterners, not attuned as they themselves were to the great, cosmopolitan affairs of Europe and Asia.

Taft (who had been denounced as a dangerous "progressive" by Mrs. Dilling only a few years before) was particularly exercised at being dismissed by the Establishment-liberal-Left alliance as an ultra-conservative. The occasion of Senator Taft's critical analysis arose from an essay published just before Pearl Harbor, by a young Arthur Schlesinger, Jr. (*Nation*, December 6, 1941). Ever ready to pin the "business" label on opposition to liberalism, Schlesinger attacked the Republican Party as reflecting a business community dragging its heels on entry into the war. Senator Taft, in a rebuttal that appeared the week after Pearl Harbor (*Nation*, December 13, 1941) sharply and keenly corrected Schlesinger's view of the true locus of "conservatism" within the Republican Party:

> Nor is Mr. Schlesinger correct in attributing the position of the majority of Republicans to their conservatism. The most conservative members of the party—the Wall Street bankers, the society group, nine-tenths of the plutocratic newspapers, and most of the party's financial contributors—are the ones who favor intervention in Europe. Mr. Schlesinger's statement that the business community in general had tended to favor appeasing Hitler is simply untrue. . . .
>
> I should say without question that it is the average man and woman—the farmer, the workman, except for a few pro-British labor leaders, and the small business man—who are opposed to the war. The war party is made up of the business community of the cities, the newspaper and magazine writers,

> the radio and movie commentators, the Communists, and the university intelligentsia.[6]

In short, in many ways the struggle was a populist one, between the mass of the populace opposed to the war and the elite groups in control of the national levers of power and of the molding of public opinion.

Thus, the drive of the New Deal toward war once again reshuffled the ideological spectrum and the meaning of Left and Right in American politics. The left and liberal opponents of war were hounded out of the media and journals of opinion by their erstwhile allies, and condemned as reactionaries and Neanderthals. These men, as well as old progressives hailed by the Left a few short years before (such as Senators Nye, LaFollette, and Wheeler) found themselves forced into a new alliance with *laissez-faire* Republicans from the Middle West. Damned everywhere as "ultra-conservatives" and "extreme Rightists," many of these allies found themselves moving "rightward" ideologically as well, moving toward the *laissez-faire* liberalism of the only mass base yet open to them. In many ways, their move rightward was a self-fulfilling prophecy by the Left. Thus, under the hammer blows of the Left-liberal Establishment, the old progressive isolationists moved *laissez-faire*-ward as well. It was under this pressure that the forging of the "old Right" was completed. And the ugly role of the Communist Party as spearhead of the smear campaign understandably turned many of these progressives not only into classical liberals but into thoroughgoing and almost fanatical anti-Communists as well. This is what happened to John T. Flynn and to John Dos Passos, what happened to some extent to Charles A. Beard, and what happened to such former sympathizers of the Soviet Union as John Chamberlain, Freda Utley, and William Henry Chamberlin. To a large extent, it was their uncomfortable "Third Camp" or isolationist position on the war that started such leading Trotskyites as Max Schachtman and James Burnham down the

---

[6]Quoted in Martin, *American Liberalism and World Politics*, p. 1278.

road to the later global anti-Communist crusade, and that led the Trotskyist-pacifist Dwight MacDonald to his bitter opposition to the Henry Wallace campaign of 1948.

The venom directed against the opponents of war by the left-liberal Establishment war coalition was almost unbelievable. Responsible publicists regularly and systematically accused the isolationists of being "fascists" and members of a "Nazi transmission belt." Walter Winchell, at the beginning of his longtime career as calumniator of all dissent against American war crusades (he was later a fervent supporter of Joe McCarthy and always, early and late, a devoted fan of the FBI), led in denouncing the opponents of war. While Communist leader William Z. Foster denounced isolationist leaders General Wood and Colonel Charles A. Lindbergh as "conscious Fascists," interventionist publicist Dorothy Thompson accused the America First Committee of being "Vichy Fascists," and Secretary of the Interior Harold C. Ickes, the bully-boy of the Roosevelt administration, denounced Wood and Lindbergh as "Nazi fellow travelers," and pinned the same label on his old friend Oswald Garrison Villard. And *Time* and *Life*, whose publisher Henry Luce was an ardent supporter not only of our entry into the war but also of the "American Century" which he envisioned as emerging after the war, stooped so low as to claim that Lindbergh's and Senator Wheeler's salutes to the American flag were similar to the fascist salute. An organization that became almost a professional vilifier of the isolationists was the left-liberal Rev. Leon M. Birkhead's Friends of Democracy, which denounced the America First Committee as a "Nazi front! It is a transmission belt by means of which the apostles of Nazism are spreading their antidemocratic ideas into millions of American homes!"[7]

The oppression of the isolationists was not confined to vilification or loss of employment. In numerous cities, such as Miami, Atlanta, Oklahoma City, Portland, Oregon, Pittsburgh, and

[7]See Wayne S. Cole, *America First* (Madison: University of Wisconsin Press, 1953), pp. 107–10.

Philadelphia, the America First Committee found it difficult or impossible to obtain halls for public meetings. Another tactic that was used systematically before, during, and immediately after the war was private espionage against the Old Right by interventionist groups. These agents employed deception, abused confidences, stole documents, and then published sensationalistic findings. Sometimes these agents acted as agents provocateurs. The most famous use of private secret agents was that of the Friends of Democracy, who sent Avedis Derounian into the isolationist groups under the name of "John Roy Carlson"; Carlson's report on his adventures was published as the bestselling *Under Cover* by Dutton in 1943. Carlson's book lumped isolationists, anti-Semites, and actual pro-Nazis together, in a potpourri of guilt by association, as constituting the "Nazi underworld of America." *Under Cover* was dedicated to the "official under cover men and women who, unnamed and unsung, are fighting the common enemy of Democracy on the military front abroad and the psychological front at home," and the book opened with a quotation from Walt Whitman:

> Thunder on! Stride on, Democracy!
> Strike with vengeful stroke!

Carlson and his cohorts were certainly being avid in pursuing Whitman's injunction.

So virulent was the smear campaign that at the end of the war John T. Flynn was moved to write an anguished pamphlet in protest called *The Smear Terror*. It was typical of the time that, while Carlson's farrago was a bestseller that received sober and favorable appraisal in the pages of the *New York Times*, Flynn's rebuttal could emerge only as a privately printed pamphlet, unknown except to what would now be called an "underground" of dedicated right-wing readers.

One of the most common accusations against the isolationists was the charge of anti-Semitism. While the ranks of the Old Right included some genuine anti-Semites, the pro-war propagandists were hardly scrupulous or interested in making subtle distinctions;

all of the isolationists were simply lumped together as anti-Semitic, despite the fact that the America First Committee, for example, included a great many Jews on its staff and research bureau. The situation was complicated by the fact that the vast bulk of American Jewry was undoubtedly in favor of American entry into the war, and virtually deified Franklin Roosevelt for entering the war, as they thought, to "save the Jews."[8]

Influential Jews and Jewish organizations helped agitate for war, and helped also to put economic pressure upon opponents of the war. This very fact of course served to embitter many isolationists against the Jews, and again create a kind of self-fulfilling prophecy; this resentment was intensified by the hysterical treatment accorded to any isolationist who dared to so much as mention these activities by Jews. In early 1942, the *Saturday Evening Post* printed an article critical of Jews by the liberal pacifist Quaker Milton Mayer, an act that was used by the Establishment to fire the conservative and isolationist editor Wesley N. Stout and his entire editorial staff (which included Garet Garrett) and replace them with conservative interventionists.

The most famous case of flak on phony charges of anti-Semitism stemmed from the celebrated speech of Charles A. Lindbergh at Des Moines on September 11, 1941. The most popular and charismatic of all opponents of the war and a man who was essentially nonpolitical, Lindbergh had been subjected to particular abuse by the Interventionist forces. The son of a progressive Congressman from Minnesota who had staunchly opposed entry into World War I, Lindbergh particularly angered the war forces not only for his charisma and popularity but also because of his obvious sincerity and his all-out position against any aid to Britain and France whatever. While most of the isolationists temporized, favoring some aid to Britain and worrying about a possible German attack on the U.S., Lindbergh clearly and consistently advocated

---

[8]In fact, Roosevelt's devotion to saving the Jews was minimal, as can be seen from such recent "revisionist" books on the subject as Arthur D. Morse, *While Six Million Died* (New York: Random House, 1968).

absolute neutrality and hoped for a negotiated peace in Europe. The matter was made still more piquant because Lindbergh was in a way a "traitor to his class," since his wife, Anne Morrow, also a distinguished opponent of the war, was the daughter of a leading Morgan partner and virtually the only member of her family and circle not enthusiastic about the war.

After many months of unremitting abuse (e.g., the ultrainterventionist playwright Robert E. Sherwood had flatly called Lindbergh a "Nazi" in the august pages of the *New York Times*), Lindbergh calmly mentioned the specific forces that were driving the United States toward war. It is obvious from his memoirs that poor, naive, honest Charles Lindbergh had no idea of the hysteria that would be unleashed when he pointed out that

> the three most important groups who have been pressing this country toward war are the British, the Jewish, and the Roosevelt administration. Behind these groups, but of lesser importance, are a number of capitalists, Anglophiles, and intellectuals who believe that their future, and the future of mankind, depends upon the domination of the British Empire.

Neither did it help Lindbergh that he added,

> It is not difficult to understand why Jewish people desire the overthrow of Nazi Germany. The persecution they suffered in Germany would be sufficient to make bitter enemies of any race. No person with a sense of the dignity of mankind can condone the persecution the Jewish race suffered in Germany.[9]

The abuse of Lindbergh was a veritable torrent now, with the White House press secretary comparing the speech to Nazi propaganda, while the *New Republic* called upon the National Association of Broadcasters to censor all of Lindbergh's future speeches.

---

[9]Quoted in Wayne S. Cole, *America First: The Battle Against Intervention, 1940–1941* (Madison: University of Wisconsin Press, 1953), p. 144).

Frightened General Robert E. Wood, head of America First, almost dissolved the organization on the spot.[10]

Calumny, social obloquy, private espionage—these were not all the hardships faced by the isolationist "Old Right." As soon as the war began, the Roosevelt administration turned to the secular arm to smash any remnants of isolationist dissent. In addition to routine FBI harassment, such isolationists as Laura Ingalls, George Sylvester Viereck, and Ralph Townsend were indicted and convicted for being German and Japanese agents respectively. William Dudley Pelley, along with 27 other isolationists, was tried and convicted in Indianapolis of "sedition" under the Espionage Act of 1917. The infamous Smith Act of 1940 was used, first to convict 18 Minneapolis Trotskyists of conspiracy to advocate overthrow of the government (to the great glee of the Communist Party), and then to move, in the mass sedition trial of 1944, against an ill-assorted collection of 26 right-wing isolationist pamphleteers with

---

[10]Lindbergh's puzzled reaction to criticisms of his speech by more politically minded isolationists was characteristic. Thus:

> John Flynn . . . says he does not question the truth of what I said at Des Moines, but feels it was inadvisable to mention the Jewish problem. It is difficult for me to understand Flynn's attitude. He feels as strongly as I do that the Jews are among the major influences pushing this country toward war. . . . He is perfectly willing to talk about it among a small group of people in private. But apparently he would rather see us get into the war than mention in public what the Jews are doing, no matter how tolerantly and moderately it is done.

Also his conversation with Herbert Hoover:

> Hoover told me he felt my Des Moines speech was a mistake. . . . I told him I felt my statements had been both moderate and true. He replied that when you had been in politics long enough you learned not to say things just because they are true. (But after all, I am not a politician—and that is one of the reasons why I don't wish to be one.) (Charles A. Lindbergh, *The Wartime Journals of Charles A. Lindbergh* [New York: Harcourt Brace Jovanovich, 1970], pp. 541, and 546–47)

the charge of contriving to cause insubordination in the armed forces. The prosecution of those who were universally described in the press as the "indicted seditionists" was pursued with great zeal by the Communist Party and its allies, the Old Left generally, and such Establishment hacks as Walter Winchell. To the chagrin of the Left and Center, the trial fizzled as a result of the spirited legal defense, especially the defense led by the brilliant defendant Lawrence Dennis, a leading isolationist intellectual who has generally, and with little foundation, been called the "leading American fascist." The death of presiding Judge Eicher—a signal for the Left to charge that he had been "murdered" by the persistent defense—provided the opportunity for the government to drop the case, despite the insistence of the Left that the persecution be resumed.[11]

All in all, the Old Right was understandably gloomy as it contemplated the inevitable approach of war. It foresaw that World War II would transform America into a Leviathan State, into a domestic totalitarian collectivism, with suppression of civil liberties at home, joined to an unending global imperialism abroad,

---

[11]An excellent and detailed account of the mass sedition trial can be found in the totally neglected book, Maximilian St. George and Lawrence Dennis, *A Trial on Trial* (National Civil Rights Committee, 1946). St. George and Dennis were astute enough to see the irony in the fact that "many of the defendants, being fanatical anti-Communists," had openly supported the Smith Act of 1940 under which they were to be indicted. "The moral," St. George and the "fascist" Dennis added,

> is one of the major points of this book: laws intended to get one crowd may well be used by them to get the authors and backers of the law. This is just another good argument for civil liberties and freedom of speech. (Ibid., p. 83)

One particularly striking parallel of this mass sedition trial with the Chicago conspiracy trial a generation later was that Justice Eicher, notably hostile to the defense, had Henry H. Klein, a lawyer for one of the defendants who had withdrawn from the case, hauled back to the court and jailed for withdrawing from the case without the judge's permission. Ibid., p. 404.

pursuing what Charles A. Beard called a policy of "perpetual war for perpetual peace." None of the Old Right saw this vision of the coming America more perceptively than John T. Flynn, in his brilliant work *As We Go Marching*, written in the midst of the war he had done so much to forestall. After surveying the polity and the economy of fascism and National Socialism, Flynn bluntly saw the New Deal, culminating in the wartime society, as the American version of fascism, the "good fascism" in sardonic contrast to the "bad fascism" we had supposedly gone to war to eradicate. Flynn saw that the New Deal had finally established the corporate state that big business had been yearning for since the end of the nineteenth century. The New Deal planners, declared Flynn,

> were thinking of a change in our form of society in which the government would insert itself into the structure of business, not merely as policeman, but as a partner, collaborator, and banker. But the general idea was first to reorder the society by making it a planned and coerced economy instead of a free one, in which business would be brought together into great guilds or an immense corporative structure, combining the elements of self-rule and government supervision with a national economic policing system to enforce these decrees. . . . This, after all, is not so very far from what business had been talking about. . . . It was willing to accept the supervision of the government. . . . Business said that orderly self-government in business would eliminate most of the causes that infected the organism with the germs of crises.[12]

The first great attempt of the New Deal to create such a society was embodied in the NRA and AAA, modeled on the fascist corporate state, and described by Flynn as "two of the mightiest engines of minute and comprehensive regimentation ever invented in any organized society." These engines were hailed by those supposedly against regimentation: "Labor unions and Chamber of Commerce officials, stockbrokers and bankers, merchants and

---

[12]John T. Flynn, *As We Go Marching* (Garden City, N.Y.: Doubleday, Doran and Co., 1944), pp. 193–94.

their customers joined in great parades in all the cities of the country in rhapsodical approval of the program."[13] After the failure of the NRA, the advent of World War II re-established this collectivist program, "an economy supported by great streams of debt and an economy under complete control, with nearly all of the planning agencies functioning with almost totalitarian power under a vast bureaucracy."[14] After the war, Flynn prophesied, the New Deal would attempt to expand this system to international affairs.

Foreseeing that the federal government would maintain vast spending and controls after the war was over, Flynn predicted that the great emphasis of this spending would be military, since this is the one form of government spending to which conservatives will never object, and which workers will welcome for its creation of jobs. "Thus militarism is the one great glamorous public-works project upon which a variety of elements in the community can be brought into agreement."[15] Hence, as part of this perpetual garrison state, conscription would also be continued on a permanent basis. Flynn declared:

> All sorts of people are for it. Numerous senators and representatives—of the Right and Left—have expressed their purpose to establish universal military training when the war ends.
>
> The great and glamorous industry is here—the industry of militarism. And when the war is ended the country is going to be asked if it seriously wishes to demobilize an industry that can employ so many men, create so much national income when the nation is faced with the probability of vast unemployment in industry. All the well-known arguments, used so long and so successfully in Europe . . . will be dusted off—America with her high purposes of world regeneration must have the power to back up her magnificent ideals; America cannot afford to grow soft, and the Army and Navy must be continued on a vast scale to toughen the moral and

[13]Ibid., p. 198.
[14]Ibid., p. 201.
[15]Ibid., p. 207.

> physical sinews of our youth; America dare not live in a world of gangsters and aggressors without keeping her full power mustered . . . and above and below and all around these sentiments will be the sinister allurement of the perpetuation of the great industry which can never know a depression because it will have but one customer—the American government to whose pocket there is no bottom.[16]

Flynn unerringly predicted that imperialism would follow in militarism's wake:

> Embarked . . . upon a career of militarism, we shall, like every other country, have to find the means when the war ends of obtaining the consent of the people to the burdens that go along with the blessings it confers upon its favored groups and regions. Powerful resistance to it will always be active, and the effective means of combating this resistance will have to be found. Inevitably, having surrendered to militarism as an economic device, we will do what other countries have done: we will keep alive the fears of our people of the aggressive ambitions of other countries and we will ourselves embark upon imperialistic enterprises of our own.[17]

Flynn noted that interventionism and imperialism had come to be called "internationalism," so that anyone who opposes imperialism "is scornfully called an isolationist." Flynn went on:

> Imperialism is an institution under which one nation asserts the right to seize the land or at least to control the government or resources of another people. It is an assertion of stark, bold aggression. It is, of course, international in the sense that the aggressor nation crosses its own borders and enters the boundaries of another nation. . . . It is international in the sense that war is international. . . . This is internationalism in a sense, in that all the activities of an aggressor are on the international stage. But it is a malignant internationalism.[18]

---

[16]Ibid., p. 212.
[17]Ibid., pp. 212–13.
[18]Ibid., p. 213.

Flynn then pointed out that countries such as Great Britain, having engaged in "extensive imperialist aggression" in the past, now try to use the hopes for world peace in order to preserve the status quo.

> This status quo is the result of aggression, is a continuing assertion of aggression, an assertion of malignant internationalism. Now they appeal to this other benevolent type of internationalism to establish a world order in which they, all leagued together, will preserve a world which they have divided among themselves. . . . Benevolent internationalism is taken over by the aggressors as the mask behind which the malignant internationalism will be perpetuated and protected. . . . I do not see how any thoughtful person watching the movement of affairs in America can doubt that we are moving in the direction of both imperialism and internationalism.[19]

Imperialism, according to Flynn, will ensure the existence of perpetual "enemies":

> We have managed to acquire bases all over the world. . . . There is no part of the world where trouble can break out where we do not have bases of some sort in which, if we wish to use the pretension, we cannot claim that our interests are menaced. Thus menaced there must remain when the war is over a continuing argument in the hands of the imperialists for a vast naval establishment and a huge army ready to attack anywhere or to resist an attack from all the enemies we shall be obliged to have. Because always the most powerful argument for a huge army maintained for economic reasons is that we have enemies. We must have enemies.[20]

A planned economy; militarism; imperialism—for Flynn what all this added up to was something very close to fascism. He warned:

---

[19]Ibid., p. 214.
[20]Ibid., pp. 225–26.

> The test of fascism is not one's rage against the Italian and German war lords. The test is—how many of the essential principles of fascism do you accept. . . . When you can put your finger on the men or the groups that urge for America the debt-supported state, the autarchial corporative state, the state bent on the socialization of investment and the bureaucratic government of industry and society, the establishment of the institution of militarism as the great glamorous public-works project of the nation and the institution of imperialism under which it proposes to regulate and rule the world and, along with this, proposes to alter the forms of government to approach as closely as possible the unrestrained, absolute government—then you will know you have located the authentic fascist.
>
> Fascism will come at the hands of perfectly authentic Americans . . . who are convinced that the present economic system is washed up . . . and who wish to commit this country to the rule of the bureaucratic state; interfering in the affairs of the states and cities; taking part in the management of industry and finance and agriculture; assuming the role of great national banker and investor, borrowing billions every year and spending them on all sorts of projects through which such a government can paralyze opposition and command public support; marshaling great armies and navies at crushing costs to support the industry of war and preparation for war which will become our greatest industry; and adding to all this the most romantic adventures in global planning, regeneration, and domination all to be done under the authority of a powerfully centralized government in which the executive will hold in effect all the powers with Congress reduced to the role of a debating society. There is your fascist. And the sooner America realizes this dreadful fact the sooner it will arm itself to make an end of American fascism masquerading under the guise of the champion of democracy.[21]

[21]Ibid., pp. 252–53.

Finally, Flynn warned that while the Communist Party was an enthusiastic supporter of his new dispensation, it would be a mistake to call the new order "communism"; it will rather be "a very genteel and dainty and pleasant form of fascism which can not be called fascism at all because it will be so virtuous and polite." In his concluding sentence, Flynn eloquently proclaimed that

> my only purpose is to sound a warning against the dark road upon which we have set our feet as we go marching to the salvation of the world and along which every step we now take leads us farther and farther from the things we want and the things that we cherish.[22]

---

[22]Ibid., pp. 255, 258.

6
World War II: The Nadir

The advent of World War II brought the Old Right to its darkest days. Harassed, reviled, persecuted, the intellectuals and agitators of the Old Right, the libertarians and the isolationists, folded their tents and disappeared from view. While it is true that the isolationist Republicans experienced a resurgence in the 1942 elections, they were no longer supported by an ideological vanguard. The America First Committee quickly dissolved after Pearl Harbor and went to war—despite the pleas of the bulk of its militants to continue being a focus of opposition to the nation's course. Charles Lindbergh totally abandoned the ideological and political arena and joined the war effort.

Among the intellectuals, there was, amidst the monolith of wartime propaganda, no room or hearing for libertarian or antiwar views. The veteran leaders of libertarianism were deprived of a voice. H.L. Mencken had retired from politics to write his charming and nostalgic autobiography. Albert Jay Nock found all the journals and magazines closed to his pen. Nock's leading disciple, Frank Chodorov, had been ousted from his post as head of the Henry George School of New York for his opposition to the war. Oswald Garrison Villard was virtually shut out of the magazines and was forced to confine himself to letters to his friends; in one of them he prophesied bitterly that "when you and I have passed off the scene the country will be called upon by some cheap poor white like Harry Truman to save the world from bolshevism and preserve the Christian religion." For the Old Right these were gloomy times indeed, and Villard was ready to select his epitaph:

He grew old in an age he condemned
Felt the dissolving throes
Of a Social order he loved
And like the Theban seer
Died in his enemies' day.[1]

For the Old Left, in contrast, World War II was a glorious age, the fulfillment and the promise of a New Dawn. Everywhere, in the United States and in western Europe, the liberal ideals of central planning, of a new planned order staffed by Brain Trusters and liberal intellectuals, seemed to be the wave of the future as well as the present. In the colleges and among the opinion molders, any conservative views seemed as dead and outmoded as the dodo, confined to the dustbin of history. And no one was more pleased at this burgeoning New Deal collectivism than the Communist Party. Its new Popular Front line of the late 1930s, a line that had replaced its old harsh revolutionary views, seemed more than vindicated by the glorious New Order a-borning. In foreign affairs, the United States was marching hand in hand with the Soviet Union in a glorious war to defeat fascism and expand democracy. Domestically, the Communists, under Earl Browder as their leader, exulted in their newfound respectability; the Browderite line of arriving at socialism through ever greater and more centralizing New Deal reforms seemed to be working in glorious fashion. The Communists trumpeted that "Communism was Twentieth-century Americanism," and they were in the forefront of the new patriotism—and of a super-identification with the American Leviathan, foreign and domestic. Communists played an exhilarating, if subordinate, role in the war effort, in planning war production, in giving orientation lectures in the armed forces, and in calling for persecution

[1]Michael Wreszin, *Oswald Garrison Villard* (Bloomington: Indiana University Press, 1965), p. 271.

of all possible opponents of the war. Earl Browder even seemed to find a willing ear at the White House. In their role as leaders in the CIO the Communists sternly put down any attempt at strikes or civil rights agitation that might deflect any energy from the glorious war. Indeed, so heady were the Communists' dreams that they took the lead in advocating a permanent no-strike pledge even after the war. As Earl Browder put it:

> [W]e frankly declare that we are ready to cooperate in making capitalism work effectively in the postwar period. . . . We Communists are opposed to permitting an explosion of class conflict in our country when the war ends . . . we are now extending the perspective of national unity for many years into the future.[2]

An eloquent cry against this wartime atmosphere arose, in a brilliant anti-New Deal novel published after the war by John Dos Passos, a lifelong radical and individualist who had been pushed from "extreme Left" to "extreme Right" by the march of war and corporate statism in America. Dos Passos wrote:

> At home we organized bloodbanks and civilian defense and imitated the rest of the world by setting up concentration camps (only we called them relocation centers) and stuffing into them American citizens of Japanese ancestry (Pearl Harbor the date that will live in infamy) without benefit of habeas corpus. . . .
>
> The President of the United States talked the sincere democrat and so did the members of Congress. In the Administration there were devout believers in civil liberty. "Now we're busy fighting a war; we'll deploy all four freedoms later on," they said. . . .
>
> War is a time of Caesars.
>
> The President of the United States was a man of great personal courage and supreme confidence in his powers of persuasion. He never spared himself a moment, flew to Brazil

[2]Art Preis, *Labor's Giant Step* (New York: Pioneer Publishers, 1964), p. 221.

> and Casablanca, Cairo to negotiate at the level of the leaders; at Teheran the triumvirate without asking anybody's leave got to meddling with history; without consulting their constituents, revamped geography, divided up the bloody globe and left the freedoms out.
>
> And the American People were supposed to say thank you for the century of the Common Man turned over for relocation behind barbed wire so help him God.
>
> We learned. There were things we learned to do but we have not learned, in spite of the Constitution and the Declaration of Independence and the great debates at Richmond and Philadelphia, how to put power over the lives of men into the hands of one man and to make him use it wisely.[3]

It was in this stifling political and ideological atmosphere that I grew to political consciousness. Economically, I had been a conservative since the eighth grade, and exclusive contact with liberals and leftists in high school and college only served to sharpen and intensify this commitment. During World War II, I was an undergraduate at Columbia University, and it seemed to my developing conservative and libertarian spirit that there was no hope and no ideological allies anywhere in the country. At Columbia, in New York generally, and in the intellectual press there was only the Center-Left monolith trumpeting the New Order. Opinion on campus ranged from Social Democratic liberals to Communists and their allies, and there seemed to be little to choose between them. Apart from the fraternity boys and the jocks who may have been instinctively conservative but had no interest in politics or ideology, I seemed to be totally alone. It was rumored that there was, indeed, one other "Republican" on campus; but he was an English major interested solely in literary matters, and so we never came into contact. All around me, the Lib-Left was echoing the same horror: "We *are* the government, so why are you so negative about government action?" "We must *learn* from Hitler, learn about planning

---

[3]John Dos Passos, *The Grand Design* (Boston: Houghton Mifflin, 1949), pp. 416–18.

the economy." And my uncle, a long-time member of the Communist Party, condescendingly told my conservative father that he would be safe in the postwar world, "provided that he kept quiet about politics." The New Order indeed seemed close at hand.

But just when the days were darkest, and just when despair seemed the order of the day for opponents of statism and despotism, individuals and little groups were stirring, unbeknownst to me or anyone else, deep in the catacombs, thinking and writing to keep alive the feeble flame of liberty. The veteran libertarians found themselves forced to find an obscure home among conservative publicists of the "extreme Right." The aging Albert Jay Nock, now in his 70s, found a home at the National Economic Council of the veteran right-wing isolationist Merwin K. Hart; in the spring of 1943, several wealthy friends induced Hart to set up a monthly *Economic Council Review of Books*, which Nock wrote and edited for the duration of the war. Frank Chodorov, ousted from the Henry George School, eked out a precarious living by founding a superbly written, one-man monthly broadsheet *analysis* in 1944, published from a dingy loft in lower Manhattan. There, Chodorov began to apply and expand the Nockian analysis of the State, and worked on a theoretical economic complement to Nock's historical *Our Enemy, the State*, a work which Chodorov issued in bound mimeographed form shortly after the end of the war.[4] John T. Flynn found a home with the long-standing right-wing outfit, the Committee for Constitutional Government, and its offshoot, America's Future, Inc. The veteran publicist Garet Garrett, ousted in the shakeup at the *Saturday Evening Post*, was able to found an obscure one-man quarterly, *American Affairs*, issued as a minor part of the operations of the statistical organization of American business, the National Industrial Conference Board. In the Los Angeles area, Leonard E. Read, general manager of the Los Angeles Chamber of Commerce, was converted to the *laissez-faire* libertarian creed by William C. Mullendore, head of

---

[4]Frank Chodorov, *The Economics of Society, Government, and State* (New York: Analysis Associates, 1946).

the Commonwealth Edison Company, while Raymond Cyrus Hoiles, anarcho-capitalist publisher of the daily *Santa Ana Register* (and later to be publisher of a string of "Freedom Newspapers"), reprinted the works of the nineteenth-century libertarian French economist Frédéric Bastiat. And, on the Left, former Trotskyist turned anarcho-pacifist Dwight Macdonald founded his virtually one-man monthly *Politics*, which tirelessly lambasted the war and its attendant statism.

What was destined to be the longest-lasting "right-wing" journalistic venture launched during the war was the Washington weekly *Human Events*, founded in 1944 as a four-page newsletter with a periodically appended four-page article of analysis. *Human Events* was founded by three veteran isolationists and conservative libertarians: Frank Hanighen, coauthor of the most famous antimilitarist muckraking book of the 1930s, *The Merchants of Death*; Felix Morley, distinguished writer and former president of the Quaker Haverford College; and Chicago businessman Henry Regnery.

But undoubtedly most important for the postwar resurgence of libertarianism were several books published during the war, books that were largely ignored and forgotten at the time, but which helped build a groundwork for a postwar renaissance. Three of the books, all published in 1943, were written by singularly independent, tough-minded, and individualistic women. Screenwriter Ayn Rand produced the novel *The Fountainhead*, a paean to individualism that had been turned down by a host of publishers and finally published by Bobbs-Merrill. Largely ignored at the time, *The Fountainhead* became a steady, "underground" bestseller over the years, spreading largely by word of mouth among its readers. (The novel had been turned down by publishers on the grounds that its theme was too "controversial," its content too intellectual, and its tough-minded hero too unsympathetic to have commercial possibilities.[5])

---

[5]See the worshipful biographical sketch by Barbara Branden in Nathaniel Branden, *Who Is Ayn Rand?* (New York: Paperback Library, 1964), pp. 158ff.

From semi-isolation in her home in Danbury, Connecticut, Rose Wilder Lane, who had been a Communist Party member in the 1920s, published *The Discovery of Freedom*,[6] an eloquent, singing prose-poem in celebration of the history of freedom and free-market capitalism.

The third important wartime libertarian book by a woman was written by Isabel Paterson, who had made her mark as an author of several flapper-type novels in the 1920s and who had been a long-time regular columnist for the New York *Herald-Tribune Review of Books*. Her nonfiction *The God of the Machine* was an eccentric but important event in libertarian thought. The book was a series of essays, some turgid and marked by the intrusive use of electrical engineering analogies in social affairs; but these essays were marked by flashes of brilliant insight and analysis. Particularly important were her chapters on the State promotion of monopoly after the Civil War, her demonstration of the impossibility of "public" ownership, and her defense of the gold standard. The two chapters with the greatest impact among libertarians were "The Humanitarian with the Guillotine," a brilliant critique of do-gooding and its consequence, the welfarist ethic; and "Our Japanized Educational System," in which Mrs. Paterson delivered a blistering philosophical critique of progressive education, a critique that was to help ignite the reaction against progressivism in the post-war era. Thus, Mrs. Paterson eloquently explained the interconnection of welfarism, parasitism, and coercion as follows:

> What can one human being actually do for another? He can give from his own funds and his own time whatever he can spare. But he cannot bestow faculties which nature has denied nor give away his own subsistence without becoming dependent himself. If he earns what he gives away, he must earn it *first*. . . . But supposing he has no means of his own, and still imagines that he can make "helping others" at once his *primary* purpose and the normal way of life, which is the central doctrine of the humanitarian creed, how is he to go about it? . . .

---

[6](New York: John Day, 1943).

> If the primary objective of the philanthropist, his justification for living, is to help others, his ultimate good *requires that others shall be in want.* His happiness is the obverse of their misery. If he wishes to help "Humanity," the whole of humanity must be in need. The humanitarian wishes to be a prime mover in the lives of others. He cannot admit either the divine or the natural order, by which men have the power to help themselves. The humanitarian puts himself in the place of God.
>
> But he is confronted by two awkward facts; first, that the competent do not need his assistance; and second, that the majority of people . . . positively do not want to be "done good" by the humanitarian. . . . Of course what the humanitarian actually proposes is that *he* shall do what he thinks is good for everybody. It is at this point that the humanitarian sets up the guillotine.
>
> What kind of world does the humanitarian contemplate as affording him full scope? It could only be a world filled with breadlines and hospitals, in which nobody retained the natural power of a human being to help himself or to resist having things done to him. And that is precisely the world that the humanitarian arranges when he gets his way. . . . There is only one way, and that is by the use of the political power in its fullest extension. Hence the humanitarian feels the utmost gratification when he visits or hears of a country in which everyone is restricted to ration cards. Where subsistence is doled out, the desideratum has been achieved, of general want and a superior power to "relieve" it. The humanitarian in theory is the terrorist in action.[7]

Equally important, and equally obscure at the time, was the publication of Albert Nock's last great work, his intellectual autobiography, *Memoirs of a Superfluous Man.*[8] In the *Memoirs* Nock expanded and wove together the themes of his previous books on history, theory, culture, and the State, and throughout all was an intensified pessimism about the prospects for a widespread adoption of

---

[7]Isabel Paterson, *The God of the Machine* (New York: G.P. Putnam's Sons, 1943), pp. 240–42.

[8](New York: Harper and Bros., 1943).

libertarianism that was all too understandable for the times in which he wrote. Gresham's Law—the bad driving out the good—worked inevitably, he felt, in the field of culture and ideas as it did in the field of coinage and money. As we marched into the new barbarism, nature would have to take its course.[9]

Meanwhile, in the field of economics, it seemed that the Keynesians and the economic planners were sweeping all before them. The most distinguished of *laissez-faire* economists, Ludwig von Mises, who had been in the front rank of the economic world on the Continent during the teens and twenties, had been largely forgotten in the wake of the "Keynesian Revolution" of the late 1930s. And this neglect came even though Mises had won fame among English-speaking economists during the early 1930s, precisely on the basis of his business-cycle theory that attributed the Great Depression to government intervention. A refugee from the Nazis, Mises had published a giant *laissez-faire* treatise on economics in Geneva in 1940, a book which got lost amidst the twin storms of the march toward collectivism in economic thought and the holocaust of World War II. Emigrating to New York in 1940, Mises, devoid of an academic post, managed to write and publish two books during the war. Both were highly important works which, again, made little or no dent in the academic world. Mises's brief *Bureaucracy*[10] is still one of the best treatments of the nature of bureaucracy, and of the inherent sharp divergence between profit-seeking management and nonprofit, or bureaucratic, management. Mises's *Omnipotent Government*[11] won some academic recognition as the most important statement of the anti-Marxian position that the essence of Nazi Germany was not the reflection of big business but was a variant of socialism and collectivism. (At

[9]For the reception of the *Memoirs*, see Robert M. Crunden, *The Mind and Art of Albert Jay Nock* (Chicago: Henry Regnery, 1964), pp. 189–91; for Nock's appreciative views of the books of Lane and Paterson, see *Selected Letters of Albert Jay Nock*, F.J. Nock, ed. (Caldwell, Id.: Caxton Printers, 1962), pp. 145–51.

[10](New Haven, Conn.: Yale University Press, 1944).

[11](New Haven, Conn.: Yale University Press, 1944).

Columbia, in those days, *Omnipotent Government* was being read as the antipode to Franz Neumann's very popular Marxian work on Nazism, *Behemoth*.)

But the wartime libertarian work that was destined to have by far the greatest immediate impact was not that of Mises, but of his most prominent Austrian free-market follower, Friedrich A. Hayek. Hayek had emigrated to England in the early 1930s, to teach at the London School of Economics, and there had considerable impact on younger economists as well as achieving prominence in English intellectual circles, and among such distinguished emigré philosophers in England as Karl Popper and Michael Polanyi. It was perhaps this prominence in England that helps to account for the smashing popular and academic success of Hayek's *The Road to Serfdom*.[12] For it was certainly not Hayek's style, heavily Germanic rather than sparkling, and far less readable than Mises, who had pursued a similar theme. Perhaps intellectuals, surfeited with years of pro-statist and pro-planning propaganda, were ripe for a statement of the other side of the coin.

Whatever the reason, *The Road to Serfdom* hit the intellectual circles of the United States and Britain like a blockbuster. Its major thesis was that socialism and central planning were incompatible with freedom, the rule of law, or democracy. The Nazi and Fascist regimes were considered one aspect of this modern collectivism, and Hayek tellingly outlined the great similarities between the statist planning of the Weimar Republic and the later economic program of Hitler. The highly touted social democracy of the Weimar Republic was but fascism in embryo.[13]

---

[12](University of Chicago Press, 1944).

[13]It is intriguing that Hayek's analysis of social democracy as totalitarianism and fascism in embryo was very similar, though of course with very different rhetoric, to the critique of the English Marxist R. Palme Dutt in the radical days before the advent of the Popular Front line, of course. Cf. R. Palme Dutt, *Fascism and Social Revolution* (New York: International Publishers, 1934).

The Road to Serfdom made its impact on all levels of opinion. The Hearst papers serialized the book, hailing its attack on socialism. It became mandatory in virtually every college course, as the case for the "other side" (although, in fact, it was scarcely consistent in its *laissez-faire* views). English intellectuals were so perturbed that two attempted refutations of Hayek by social democrats were rushed into print: Hermann Finer's vituperative *Road to Reaction* and Barbara Wootton's *Plan or No Plan* (to which Mises would retort that free-market economists favored each man's planning for *himself*). And Hayek's work had incalculable effect in converting or helping to convert many socialist intellectuals to the individualist, capitalist ranks. John Chamberlain, one of the leading Left writers and critics of the 1930s and author of the noted *Farewell to Reform*, found his conversion to conservative-individualism greatly accelerated by the book, and Chamberlain contributed the preface to *The Road to Serfdom*. F.A. Harper, a free-market professor of agricultural economics at Cornell, found his dedication to libertarian views redoubled. And Frank S. Meyer, one of the leading theoreticians of the Communist Party, member of its national committee and head of its Workers' School in Chicago, found disturbingly convincing Hayek's portrayal of the incompatibility of socialism and freedom. It is an ironic and fascinating footnote to the ideological history of our time that *The Road to Serfdom* had one of its most sympathetic reviews in the *Communist New Masses*—a review that constituted one of Frank Meyer's last contributions to the Communist movement. And surely these were but a few instances of the vital impact of Hayek's work.

But this impact, and indeed the quieter ripples made by the other libertarian works during the war, was visible only as a success of the day. There did not *seem* to be any lasting result, any sort of movement to emerge out of the black days on which the libertarian creed had fallen. On the surface, as the war came to an end, there seemed to be as little hope as ever for the individualist, free-market cause as there had been during the war.

7
The Postwar Renaissance I: Libertarianism

For a while the postwar ideological climate seemed to be the same as during the war: internationalism, statism, adulation of economic planning and the centralized state, were rampant everywhere. During the first postwar year, 1945–46, I entered Columbia Graduate School, where the intellectual atmosphere was oppressively just more of the same. By early 1946 the veterans had come back from the war, and the atmosphere on campus was rife with the heady plans and illusions of various wings of the Old Left. Most of the veterans had joined the newly formed American Veterans Committee (AVC), a group confined to World War II vets with the high hope of replacing the old and reactionary American Legion and Veterans of Foreign Wars. During these years, the AVC on campus was split between the Social Democrats on the right and the Communists and their allies on the left, and these factions set the parameters of political debate on campus.

It was in this stifling atmosphere that I first became aware that I was not totally alone; that there was such a thing as a libertarian "movement," however small and embryonic. A young economics professor from Brown University began to teach at Columbia in the fall of 1946: George J. Stigler, later to become a distinguished member of the free-market "Chicago School" of economics. Tall, witty, self-assured, Stigler strode in to a huge class in price theory, and proceeded to confound the assorted leftists by devoting his first two lectures to an attack on rent control, and to a refutation of minimum wage laws. As Stigler left the classroom, he would be surrounded by moving circles of amazed and bewildered students, arguing with his point of view that seemed to them to be deposited all of a sudden from the Neanderthal Age. I was of course delighted; here at last was a free-market viewpoint of intellectual substance, and not simply couched in the lurid and confused tones of the Hearst Press! Professor Stigler referred us to a pamphlet (now long out of print, and *still* one of the few studies of rent control) jointly written by himself and another young free-market economist, Milton Friedman, "Roofs or Ceilings?" and published by an outfit called the Foundation for Economic Education (FEE), in Irvington-on-Hudson, New York. Stigler explained that he and Friedman had published the pamphlet with this obscure outfit because "nobody else would publish it." Enchanted, I wrote away for the pamphlet, and for information about the organization; and by that act I had unwittingly "entered" the libertarian movement.

FEE had been founded during 1946 by Leonard E. Read, who for many years was its president, ruler, line-setter, fundraiser, and guiding light. In those years and for many years thereafter, FEE served as the major focus and the open center for libertarian activity in the United States. Not only has virtually every prominent libertarian in the country of middle age or over served at one time or another on its staff; but by its activities FEE served as the first beacon light for attracting innumerable young libertarians into the movement. Its earliest staff was focused around a group of free-market agricultural economists led by Dr. F.A. ("Baldy") Harper, who had come down from Cornell, and who had already written an antistatist pamphlet, "The Crisis of the Free Market," for the National Industrial Conference Board, for whom Leonard Read had worked after leaving the Los Angeles Chamber of Commerce. Among the young economists coming to FEE from Cornell with Harper were Doctors Paul Poirot, William Marshall Curtiss, Ivan Bierly, and Ellis Lamborn. Coming to FEE from Los Angeles along with Read was Dr. V. Orval Watts, who had been the economist for the Los Angeles Chamber.

One of the important but unsung figures in the early postwar libertarian movement was Loren ("Red") Miller, who had been active in municipal reform movements in Detroit and elsewhere.

In Kansas City, Miller joined with William Volker, head of the William Volker Company, a leading wholesale furniture specialty distributing house for the Western states, in battling against the corrupt Pendergast machine. The charismatic Miller was apparently instrumental in converting many municipal reformers throughout the country to *laissez-faire*; these included Volker and his nephew and heir Harold W. Luhnow.[1]

Luhnow, now head of the Volker Company and his uncle's William Volker Charities Fund, had been an active isolationist before the war. Now he became an active supporter of FEE, and was particularly eager to advance the almost totally neglected cause of libertarian scholarship. Another Red Miller convert was the young administrative genius Herbert C. Cornuelle, who for a short while was executive vice president of FEE. After the death of Volker in 1947, Luhnow began to change the orientation of the Volker Fund from conventional Kansas City charities to promoting libertarian and *laissez-faire* scholarship. He began valiant efforts in the later 1940s to obtain prestigious academic posts for the leaders of the Austrian School of economics, Ludwig von Mises and F.A. Hayek. The best he could do for Mises, who had been languishing in New York, was to find him a post as "Visiting Professor" at New York University Graduate School of Business. Mises also became a part-time staff member at FEE. Luhnow was more successful with Hayek, arranging for a professorship at the newly established graduate Committee on Social Thought at the University of Chicago—after the economics department at Chicago had rejected a similar arrangement. In both cases, however, the university refused to pay any salary to these eminent scholars. For the rest of their careers in American academia, the salaries of both Mises and Hayek were paid for by the William Volker Fund. (After the Fund collapsed in 1962, the task of financing Mises's post at NYU was taken up by Read and a consortium of businessmen.)

---

[1]On William Volker, see Herbert C. Cornuelle, *"Mr. Anonymous": The Story of William Volker* (Caldwell, Id.: Caxton Printers, 1951).

After a couple of years of acting alone at the Volker Fund, Harold Luhnow decided to expand the activity of the Fund in stimulating conservative and libertarian scholarship, and Herb Cornuelle went from FEE to the Volker Fund as its first liaison officer.

After a brief flurry in political agitation against rent control, Read decided to keep FEE as a purely educational organization. For its first decade, FEE published pamphlets by staff members and others, many of which were collected in a book-form series, *Essays on Liberty*; but probably more important was its role as an open center for the movement, in its sponsoring of seminars, meetings, and soirees, and in its hospitality to visiting and budding libertarians. It was at and through FEE that I met or discovered all the previously "underground" channels of libertarian thought and expression: the books published during the war, the Nockians (Nock himself had died in the summer of 1945), and the continuing activities of John T. Flynn and Rose Wilder Lane (who had succeeded Nock as editor of the *Economic Council Review of Books*), and *Human Events*.

It was in the midst of this new and exhilarating milieu that I emerged from my previous rather vague "Chamber of Commerce conservatism" and became a hard-nosed and "doctrinaire" *laissez-faire* libertarian, believing that no man and no government had the right to aggress against another man's person or property. It was also in this period that I became an "isolationist." During the years when I was becoming ever more "conservative" economically, I had done little or no independent thinking on foreign affairs; I was literally content to take my foreign policy thinking from the editorials of the good grey *New York Times*. It now became clear to me, however, that "isolationism" in foreign affairs was but the foreign counterpart of strictly limited government within each nation's borders.

One of the most important influences upon me was Baldy Harper, whose quiet and gentle hospitality toward young newcomers attracted many of us to the pure libertarian creed that he espoused and exemplified—a creed all the more effective for his stressing the philosophical aspects of liberty even more than the narrowly economic. Another was Frank Chodorov, whom I met at FEE, and thereby discovered his superb broadsheet *analysis*. More than any single force, Frank Chodorov—that noble, courageous, candid, and spontaneous giant of a man who compromised not one iota in his eloquent denunciations of our enemy the State—was my entree to uncompromising libertarianism.

The first time I came across Frank's work was a true—and infinitely exhilarating—culture shock. I was at the Columbia University bookstore one day in 1947, when, amidst a raft of the usual Stalinist, Trotskyist, etc. leaflets, one pamphlet was emblazoned in red letters with its title: "Taxation Is Robbery," by Frank Chodorov.[2] This was it. Once seeing those shining and irrefutable words, my ideological outlook could never be the same again. What else, indeed, was taxation if not an act of theft? And it became clear to me that there was no way whatever of defining taxation that was not also applicable to the tribute exacted by a robber gang.

Chodorov began his pamphlet by stating that there were only two basic alternative moral positions on the State and taxation. The first holds that "political institutions stem from 'the nature of man,' thus enjoying vicarious divinity," or that the State is "the keystone of social integrations." Adherents of this position have no difficulty in favoring taxation. People in the second group "hold to the primacy of the individual, whose very existence is his claim to inalienable rights"; they believe that "in the compulsory collection of dues and charges the state is merely exercising power, without regard to morals." Chodorov unhesitatingly placed himself in this second group:

> If we assume that the individual has an indisputable right to life, we must concede that he has a similar right to the enjoyment of the products of his labor. This we call a property

[2]Frank Chodorov, *Taxation Is Robbery* (Chicago: Human Events Associates, 1947), reprinted in Chodorov, *Out of Step* (New York: Devin-Adair, 1962).

> right. The absolute right to property follows from the original right to life because one without the other is meaningless; the means to life must be identified with life itself. If the state has a prior right to the products of one's labor, his right to existence is qualified . . . no such prior rights can be established, except by declaring the state the author of all rights. . . . We object to the taking of our property by organized society just as we do when a single unit of society commits the act. In the latter case we unhesitatingly call the act robbery, a *malum in se*. It is not the law which in the first instance defines robbery, it is an ethical principle, and this the law may violate but not supersede. If by the necessity of living we acquiesce to the force of law, if by long custom we lose sight of the immorality, has the principle been obliterated? Robbery is robbery, and no amount of words can make it anything else.[3]

The idea that taxes are simply a payment for social services rendered received only scorn from Chodorov:

> Taxation for social services hints at an equitable trade. It suggests a *quid pro quo*, a relationship of justice. But the essential condition of trade, that it be carried on willingly, is absent from taxation; its very use of compulsion removes taxation from the field of commerce and puts it squarely into the field of politics. Taxes cannot be compared to dues paid to a voluntary organization for such services as one expects from membership, because the choice of withdrawal does not exist. In refusing to trade one may deny oneself a profit, but the only alternative to paying taxes is jail. The suggestion of equity in taxation is spurious. If we get anything for the taxes we pay it is not because we want it; it is forced on us.[4]

On the "ability to pay" principle of taxation, Chodorov acidly noted: "What is it but the highwayman's rule of taking where the

---

[3]Chodorov, *Out of Step*, p. 217.

[4]Ibid., pp. 228–29.

taking is best?" He concluded trenchantly: "There cannot be a good tax or a just one; every tax rests its case on compulsion.[5]

Or take another headline that screamed at me from Chodorov's *analysis*: DON'T BUY BONDS! In an age in which government savings bonds were being universally sold as a badge of patriotism, this too came as a shock. In the article, Chodorov concentrated on the basic immorality, not simply the fiscal shakiness of the federal tax-and-bond paying process.

It is typical of Frank Chodorov that his consistency, his very presence exposed the far more numerous "free-enterprise" groups for the time-servers or even charlatans that they tended to be. While other conservative groups called for a lessening of the tax burden, Chodorov called for its abolition; while others warned of the increasing burden of the public debt, Chodorov alone—and magnificently—called for its *repudiation* as the only moral course. For if the public debt is burdensome and immoral, then outright repudiation is the best and most moral way of getting rid of it. If the bondholders, as seemed clear, were living coercively off the taxpayer, then this legalized expropriation would have to be ended as quickly as possible. Repudiation, Chodorov wrote, "can have a salutary effect on the economy of the country, since the lessening of the tax burden leaves the citizenry more to do with. The market place becomes to that extent healthier and more vigorous." Furthermore, "Repudiation commends itself also because it weakens faith in the State. Until the act is forgotten by subsequent generations, the State's promises find few believers; its credit is shattered."[6]

As for the argument that buying bonds is the public's patriotic expression of support for fighting a war, Chodorov retorted that the true patriot would give, not lend, money to the war effort.

As a disciple of Albert Jay Nock and thus an uncompromising and consistent opponent of State power and privilege, Frank

---

[5]Ibid., pp. 237, 239.

[6]Ibid., p. 2.

Chodorov was keenly aware of the gulf between himself and the run-of-the-mill free-enterprise and antisocialist groups. He pinpointed the difference brilliantly in his "Socialism by Default":

> The cause of private property has been championed by men who had no interest in it; their main concern has always been with the institution of privilege which has grown up alongside private property. They start by defining private property as anything that can be got by law; hence, they put their cunning to the control of the lawmaking machinery, so that the emerging laws enable them to profit at the expense of producers. They talk about the benefits of competition and work toward monopolistic practices. They extol individual initiative and support legal limitations on individuals who might challenge their ascendancy. In short, they are for the State, the enemy of private property, because they profit by its schemes. Their only objection to the State is its inclination to invade their privileged position or to extend privileges to other groups.[7]

Specifically, Chodorov pointed out that if the "free-enterprise" groups sincerely favored freedom, they would call for the abolition of: tariffs, import quotas, government manipulation of money, subsidies to railroads, airlines and shippers, and farm price supports. The only subsidies which these groups will attack, he added, are those "which cannot be capitalized" into the value of corporate stocks, such as handouts to veterans or the unemployed. Neither do they oppose taxation; for one thing, government bondholders cannot attack the income tax, and for another, the liquor interests oppose the abolition of taxes on stills because then "every farmer could open a distillery." And, above all,

> militarism is undoubtedly the greatest waste of all, besides being the greatest threat to the freedom of the individual, and yet it is rather condoned than opposed by those whose hearts bleed for freedom, according to their literature.[8]

---

[7]Frank Chodorov, *One Is a Crowd* (New York: Devin-Adair, 1952), pp. 93–94.

[8]Ibid., p. 95.

It was largely through Chodorov and *analysis* that I discovered Nock, Garrett, Mencken, and the other giants of libertarian thought. In fact, it was Chodorov who gave this young and eager author his first chance to break into print—apart from letters to the press—in a delighted review of H.L. Mencken's *Chrestomathy* in the August 1949 issue of *analysis*. It was also my first discovery of Mencken, and I was dazzled permanently by his brilliant style and wit; and I spent many months devouring as much of H.L.M. as I could get my hands on. And as a result of my article, I began to review books for Chodorov for some months to come.

The winter of 1949–50, in fact, witnessed the two most exciting and shattering intellectual events of my life: my discovery of "Austrian" economics, and my conversion to individualist anarchism. I had gone through Columbia College and to Columbia's graduate school in economics, passing my Ph.D. orals in the spring of 1948, and not once had I heard of Austrian economics, except as something that had been integrated into the main body of economics by Alfred Marshall sixty years before. But I discovered at FEE that Ludwig von Mises, whom I had heard of only as contending that socialism could not calculate economically, was teaching a continuing open seminar at New York University. I began to sit in on the seminar weekly, and the group became a kind of informal meeting ground for free-market-oriented people in New York City. I had also heard that Mises had written a book covering "everything" in economics, and when his *Human Action* was published that fall it came as a genuine revelation. While I had always enjoyed economics, I had never been able to find a comfortable home in economic theory: I tended to agree with institutionalist critiques of Keynesians and mathematicians, but also with the latters' critiques of the institutionalists. No positive system seemed to make sense or to hang together. But in Mises's *Human Action* I found economics as a superb architectonic, a mighty edifice with each building block related to and integrated with every other. Upon reading it, I became a dedicated "Austrian" and Misesian, and I read as much Austrian economics as I could find.

While I was an economist and had now found a home in Austrian theory, my basic motivation for being a libertarian had never been economic but moral. It is all too true that the disease of most economists is to think solely in terms of a phantom "efficiency," and to believe that they can then make political pronouncements as pure value-free social technicians, divorced from ethics and the moral realm. While I was convinced that the free market was more efficient and would bring about a far more prosperous world than statism, my major concern was moral: the insight that coercion and aggression of one man over another was criminal and iniquitous, and must be combated and abolished.

My conversion to anarchism was a simple exercise in logic. I had engaged continually in friendly arguments about *laissez-faire* with liberal friends from graduate school. While condemning taxation, I had still felt that taxation was required for the provision of police and judicial protection and for that only. One night two friends and I had one of our usual lengthy discussions, seemingly unprofitable; but this time when they'd left, I felt that for once something vital had actually been said. As I thought back on the discussion, I realized that my friends, as liberals, had posed the following challenge to my *laissez-faire* position:

> *They*: What is the legitimate basis for your *laissez-faire* government, for this political entity confined solely to defending person and property?
>
> *I*: Well, the people get together and decide to establish such a government.
>
> *They*: But if "the people" can do that, why can't they do exactly the same thing and get together to choose a government that will build steel plants, dams, etc.?

I realized in a flash that their logic was impeccable, that *laissez-faire* was logically untenable, and that either I had to become a liberal, or move onward into anarchism. I became an anarchist. Furthermore, I saw the total incompatibility of the insights of Oppenheimer and Nock on the nature of the State as conquest, with the vague "social contract" basis that I had been postulating for a *laissez-faire* government. I saw that the only *genuine* contract had to be an individual's specifically disposing of or using his own property.

Naturally, the anarchism I had adopted was individualist and free-market, a logical extension of *laissez-faire*, and not the woolly communalism that marked most of contemporary anarchist thought. On top of Mencken and Austrian economics, I now began to devour all the individualist anarchist literature I could dig up—fortunately as a New Yorker I was close to two of the best anarchist collections in the country, at Columbia and the New York Public Library. I raced through the sources not simply for scholarly interest but also to help me define my own ideological position. I was enchanted particularly with Benjamin R. Tucker's *Liberty*, the great individualist anarchist magazine published for nearly three decades in the latter part of the nineteenth century. I was particularly delighted by Tucker's incisive logic, his clear and lucid style, and his ruthless dissection of numerous "deviations" from his particular line. And Lysander Spooner, the anarchist constitutional lawyer and associate of Tucker, enchanted me by his brilliant insight into the nature of the State, his devotion to morality and justice, and his couching of anarchistic invective in a delightful legal style.

Spooner's *Letter to Grover Cleveland* I discovered to be one of the greatest demolitions of statism ever written.[9] And for my own personal development, I found the following passage in Spooner's *No Treason* decisive in confirming and permanently fixing my hatred of the State. I was convinced that no one could read these beautifully clear lines on the nature of the State and remain unshaken:

> The fact is that the government, like a highwayman, says to a man: "Your money, or your life." And many, if not most, taxes are paid under the compulsion of that threat.

---

[9]Lysander Spooner, *A Letter to Grover Cleveland, On His False Inaugural Address, the Usurpations and Crimes of Lawmakers and Judges, and the Consequent Poverty, Ignorance and Servitude of the People* (Boston: Benjamin R. Tucker, 1886).

> The government does not, indeed, waylay a man in a lonely place, spring upon him from the roadside and, holding a pistol to his head, proceed to rifle his pockets. But the robbery is none the less a robbery on that account, and it is far more dastardly and shameful.
>
> The highwayman takes solely upon himself the responsibility, danger, and crime of his own act. He does not pretend that he has any rightful claim to your money, or that he intends to use it for your own benefit. He does not pretend to be anything but a robber. He has not acquired impudence enough to profess to be merely a "protector," and that he takes men's money against their will, merely to enable him to "protect" those infatuated travelers, who feel perfectly able to protect themselves, or do not appreciate his peculiar system of protection. He is too sensible a man to make such professions as these. Furthermore, having taken your money, he leaves you as you wish him to do. He does not persist in following you on the road, against your will; assuming to be your rightful "sovereign," on account of the "protection" he affords you. He does not keep "protecting" you by commanding you to bow down and serve him; by requiring you to do this, and forbidding you to do that; by robbing you of more money as often as he finds it for his interest or pleasure to do so; and by branding you as a rebel, a traitor, and an enemy to your country, and shooting you down without mercy, if you dispute his authority, or resist his demands. He is too much of a gentleman to be guilty of such impostures, and villainies as these. In short, he does not, in addition to robbing you, attempt to make you either his dupe or his slave.[10]

Anarchism, in fact, was in the air in our little movement in those days. My friend and fellow Mises-student, Richard Cornuelle, younger brother of Herb, was my first, and willing, convert. Anarchist ferment was also brewing at no less a place than FEE. Ellis Lamborn, one of the staff members, was openly referring to himself as an "anarchist," and Dick smilingly reported from

[10]Lysander Spooner, *No Treason* (Larkspur, Colo.: Pine Tree Press, 1966), p. 17.

his own stay at FEE that he was "having increasing difficulty in coping with the anarchist's arguments." Dick also delightedly reported that, amidst a lengthy discussion about what name to call this newly found pure-libertarian creed—"libertarian," "voluntaryist," "individualist," "true liberal," etc.—this pioneering staff member cut in, with his Midwestern twang: "Hell, 'anarchist' is good enough for me." Another leading staff member, F.A. Harper, on one of my visits to Irvington, softly pulled a copy of Tolstoy's *The Law of Love and the Law of Violence* from under his desk, and thereby introduced me to the absolute pacifist variant of anarchism. Indeed, it was rumored that almost the entire staff of FEE had become anarchists by this time, with the exception of Mr. Read himself—and that even he was teetering on the brink. The closest Read ever came publicly to the brink was in his pamphlet "Students of Liberty," written in 1950. After expounding on the necessity of keeping the violence of government strictly limited to defense of person and property, Read confessed that even these proposed limits left him with two telling questions to which he had not been able to find satisfactory answers. First, "can violence be instituted, regardless of how official or how limited in intention, without begetting violence outside officialdom and beyond the prescribed limitation?" And second,

> Is not limitation of government, except for relatively short periods, impossible? Will not the predatory instincts of some men, which government is designed to suppress, eventually appear in the agents selected to do the suppressing? These instincts, perhaps, are inseparable companions of power. . . . If there be criminals among us, what is to keep them from gaining and using the power of government?[11]

It is scarcely a coincidence, in fact, that the Tolstoyan influence, the contrasting of the "law of love" with the "law of violence" that

[11]Leonard E. Read, *Students of Liberty* (Irvington-on-Hudson, N.Y.: Foundation for Economic Education, 1950), p. 14.

constitutes government, appears as a leitmotif throughout the essay.[12]

The libertarian idyll at FEE came abruptly to an end in 1954, with the publication of Leonard Read's booklet *Government—An Ideal Concept.* The book sent shockwaves reverberating through libertarian circles, for with this work Read moved decisively back into the pro-government camp. Read had abandoned the leadership of the anarcho-capitalist camp, which could have been his for the asking, in order to take up the cudgels for the Old Order.

Before the publication of this book, not one of the numerous essays from FEE had ever said a single word in praise of government; all of their thrust had been in opposition to illegitimate government action. While anarchism had never been explicitly advocated, all of FEE's material had been *consistent* with an anarchist ideal, because FEE had never positively advocated government or declared that it was a noble ideal. But now that tradition had been liquidated.

Numerous letters and lengthy manuscripts poured into FEE in protest from anarchist friends across the country. But Read was unheeding;[13] among the anarchists, the cry went up that Leonard

---

[12]Read's "On That Day Began Lies," written around the same period, begins explicitly with a quotation from Tolstoy and is written as a Tolstoyan critique of organizations that repress or violate the consciences of individual members. See "On That Day Began Lies," *Essays on Liberty* (Irvington-on-Hudson, N.Y.: Foundation for Economic Education, 1952), vol. 1, pp. 231–52.

[13]One of the protesting manuscripts circulating among libertarians at the time was written by Mr. Mercer Parks. Parks wrote,

> To defend the use of coercion to collect any reluctant taxes by contending that government "is merely performing its proper role of defending its members" . . . is evasively inconsistent with the published beliefs of FEE staff members. So, coercion is no longer coercion, says this essay. But coercion is always coercion if it uses force to make one do something unwillingly. No matter whether the tax is equitable or inequitable, if it is taken from an unwilling person through force or threats of

had literally "sold out," and gossip had it that a major factor in Leonard's backsliding was an objective and thorough report on FEE by an organization that studied and summed up institutes and foundations for potential business contributors. The outfit had cogently called FEE a "Tory anarchist" or "right-wing anarchist" organization, and the rumor was that Leonard was reacting in fear of the effect of the "anarchist" label on the tender sensibilities of FEE's wealthy contributors.

FEE's publication of Read's book also had a long-lasting impact on the productivity and scholarship at FEE. For until this point, one of the working rules had been that nothing got published under FEE's imprint except with the unanimous consent of the staff—thus insuring that the Tolstoyan concern for individual conscience would be preserved as opposed to its suppression and misrepresentation by any social organization. But here, despite heavy and virtually unanimous staff opposition, Read had highhandedly broken this social compact and had gone ahead and published his praise of government under FEE's imprimatur. It was this attitude that launched a slow, but long and steady decline of FEE as a center of libertarian productivity and research, as well as an exodus from FEE of all its best talents, led by F.A. Harper. Read had pledged to Harper at the start of FEE in 1946 that the organization would become an institute or think-tank of advanced libertarian study. These hopes had now gone a-glimmering, though Read was later to deny his failure by serenely calling FEE a designed "high school of liberty."

The winter of 1949–50 was indeed a momentous one for me, and not only because I was converted to anarchism and Austrian

---

> force by government, no matter if it be only one cent, it is secured by the use of coercion. (Mercer H. Parks, "In Support of Limited Government" [unpublished ms., March 5, 1955])

A sad commentary on the size and influence of the anarcho-capitalists at the time is the fact that such critiques as Parks's could not be published for lack of any sort of outlet, outside of FEE, for the publication of libertarian writings.

economics. My adoption of Austrianism and my attendance at Mises's seminar were to determine the course of my career for many years to come. Herb Cornuelle, now of the William Volker Fund, suggested in the fall of 1949 that I write a college textbook boiling down Mises's *Human Action* into a form suitable for students. Since Mises didn't know of me at the time, he suggested that I write a sample chapter; I did a chapter on money during the winter, and Mises's approval led the Volker Fund to give me a multi-year grant for an Austrian textbook—a project which eventually snowballed into a large-scale treatise on Austrian economics, *Man, Economy, and State*, on which I began to work in early 1952. Thus began my association with the William Volker Fund, which continued for a decade, and included consulting work for the fund as a reviewer and analyst of books, journals, and manuscripts.

Indeed as FEE slipped from its high promise of productivity and scholarship, the Volker Fund began to take up the slack. Herb Cornuelle soon left the Fund to launch a brilliant career in top industrial management—a gain to industry but a great loss to the libertarian movement. His place at Volker (which by now had moved from Kansas City to Burlingame, California) was taken by his younger brother Dick, and soon other liaison officers were added, as the unique Volker Fund concept took shape. This concept involved not only the subsidizing of conservative and libertarian scholarship—conferences, fellowships, book distributions to libraries, and eventually direct book publishing—but also the granting of funds to individual scholars rather than the usual foundation technique of granting funds *en masse* to Establishment-type organizations and universities (such as the Social Science Research Council). Granting funds to individuals meant that the Volker Fund had to have a liaison staff far larger than funds many times its comparatively modest size (approximately $17 million).

And so the Volker Fund eventually added Kenneth S. Templeton, Jr., a young historian teaching at Kent School, Connecticut; F.A. Harper, one of the exodus from FEE; Dr. Ivan R. Bierly, a doctoral student of Harper's at Cornell and later at FEE; and H. George Resch, a recent graduate of Lawrence College and a specialist in World War II revisionism. Working within a framework of old Mr. Volker's injunction for anonymous philanthropy, the Volker Fund never courted or received much publicity, but its contributions were vital in promoting and bringing together a large body of libertarian, revisionist, and conservative scholarship. In the field of revisionism, the Fund played a role in financing Harry Elmer Barnes's mammoth project for a series of books on the revisionism of World War II.

By the early 1950s, all this libertarian activity forced mainstream opinion to sit up and take notice. In particular, in 1948 Herb Cornuelle and the William Volker Fund had helped Spiritual Mobilization, a right-wing Los Angeles-based organization headed by the Reverend James W. Fifield, to establish a monthly magazine, *Faith and Freedom*. Cornuelle installed William Johnson, a libertarian who had been his assistant in the Navy, as editor of the new magazine. Chodorov, who merged his *analysis* into *Human Events* in March 1951 and moved to Washington to become an associate editor of the latter publication, began to write a regular column for *Faith and Freedom*, "Along Pennsylvania Avenue."

In 1953, the first mainstream recognition of the new libertarian movement appeared, in the form of a vituperative "brown-baiting" book by a young Methodist minister denouncing "extremists" in the Protestant churches. The book, Ralph Lord Roy's *Apostles of Discord: A Study of Organized Bigotry and Disruption on the Fringes of Protestantism*,[14] had been a thesis written under the high priest of Left-liberalism at Union Theological Seminary in New York, Dr. John C. Bennett. This work was part of a popular genre of the time that might be termed "extremist-baiting," in which the self-evidently proper and correct "vital center" is defended against extremists of all sorts, but most particularly right-wingers. Thus, Roy, devoting one perfunctory chapter to attacking pro-Communist Protestants, spent the rest of the book on various kinds of right-wingers, whom he divided into two baleful groups: Apostles of Hate, and Apostles of Discord. In the slightly less menacing

---

[14](Boston: Beacon Press, 1953).

Ministry of Discord (along with pro-Communists and various rightists) was, in chapter 12, "God and the 'Libertarians,'" placed for some reason in quotation marks. But, quotation marks or not, under attack or not, we had at least gained general attention, and I suppose we should have been grateful to be placed in the Discord rather than the Hate category.

Roy denounced the intellectual "façade" of Spiritual Mobilization and its *Faith and Freedom*, as well as FEE, Nock, and Chodorov. His treatment was fairly accurate, although the Volker Fund managed to elude his notice; however, his inclusion of FEE under Protestantism was highly strained, based only on the fact that Leonard Read was a member of Spiritual Mobilization's advisory committee. Also attacked in the Roy chapter was *Christian Economics* (*CE*), a bimonthly free-market tabloid edited by the veteran Howard E. Kershner, who had set up the Christian Freedom Foundation and begun publishing the *CE* in 1950. Kershner had been a deputy to Herbert Hoover's food relief program after World War I, and a long-time friend of his fellow Quaker. Working as columnist in *CE*'s New York office was long-time economic journalist Percy L. Greaves, Jr., who was becoming a faithful follower of Ludwig von Mises in Mises's seminar. Before coming to New York to join *CE* in 1950, Percy had been a leading staffer of the Republican National Committee in Washington, and was the minority counsel to Senator Brewster of Maine, and the Pearl Harbor Congressional investigating committee. This experience made Percy one of the outstanding Pearl Harbor revisionists in the country. Percy was a rare example of someone with both political experience and interest in economic scholarship. While still in Washington in 1950, he thought seriously of running for U.S. Senate from Maryland in the Republican primary. Since that turned out to be the year in which the seemingly impregnable Senator Millard E. Tydings lost to the unknown John Marshall Butler because of Joe McCarthy's battle against him, Percy could well have become Senator that year instead of Butler. As a result, and because of his general demeanor, our group in the Mises seminar affectionately referred to Percy as "the Senator."

One gratifying aspect of our rise to some prominence is that, for the first time in my memory, we, "our side," had captured a crucial word from the enemy. Other words, such as "liberal," had been originally identified with *laissez-faire* libertarians, but had been captured by left-wing statists, forcing us in the 1940s to call ourselves rather feebly "true" or "classical" liberals.[15] "Libertarians," in contrast, had long been simply a polite word for left-wing anarchists, that is for anti-private property anarchists, either of the communist or syndicalist variety. But now we had taken it over, and more properly from the view of etymology; since we were proponents of individual liberty and therefore of the individual's right to his property.

Some libertarians, such as Frank Chodorov, continued to prefer the word "individualist." Indeed, what Frank thought of as his major legacy to the cause, was his founding of an educational Intercollegiate Society of Individualists. Frank devoted a special October 1950 issue of *analysis* to "A Fifty-Year Project" to take back intellectual life from the predominant statism in America. Chodorov attributed the "transmutation of the American character from individualist to collectivist" to such turn of the twentieth century organizations as the Intercollegiate Socialist Society; what was needed was an antipode to educate and take back college youth, the future of the country. Chodorov reworked his approach in "For Our Children's Children" to a wider audience in the September 6, 1950 issue of *Human Events*. As a result the Intercollegiate Society of Individualists was founded in 1953, with the aid of a $1,000 donation from J. Howard Pew of Sun Oil, in those days the leading contributor to Old Right causes, and with the help of the mailing list of FEE. After the first year in *Human Events*'

[15]Another word captured by statists was "monopoly." From the seventeenth through the nineteenth centuries, "monopoly" meant simply a grant of exclusive privilege by the State to produce or sell a product. By the end of the nineteenth century, however, the word had been transformed into virtually its opposite, coming to mean instead the achievement of a price on the free market that was in some sense "too high."

offices, Chodorov moved the headquarters of ISI to the Foundation for Economic Education, when he left *Human Events* in the summer of 1954 to take up his duties as editor of a new monthly magazine, *The Freeman*, published by FEE.

8

The Postwar Renaissance II: Politics and Foreign Policy

In the realm of direct politics, it seemed clear that there was only one place for those of us not totally disillusioned with political action: the "extreme right wing" of the Republican Party. It was the extreme right, particularly well represented in the House, and including such men as Rep. Howard H. Buffett of Omaha, Rep. Ralph W. Gwinn of New York, Frederick C. Smith of Ohio, and H.R. Gross of Iowa (virtually the only one of the group now remaining), who were solidly isolationist and opposed to foreign wars and interventions, and roughly free-market and libertarian in domestic affairs. They were, for example, staunchly opposed to conscription, which was put through by a coalition of liberals and what used to be called "enlightened" conservatives and internationalists. The extreme right also included Colonel McCormick's *Chicago Tribune*, to which I delightedly subscribed for a while, and which continued excellent anti-Wall Street and anti-interventionist muckraking, as well as continuing articles in behalf of national liberation of the Welsh and the Scots from McCormick's hated England. Senator Taft was the major political figure of that wing of the party, but the confusion—then and since—came from Taft's philosophical devotion to compromise as a good in itself. As a result, Taft was always compromising and "selling out" the individualist cause: the free market at home and nonintervention abroad. In the parlance of that time, then, Taft was really on the "extreme left" of the extreme right wing of the Republicans, and his surrenders of principle were constantly thrown at us by the liberals: "Why, even Senator Taft favors" federal aid to education, or defense of Chiang, or whatever.

At any rate, I quickly identified myself with the right-wing Republicans as soon as I became politically active at the end of World War II. I joined the Young Republican Club of New York, where I wrote a campaign report in 1946 attacking the Office of Price Administration (OPA) and price controls, and took the *laissez-faire* side in a series of internal debates on the future of the Republican Party. It was a lone minority position, especially among the YR's, who were largely opportunistic lawyers looking for place and patronage within the Dewey machine. (Bill Rusher, who later became publisher of *National Review*, was in those days a regular Dewey Republican with the YR's.) However, my enthusiasm was unbounded when the Republicans, largely conservative, swept Congress in 1946. At last, socialism and internationalism would be rolled back. One of my first published writings was a "Hallelujah" letter that I sent to the New York *World-Telegram* celebrating the glorious victory. However, an evil worm soon appeared in the apple; true to his compromising nature, Bob Taft turned over the leadership of foreign policy in the Senate to the renegade isolationist Arthur Vandenberg, now a hero of the *New York Times*-Eastern Establishment circuit. (The bitter rumor on the Right was that Vandenberg had literally been seduced into changing his foreign policy stance by an English mistress.) It was Vandenberg, overriding the fervent opposition of the isolationist right wing of the party, who mobilized support for the launching of the Cold War, the loan to Britain, the Marshall Plan, and aid to Greece and Turkey, to take over the old British imperial role and crush the Greek revolution.

Another severe blow to the Old Right cause in the Republican Party was the nomination of Tom Dewey for the presidency in 1948, Dewey now being a representative of the Eastern Wall Street internationalist, statist, "leftish" Establishment. Dewey refused to defend the conservative record of the 80th Congress against Harry Truman's sneers at being "do-nothings" (actually, they had done far too much). I could not support Dewey for President, and was the only Northerner at Columbia to join the short-lived Students for Thurmond Club, basing my support on Strom Thurmond's decentralist, states' rights program. Taft and the Taftites were isolationist, and therefore far more anti-interventionist and hence anti-imperialist than Henry Wallace in the 1948 campaign. The proof of this pudding is that Wallace himself and the bulk of his Progressive Party supported our Korean imperial adventure in the name of "collective security" two years later, while the isolationist extreme-right Republicans constituted the only political opposition to the war.[1]

The most important fact to realize about the Old Right in the postwar era is that it staunchly and steadfastly opposed both American imperialism and interventionism abroad and its corollary in militarism at home. Conscription was vigorously opposed as far worse than other forms of statist regulation; for the draft, like slavery, conscripted the draftee's most precious "property"—his own person and being. Day in and day out, for example, the veteran publicist John T. Flynn, now a speaker and writer for the conservative America's Future, Inc.—a spinoff of the Committee for Constitutional Government—inveighed against militarism and the draft. And this despite his increasing support for the Cold War abroad. Even the Wall Street weekly, the *Commercial and Financial Chronicle*, published a lengthy attack on conscription. And Frank Chodorov, praising in his *analysis* a pamphlet issued by the National Council Against Conscription, wrote that "the State cannot intervene in the economic affairs of society without building up its coercive machinery, and that, after all, is militarism. Power is the correlative of politics."

In foreign policy, it was the extreme right-wing Republicans, who were particularly strong in the House of Representatives, who staunchly battled conscription, NATO, and the Truman Doctrine.

---

[1]For a revisionist interpretation of Henry Wallace as internationalist, see Leonard Liggio and Ronald Radosh, "Henry A. Wallace and the Open Door," in *Cold War Critics*, Thomas Paterson, ed. (Chicago: Quadrangle, 1971), pp. 76–113.

Consider, for example, Omaha's Representative Howard Buffett, Senator Taft's midwestern campaign manager in 1952, one of the most "extreme" of the extremists, a man who consistently received a zero rating from such liberal raters of Congressmen as ADA and the *New Republic*, and whom the *Nation* characterized in that era as "an able young man whose ideas have tragically fossilized." I came to know Howard as a genuine, consistent, and thoughtful libertarian. Attacking the Truman Doctrine on the floor of Congress, Buffett declared:

> Even if it were desirable, America is not strong enough to police the world by military force. If that attempt is made, the blessings of liberty will be replaced by coercion and tyranny at home. Our Christian ideals cannot be exported to other lands by dollars and guns. . . . We cannot practice might and force abroad and retain freedom at home. We cannot talk world cooperation and practice power politics.[2]

Also in 1947, Representative George Bender of Ohio, who was to be Taft's floor manager in 1952 and later Taft's successor in the Senate, kept up a drumfire of criticism of the Truman Doctrine. Attacking the corrupt Greek government and the fraudulent elections that had maintained it in power, Bender declared:

> I believe that the White House program is a reaffirmation of the nineteenth-century belief in power politics. It is a refinement of the policy first adopted after the Treaty of Versailles in 1919 designed to encircle Russia and establish a "Cordon Sanitaire" around the Soviet Union. It is a program which points to a new policy of interventionism in Europe as a corollary to our Monroe Doctrine in Southern America. Let there be no mistake about the far-reaching implications of this plan. Once we have taken the historic step of sending financial aid, military experts and loans to Greece and Turkey, we shall be irrevocably committed to a course of action from which it will be impossible to withdraw. More

---

[2] *Congressional Record*, 80th Congress, First Session, March 18, 1947, p. 2217.

> and larger demands will follow. Greater needs will arise throughout the many areas of friction in the world.[3]

Bender, moreover, was one of the few Congressional defenders of Henry Wallace when Wallace spoke abroad in opposition to the Truman Doctrine. In answer to such attacks as Deweyite Representative Kenneth Keating's denunciation of Wallace for "treason," and to Winston Churchill's attacks on Wallace for voicing his opposition abroad, Bender replied that if Churchill could attempt to launch the Cold War by speaking in the United States, Wallace could certainly seek to prevent that war by speaking in Europe.

Launching an overall criticism of Truman's foreign policy in June, 1947, Bender charged:

> Mr. Truman urged the Congress to authorize a program of military collaboration with all the petty and not so petty dictators of South America. Mr. Truman submitted a draft bill which would authorize the United States to take over the arming of South America on a scale far beyond that involved in the $400,000,000 handout to Greece and Turkey.
>
> Mr. Truman continued his campaign for universal peacetime military training in the United States.
>
> But military control at home is a part of the emerging Truman program. The Truman administration is using all its propaganda resources in an attempt to soften up the American people to accept this idea.
>
> Yes; the Truman administration is busy in its attempt to sell the idea of military control to the people of America. And hand in hand with the propaganda campaign go secret meetings for industrial mobilization.
>
> This is the kind of thing which is taking place behind barred doors in the Pentagon Building, about which the people of the United states [sic] learn only by accident. This is a part of the emerging Truman program . . . a part of the whole

---

[3] *Congressional Record*, 80th Congress, First Session March 28, 1947, pp. 2831–32. See in particular Leonard P. Liggio, "Why the Futile Crusade?" *Left and Right* 1, no. 1 (Spring, 1965): 43–44.

> Truman doctrine of drawing off the resources of the United States in support of every reactionary government in the world.[4]

While Senator Taft himself waffled and compromised on foreign affairs, especially in regard to China and the support of Chiang, Representative Bender did not waver. Warning Congress of the "intense pressure" of the China Lobby in May 1947, Bender charged

> that the Chinese Embassy here has had the arrogance to invade our State Department and attempt to tell our State Department that the Truman Doctrine has committed our Government and this Congress to all-out support of the present Fascist Chinese Government.[5]

Even Taft himself took a generally isolationist and anti-interventionist stance. Thus, the Senator opposed the Marshall Plan, for one reason because "granting aid to Europe would only furnish the Communists with further arguments against the 'imperialist' policy of the United States." Furthermore, Taft declared that if the countries of Western Europe should decide to include Communists in their governments, this would be proof that competitive capitalism had not been approved in Europe, which instead was ridden with cartels and privileges. Particularly commendable was Taft's courage in refusing to be stamped by the Trumanite liberals and Republican interventionists into favoring Cold War measures in response to the Communist "takeover" in Czechoslovakia in 1948—a "coup" which actually consisted of the resignation of rightist members of the Czech cabinet, leaving a leftist government in power. Taft stoutly denied that Russia had any plans for initiating aggression or conquering additional territory: the Russian influence, Taft pointed out, "has been predominant in Czechoslovakia since the

---

[4]*Congressional Record*, 80th Congress, First Session, June 6, 1947, pp. 6562-63. Quoted in Liggio, "Why the Futile Crusade?" pp. 45–46.

[5]Ibid., pp. 46–47.

end of the war. The Communists are merely consolidating their position in Czechoslovakia but there has been no military aggression."

Senator Taft also opposed the Cold War creation of NATO in 1949. He warned that

> the building up of a great army surrounding Russia from Norway to Turkey and Iran might produce a fear of the invasion of Russia or some of the satellite countries regarded by Russia as essential to the defense of Moscow.

NATO, Taft warned, violated the entire spirit of the UN Charter:

> An undertaking by the most powerful nation in the world to arm half the world against the other half goes far beyond any "right of collective defense if an armed attacked occurs." It violates the whole spirit of the United Nations Charter. . . . The Atlantic Pact moves in exactly the opposite direction from the purposes of the charter and makes a farce of further efforts to secure international justice through law and justice. It necessarily divides the world into two armed camps. . . . This treaty, therefore, means inevitably an armament race, and armament races in the past have led to war.[6]

In a debate with Senator John Foster Dulles, scion of Wall Street and the Rockefeller interests, in July 1949, Taft affirmed that "I cannot vote for a treaty which, in my opinion, will do far more to bring about a third world war than it ever will to maintain the peace of the world."

Even on Asia, Taft, in January 1950, opposed the Truman policy of supplying aid to the French army in suppressing the Indo-Chinese national revolution; he also warned that he would not support any commitment to back Chiang in a war against China, and he called for the removal of Chiang, his bureaucrats, and his

---

[6]Robert A. Taft, *A Foreign Policy for Americans* (New York: Doubleday & Co., 1951), pp. 89–90, 113. Quoted in Liggio, "Why the Futile Crusade?" pp. 49–50.

army of occupation on Formosa in order to permit the Formosan people a free vote on their own self-determination:

> [A]s I understand it, the people of Formosa, if permitted to vote, would probably vote to set up an independent republic of Formosa. . . . If, at the peace conference, it is decided that Formosa be set up as an independent republic, we certainly have the means to force the Nationalists' surrender of Formosa.[7]

Furthermore, in early 1950 many internationalist Republicans joined with the isolationists to deal a severe blow to our mounting intervention in Asia—a defeat of the Truman administration's $60 million aid bill for South Korea by one vote. It was generally agreed by the opponents that aid to the Rhee regime was a complete waste and that Korea was beyond the American defense interest. The historian Tang Tsou noted that "this was the first major setback in Congress for the administration in the field of foreign policy since the end of the war."[8]

It was only the efforts of Representative Walter Judd (R., Minn.), veteran internationalist, former missionary in China, and leader of the China lobby in Congress, that induced the House, in a fateful shift, to reverse its decision.

The Korean War was the last great stand of the antiwar isolationism of the Old Right. This was a time when virtually the entire Old Left, with the exception of the Communist Party and of I.F. Stone, surrendered to the global mystique of the United Nations and its "collective security against aggression," and backed Truman's imperialist aggression in that war. The fact that the UN was

---

[7]Robert A. Taft, "'Hang On' To Formosa: Hold Until Peace Treaty with Japan Is Signed," *Vital Speeches* 16, no. 8 (February 1, 1950): 236–37. Quoted in Liggio, "Why the Futile Crusade?" p. 52.

[8]Tang Tsou, *America's Failure in China, 1941–50* (Chicago: University of Chicago Press, 1963), pp. 537–38. Quoted in Liggio, "Why the Futile Crusade?" p. 53.

and has continued to be a tool of the United States was scarcely considered. Even Corliss Lamont supported the American stand in Korea, along with virtually the entire leadership of the Progressive Party. Only the extreme right-wing Republicans valiantly opposed the war.

Howard Buffett, for example, was convinced that the United States was largely responsible for the eruption of conflict in Korea, for he had been told by Senator Stiles Bridges (R., N.H.) that Admiral Roscoe Hillenkoeter, head of the CIA, had so testified in secret before the Senate Armed Services Committee at the outbreak of the war. For his indiscretion in testifying, Admiral Hillenkoeter was soon fired by President Truman and was little heard from again in Washington. For the rest of his life, Buffett carried on a crusade to have Congress declassify the Hillenkoeter testimony, but without success. Buffett recalled to me with pleasure in later years that I.F. Stone had sent him a warm note, commending him for his leadership in Congress in opposing the Korean conflict. In retrospect, it is unfortunate that Howard did not follow up the Stone feeler and move to establish a Left-Right alliance against the war—although, as I have said, there was precious little Left sentiment in opposition.

Senator Taft attacked the Truman intervention in Korea; he insisted that Korea was not vital to the Untied States, that the intervention could be construed as a threat to the security of the Soviet bloc, and that the "police action" violated the UN Charter and was an unconstitutional aggrandizement of the war powers of the President. "If the President can intervene in Korea without congressional approval," Taft charged, "he can go to war in Malaya or Indonesia or Iran or South America." In contrast, the *Nation* and the *New Republic*, which had previously been critical of the Truman Doctrine and the Cold War, now joined up with enthusiasm. These two liberal journals denounced Taft and Colonel McCormick's *Chicago Tribune* for joining the Communists in their "defeatism," in opposing the war. The savage campaign against Taft's re-election in 1950 was the occasion of a massive assault on Taft by organized liberalism, with the Truman administration attacking Taft's isolationism and alleged softness toward the Soviet

Union. The *New Republic*, in its September 4 analysis of congressional voting, hailed the Democrats for their staunchly "anti-Communist" voting record in foreign affairs (87 percent); Senator Taft, on the other hand, had only a 53 percent score for the *New Republic*, while such more consistent isolationists as Senator Kenneth Wherry (R., Neb.) had only a 23 percent "anti-Communist" mark. And the *New Republic* sourly noted the consistency of Taft's isolationism and "legalistic" devotion to nonaggression and international law:

> There has historically been a working affinity between isolationists and legalists—the former attacked Roosevelt's 1941 destroyer deal as warmongering, the latter as dictatorship. There are signs that this coalition is again tightening.[9]

At the opening of the new Congress in early 1951, the isolationist forces, led by Senators Wherry and Taft, launched an attack on the war by submitting a resolution prohibiting the President from sending any troops abroad without prior approval of Congress. They attacked Truman's refusal to accept a ceasefire or to agree to peace in Korea, and warned that the United Sates did not have enough troops for a stalemated land war on the Asian continent. Taft also attacked the President's assertion of the right to use atomic weapons and to send troops out of the country on his own authority.

An intriguing attack on Senator Taft's foreign policy was launched by the highly influential war-liberal McGeorge Bundy. Bundy expressed worry that Taft's solid re-election victory indicated popular support for limiting the executive's power to lead the United States into conflict without congressional sanction. As Leonard Liggio puts it,

> Taft's preference for negotiations rather than wastage of blood in military interventions appeared to Bundy as a failure to assert America's global leadership against Communism

---

[9] "The Hoover Line Grows," *New Republic* 124 (January 15, 1951): 7. Quoted in Liggio, "Why the Futile Crusade?" p. 57.

> and as a defective attitude of doubt, mistrust and fear towards America's national purpose in the world.[10]

Bundy declared that the normal statesman's pursuit of peace must be discarded and replaced by the power-wielder who applies diplomacy and military might in a permanent struggle against world communism in limited wars alternating with limited periods of peace. Hence Bundy criticized Taft for "appeasement" in opposing the encircling of the Soviet Union by military alliances, and the intervention in Korea, and finally for Taft's willingness to compromise with Communist China in order to extricate ourselves from the Korean debacle.

Bundy also differed strongly with Taft over the latter's launching of an open debate on the Korean War. For Taft had denounced the idea of unquestioning support for the President in military adventures:

> Anyone [who] dared to suggest criticism or even a thorough debate . . . was at once branded as an isolationist and a saboteur of unity and the bipartisan foreign policy.[11]

Bundy, in contrast, denounced the idea of any recriminations or even public questioning of the decisions of the executive policymakers, for the public merely reacted *ad hoc* to given situations without being committed to the policymakers' rigid conception of the national purpose.[12]

The last famous isolationist Old Right political thrust came in a Great Debate that ensued upon the heels of our crushing defeat at the hands of the Chinese in late 1950, a defeat in which the Chinese had driven the American forces out of North Korea. The

---

[10]Liggio, "Why the Futile Crusade?" p. 57.

[11]*Congressional Record*, 82nd Congress, 1st Session, January 5, 1951, p. 55.

[12]McGeorge Bundy, "The Private World of Robert Taft," *The Reporter*, December 11, 1951; Bundy, "Appeasement, Provocation, and Policy," *The Reporter*, January 9, 1951. See Liggio, "Why the Futile Crusade?" pp. 57–60.

Truman administration stubbornly refused to acknowledge the new realities and to make peace in Korea on the basis of the 38th parallel, thereby condemning American troops to years of heavy casualties. In response, two well-known isolationist elder statesmen, Herbert Hoover and Joseph P. Kennedy, delivered ringing and obviously coordinated back-to-back speeches in December 1950 calling for American evacuation of Korea and an end to the war in Asia.

On December 12, former Ambassador Kennedy noted the decades-long continuity of his own isolationist antiwar stand, and declared:

> From the start I had no patience with a policy that without due regard to our resources—human and material—would make commitments abroad that we could not fulfill. As Ambassador to London in 1939 I had seen the folly of this when the British made their commitment to Poland that they could not fulfill and have not yet fulfilled—a commitment that brought them into war.
>
> I naturally opposed Communism, but said if portions of Europe or Asia were to go Communistic or even had Communism thrust upon them, we cannot stop it. Instead we must make sure of our strength and be certain not to fritter it away in battles that could not be won.
>
> But where are we now? Beginning with intervention in the Italian elections and financial and political aid to Greece and Turkey, we have expanded our political and financial programs on an almost unbelievably wide scale. Billions have been spent in the Marshall plan, further billions in the occupation of Berlin, Western Germany and Japan. Military aid has been poured into Greece, Turkey, Iran, the nations of the North Atlantic Pact, French Indo-China, and now in Korea we are fighting the fourth-greatest war in our history.
>
> What have we in return for this effort? Friends? We have far fewer friends than we had in 1945. . . .
>
> To engage those vast armies [of the Communist countries] on the European or Asian continent is foolhardy, but that is the direction towards which our policy has been tending.
>
> That policy is suicidal. It has made us no foul weather friends. It has kept our armament scattered over the globe. It

> has picked one battlefield and threatens to pick others impossibly removed from our sources of supply. It has not contained Communism. By our methods of opposition it has solidified Communism, where otherwise Communism might have bred within itself internal dissensions. Our policy today is politically and morally a bankrupt policy.

Kennedy concluded that the only alternative was for America to abandon the entire policy of global intervention and adopt isolationism once more:

> I can see no alternative other than having the courage to wash up this policy and start with the fundamentals I urged more than five years ago. . . .
>
> A first step in the pursuit of this policy is to get out of Korea—indeed, to get out of every point in Asia which we do not plan to hold in our own defense. Such a policy means that in the Pacific we will pick our own battlegrounds if we are forced to fight and not have them determined by political and ideological considerations that have no relationship to our own defense.
>
> The next step in pursuit of this policy is to apply the same principle to Europe. Today it is idle to talk of being able to hold the line of the Elbe or the line of the Rhine. Why should we waste valuable resources in making such an attempt? . . . To pour arms and men into a Quixotic military adventure makes no sense whatever. What have we gained by staying in Berlin? Everyone knows we can be pushed out the moment the Russians choose to push us out. . . .
>
> The billions that we have squandered on these enterprises could have been far more effectively used in this hemisphere and on the seas that surround it. . . .
>
> People will say, however, that this policy will not contain Communism. Will our present policy do so? Can we possibly contain Communist Russia, if she chooses to march, by a far-flung battle line in the middle of Europe? The truth is that our only real hope is to keep Russia, if she chooses to march, on the other side of the Atlantic and make Communism much too costly for her to try to cross the seas. It may be that Europe for a decade or a generation or more will turn Communistic. But in doing so, it may break of itself as a unified

> force. Communism still has to prove itself to its peoples as a government that will achieve for them a better way of living. The more people that it will have to govern, the more necessary it becomes for those who govern to justify themselves to those being governed. The more peoples that are under its yoke, the greater are the possibilities of revolt. Moreover, it seems certain that Communism spread over Europe will not rest content with being governed by a handful of men in the Kremlin. Tito in Jugoslavia is already demonstrating this fact. Mao in China is not likely to take his orders from Stalin. . . .

After this highly prophetic forecast—greatly derided at the time—of the inevitable breaking up of the international Communist monolith, Kennedy courageously added:

> This policy will, of course, be criticized as appeasement. No word is more mistakenly used. Is it appeasement to withdraw from unwise commitments . . . and to make clear just exactly how and for what you will fight? If it is wise in our interest not to make commitments that endanger our security, and this is appeasement, then I am for appeasement. I can recall only too well the precious time bought by Chamberlain at Munich. I applauded that purchase then; I would applaud it today. Today, however, while we have avoided a Munich, we are coming perilously close to another Dunkirk. Personally, I should choose to escape the latter.

And Kennedy concluded, on the current mess in Asia and foreign affairs generally:

> Half of this world will never submit to dictation by the other half. The two can only agree to live next to each other because for one to absorb the other becomes too costly.
>
> An attitude of realism such as this is, I submit, in accord with our historic traditions. We have never wanted a part of other peoples' scrapes. Today we have them and just why, nobody quite seems to know. What business is it of ours to support French colonial policy in Indo-China or to achieve Mr. Syngman Rhee's concepts of democracy in Korea? Shall we now send the Marines into the mountains of Tibet to keep the Dalai Lama on his throne? We can do well to mind our

> business and interfere only where somebody threatens our business and our homes.
>
> The policy I suggest, moreover, gives us a chance economically to keep our heads above water. For years, I have argued the necessity for not burdening ourselves with unnecessary debts. There is no surer way to destroy the basis of American enterprise than to destroy the initiative of the men who make it. . . . Those who recall 1932 know too easily the dangers that can arise from within when our own economic system fails to function. If we weaken it with lavish spending either on foreign nations or in foreign wars, we run the danger of precipitating another 1932 and of destroying the very system which we are trying to save.
>
> An Atlas, whose back is bowed and whose hands are busy holding up the world, has no arms to lift to deal with his own defense. Increase his burdens and you will crush him. . . . This is our present posture. . . . The suggestions I make . . . would . . . conserve American lives for American ends, not waste them in the freezing hills of Korea or on the battle-scarred plains of Western Germany.[13]

Eight days later, Herbert Hoover backed up the Kennedy speech with one of his own on nationwide network radio. While refusing to go as far as Kennedy, and indeed attacking "appeasement" and "isolationism" and scorning fears of "Dunkirks," Hoover insisted:

> We must face the fact that to commit the sparse ground forces of the non-Communist nations into a land war against this Communist land mass would be a war without victory, a war without a successful terminal. Any attempt to make war on the Communist mass by land invasion, through the quicksands of China, India or Western Europe, is sheer folly. That would be the graveyard of millions of American boys and

---

[13]Joseph P. Kennedy, "Present Policy is Politically and Morally Bankrupt," *Vital Speeches* 17, no. 6 (January 1, 1951): 170–73.

> would end in the exhaustion of this Gibraltar of Western Civilization.[14]

It is instructive to note the reactions of organized Liberalism to the Kennedy-Hoover thesis, a position supported by Senator Taft. Along with the Truman administration and such Wall Street-oriented Republicans as Governor Dewey and John Foster Dulles, the *Nation* and the *New Republic* proceeded to red-bait these distinguished right-wing leaders. The *Nation* charged:

> The line they are laying down for their country should set the bells ringing in the Kremlin as nothing has since the triumph of Stalingrad. Actually the line taken by *Pravda* is that the former President did not carry isolationism far enough.

And the *New Republic* summarized the isolationist position as holding that the Korean War "was the creation not of Stalin, but of Truman, just as Roosevelt, not Hitler, caused the Second World War." And in the desire of Taft, Hoover, and Kennedy to accept Soviet offers of negotiating peace, the *New Republic* saw an

> opposition who saw nothing alarming in Hitler's conquest of Europe (and who would clearly grab at the bait). Stalin, after raising the ante, as he did with Hitler, and sweeping over Asia, would move on until the Stalinist caucus in the *Tribune* tower would bring out in triumph the first Communist edition of the *Chicago Tribune*.

The *New Republic* was particularly exercised over the fact that the isolationists

> condemned U.S. participation in Korea as unconstitutional and provided that the only funds available for overseas troops shipment should be funds necessary to facilitate the extrication of U.S. forces now in Korea.[15]

---

[14]Herbert Hoover, "Our National Policies in This Crisis," in ibid., pp. 165–67.

[15]"Hoover's Folly," *Nation* 171, no. 27 (December 30, 1950): 688; "Korea: Will China Fight the UN?" *New Republic* 123 (November 20,

One of the people whom the *New Republic* was undoubtedly referring to as part of the "Stalinist caucus" at Colonel McCormick's valiantly isolationist *Chicago Tribune* was George Morgenstern, editorial writer for the *Tribune* and author of the first great, and still the basic, revisionist work on Pearl Harbor, *Pearl Harbor: Story of a Secret War.*[16] During the Korean War, Morgenstern published a blistering article, summing up the century of American imperialism, in the right-wing Washington weekly *Human Events*, then open to isolationist material but having become, since the resignation of Felix Morley, a hack tabloid for the warmongering New Right. Morgenstern wrote:

> At the end of the 19th century the United States began to stir with those promptings of imperialism and altruism which have worked to the mischief of so many puissant states. The sinister Spaniard provided a suitable punching bag. Two days before McKinley went to Congress with a highly misleading message which was an open invitation to war, the Spanish government had agreed to the demands for an armistice in Cuba and American mediation. There was no good reason, but there was war anyway. We wound up the war with a couple of costly dependencies, but this was enough to intoxicate the precursors of those who now swoon on very sight of the phrase "world leadership."
>
> McKinley testified that in lonely sessions on his knees at night he had been guided to the realization that we must "uplift and civilize and Christianize" the Filipinos. He asserted that the war had brought new duties and responsibilities "which we must meet and discharge as becomes a great nation on whose growth and career from the beginning the Ruler of Nations has plainly written the high command and pledge of civilization." This sort of exalted nonsense is familiar to anyone who later attended the evangelical rationalizations of Wilson for intervening in the European war, of

---

1950): 5–6; "Can We Save World Peace?" *New Republic* 124 (January 1, 1951): 5 and January 15, 1951, p. 7. Cited in Liggio, "Why the Futile Crusade?" p. 56.

[16](New York: Devin-Adair, 1947).

Roosevelt promising the millennium . . . of Eisenhower treasuring the "crusade in Europe" that somehow went sour, or of Truman, Stevenson, Paul Douglas, or the New York *Times* preaching the holy war in Korea. . . .

An all-pervasive propaganda has established a myth of inevitability in American action: all wars were necessary, all wars were good. The burden of proof rests with those who contend that America is better off, that American security has been enhanced, and that prospects of world peace have been improved by American intervention in four wars in half a century. Intervention began with deceit by McKinley; it ends with deceit by Roosevelt and Truman.

Perhaps we would have a rational foreign policy . . . if Americans could be brought to realize that the first necessity is the renunciation of the lie as an instrument of foreign policy.[17]

---

[17]George Morgenstern, "The Past Marches On," *Human Events* (April 22, 1953).

9
The Postwar Renaissance III: Libertarians and Foreign Policy

One of the most brilliant and forceful attacks on Cold War foreign policy in this era came from the pen of the veteran conservative and free-market publicist Garet Garrett. In his pamphlet "The Rise of Empire," published in 1952, Garrett began by declaring: "We have crossed the boundary that lies between Republic and Empire." Linking his thesis with his pamphlet of the 1930s, "The Revolution Was," denouncing the advent of domestic executive and statist despotism within the republican form under the New Deal, Garrett saw once more a "revolution within the form" of the old constitutional republic:

> After President Truman, alone and without either the consent or knowledge of Congress, had declared war on the Korean aggressor, 7,000 miles away, Congress condoned his usurpation of its exclusive Constitutional power to declare war. More than that, his political supporters in Congress argued that in the modern case that sentence in the Constitution conferring upon Congress the sole power to declare war was obsolete. . . .
>
> Mr. Truman's supporters argued that in the Korean instance his act was defensive and therefore within his powers as Commander-in-Chief. In that case, to make it Constitutional, he was legally obliged to ask Congress for a declaration of war afterward. This he never did. For a week Congress relied upon the papers for news of the country's entry into war; then the President called a few of its leaders to the White House and told them what he had done. . . .

> A few months later Mr. Truman sent American troops to Europe to join an international army, and did it not only without a law, without even consulting Congress, but challenged the power of Congress to stop it.[1]

Garrett noted that the Senate Foreign Relations Committee then asked the State Department to set forth the position of the executive branch on the powers of the President to send troops abroad. The State Department declared that "constitutional doctrine has been largely molded by practical necessities. Use of the congressional power to declare war, for example, has fallen into abeyance because wars are no longer declared in advance." Garrett added that "Caesar might have said it to the Roman Senate," and that this statement "stands as a forecast of executive intentions, a manifestation of the executive mind, a mortal challenge to the parliamentary principle."

What, then, were the hallmarks of Empire? The first requisite, Garrett declared, was that "the executive power of government shall be dominant." For

> what Empire needs above all in government is an executive power that can make immediate decisions, such as a decision in the middle of the night by the President to declare war on the aggressor in Korea.[2]

In previous years, he added, it was assumed that the function of the Congress was to speak for the American people. But now

> it is the President, standing at the head of the Executive Government, who says: "I speak for the people" or "I have a mandate from the people.". . . Now much more than Congress, the President acts directly upon the emotions and passions of the people to influence their thinking. As he controls Executive Government, so he controls the largest propaganda machine in the world. The Congress has no propaganda

---

[1]Garet Garrett, *The People's Pottage* (Caldwell, Id.: Caxton Printers, 1953), pp. 122–23.

[2]Ibid., p. 129.

> apparatus at all and continually finds itself under pressure from the people who have been moved for or against something by the ideas and thought material broadcast in the land by the administrative bureaus in Washington.

The powers of the executive are aggrandized by delegation from Congress, by continual reinterpretation of the language of the Constitution, by the appearance of a large number of administrative bureaus within the executive, by usurpation, and as a natural corollary of the country's intervening more and more into foreign affairs.

A second hallmark of the existence of Empire, continued Garrett, is that "Domestic policy becomes subordinate to foreign policy." This is what happened to Rome, and to the British Empire. It is also happening to us, for

> as we convert the nation into a garrison state to build the most terrible war machine that has ever been imagined on earth, every domestic policy is bound to be conditioned by our foreign policy. The voice of government is saying that if our foreign policy fails we are ruined. It is all or nothing. Our survival as a free nation is at hazard. That makes it simple, for in that case there is no domestic policy that may not have to be sacrificed to the necessities of foreign policy—even freedom. . . . If the cost of defending not ourselves alone but the whole non-Russian world threatens to wreck our solvency, still we must go on.[3]

Garrett concluded,

> We are no longer able to choose between peace and war. We have embraced perpetual war. . . . Wherever and whenever the Russian aggressor attacks, in Europe, Asia, or Africa, there we must meet him. We are so committed by the Truman Doctrine, by examples of our intention, by the global posting of our armed forces, and by such formal engagements as the North Atlantic Treaty and the Pacific Pact.

---

[3]Ibid., p. 139.

And, furthermore,

> Let it be a question of survival, and how relatively unimportant are domestic policies—touching, for example, the rights of private property, when if necessary, all private property may be confiscated; or touching individual freedom, when, if necessary, all labor may be conscripted. . . . The American mind is already conditioned.

Garrett then—himself prophetically—pointed to the keen prophetic insight of a *New York Times* editorial of October 31, 1951, in detailing the permanent changes in American life wrought by the Korean War. Wrote the *Times*:

> We are embarking on a partial mobilization for which about a hundred billion dollars have been already made available. We have been compelled to activate and expand our alliances at an ultimate cost of some twenty-five billion dollars, to press for rearmament of former enemies and to scatter our own forces at military bases throughout the world. Finally, we have been forced not only to retain but to expand the draft and to press for a system of universal military training which will affect the lives of a whole generation. The productive effort and the tax burden resulting from these measures are changing the economic pattern of the land.
>
> What is not so clearly understood, here or abroad, is that these are not temporary measures for a temporary emergency but rather the beginning of a whole new military status for the United States, which seems certain to be with us for a long time to come.

Garrett, endorsing this insight, added sardonically that "probably never before in any history, could so dire a forecast have been made in these level tones"—tones made possible by the myth that this new state of affairs was "not the harvest of our foreign policy but Jehovah acting through the Russians to afflict us—and nobody else responsible."[4]

---

[4]Ibid., pp. 140–41.

A third brand of Empire, continued Garrett, is the "ascendancy of the military mind." Garrett noted that the great symbol of the American military mind is the Pentagon Building in Washington, built during World War II, as a "forethought of perpetual war." There at the Pentagon, "global strategy is conceived; there, nobody knows how, the estimates of what it will cost are arrived at; and surrounding it is our own iron curtain." The Pentagon allows the public to know only the information that it wills it to learn;

> All the rest is stamped "classified" or "restricted," in the name of national security, and Congress itself cannot get it. That is as it must be of course; the most important secrets of Empire are military secrets.

Garrett went on to quote the devastating critique of our garrison state by General Douglas MacArthur:

> Talk of imminent threat to our national security through the application of external force is pure nonsense. . . . Indeed, it is a part of the general patterns of misguided policy that our country is now geared to an arms economy which was bred in an artificially induced psychosis of war hysteria and nurtured upon an incessant propaganda of fear. While such an economy may produce a sense of seeming prosperity for the moment, it rests on an illusionary foundation of complete unreliability and renders among our political leaders almost a greater fear of peace than is their fear of war.

Garrett then interprets that quotation as follows:

> War becomes an instrument of domestic policy. . . . [The government may] increase or decrease the tempo of military expenditures, as the planners decide that what the economy needs is a little more inflation or a little less. . . . And whereas it was foreseen that when Executive Government is resolved to control the economy it will come to have a vested interest in the power of inflation, so now we may perceive that it will come also to have a kind of proprietary interest in the institution of perpetual war.[5]

---

[5]Ibid., pp. 148–49.

A fourth mark of Empire, continued Garrett, is "a system of satellite nations." We speak only of Russian "satellites," and with contempt, but "we speak of our own satellites as allies and friends or as freedom loving nations." The meaning of satellite is a "hired guard." As Garrett notes:

> When people say we have lost China or that if we lose Europe it will be a disaster, what do they mean? How could we lose China or Europe, since they never belonged to us? What they mean is that we have lost or may lose a following of dependent people who act as an outer guard.

Armed with a vast array of satellites, we then find that "for any one of them to involve us in war it is necessary only for the Executive Power in Washington to decide that its defense is somehow essential to the security of the United States." The system had its origins in the Lend-Lease Act of 1941. Garrett concludes that the Imperial Center is pervaded by a fear of standing alone in the world, without satellites.

> Fear at last assumes the phase of a patriotic obsession. It is stronger than any political party. . . . The basic conviction is simple. We cannot stand alone. A capitalistic economy, though it possesses half the industrial power of the whole world, cannot defend its own hemisphere. It may be able to save the world; alone it cannot save itself. It must have allies. Fortunately, it is able to buy them, bribe them, arm them, feed and clothe them; it may cost us more than we can afford, yet we must have them or perish.[6]

The final hallmark of Empire is "a complex of vaunting and fear." Here Garrett cuts to the heart of the imperial psychology. On the one hand vaunting:

> The people of Empire . . . are mighty. They have performed prodigious works. . . . So those must have felt who lived out the grandeur that was *Rome*. So the British felt while they ruled the world. So now Americans feel. As we assume

---

[6]Ibid., pp. 150, 155.

> unlimited political liabilities all over the world, as billions in multiples of ten are voted for the ever expanding global intention, there is only scorn for the one who says: "We are not infinite." The answer is: "What we will to do, that we can do'."

But in addition to vaunting is the fear.

> Fear of the barbarian. Fear of standing alone. . . . A time comes when the guard itself, that is, your system of satellites, is a source of fear. Satellites are often willful and the more you rely upon them the more willful and demanding they are. There is, therefore, the fear of offending them. . . . How will they behave when the test comes?—when they face . . . the terrible reality of becoming the European battlefield whereon the security of the United States shall be defended? If they falter or fail, what will become of the weapons with which we have supplied them?[7]

Having concluded that we now have all the hallmarks of Empire, Garrett then points out that the United States, like previous empires, feels itself "a prisoner of history." Americans feel somehow obliged to play their supposed role on the world stage. For beyond fear lies "collective security" and beyond that lies "a greater thought." In short:

> It is our turn.
>
> Our turn to do what?
>
> Our turn to assume the responsibilities of moral leadership in the world.
>
> Our turn to maintain a balance of power against the forces of evil everywhere—in Europe and Asia and Africa, in the Atlantic and in the Pacific, by air and by sea—evil in this case being the Russian barbarian.
>
> Our turn to keep the peace of the world.

---

[7]Ibid., pp. 155–57.

> Our turn to save civilization.
>
> Our turn to serve mankind.
>
> But this is the language of Empire. The Roman Empire never doubted that it was the defender of civilization. Its good intentions were peace, law and order. The Spanish Empire added salvation. The British Empire added the noble myth of the white man's burden. We have added freedom and democracy. Yet the more that may be added to it the more it is the same language still. A language of power.[8]

Garrett ends his splendid work by calling for the recapture of the "lost terrain" of liberty and republicanism from executive tyranny and Empire. But, as he pointed out, we must face the fact

> that the cost of saving the Republic may be extremely high. It could be relatively as high as the cost of setting it up in the first place, one hundred and seventy-five years ago, when love of political liberty was a mighty passion, and people were willing to die for it. . . . [D]eceleration will cause a terrific shock. Who will say, "Now?" Who is willing to face the grim and dangerous realities of deflation and depression? . . . No doubt the people know they can have their Republic back if they want it enough to fight for it and to pay the price. The only point is that no leader has yet appeared with the courage to make them choose.[9]

No less enthusiastic was the devotion to peace and the opposition to the Korean War and militarism on the part of the more narrowly libertarian wing of the Old Right movement. Thus, Leonard Read published a powerful pamphlet, "Conscience on the Battlefield" (1951), in which he imagined himself as a young American soldier dying on a battlefield in Korea and engaged in a dialogue with his own conscience. The Conscience informs the soldier that

---

[8]Ibid., pp. 158–59.

[9]Ibid., pp. 173–74.

> while in many respects you were an excellent person, the record shows that you killed many men—both Korean and Chinese—and were also responsible for the death of many women and children during this military campaign.

The soldier replies that the war was "good and just," that "we had to stop Communist aggression and the enslavement of people by dictators." Conscience asks him, "Did you kill these people as an act of self-defense? Were they threatening your life or your family? Were they on your shores, about to enslave you?" The soldier again replies that he was serving the clever U.S. foreign policy, which anticipates our enemies' actions by defeating them first overseas.

Read's Conscience then responds:

> Governments and such are simply phrases, mere abstractions behind which persons often seek to hide their actions and responsibilities. . . . In the Temple of Judgment which you are about to enter, Principles only are likely to be observed. It is almost certain that you will find there no distinction between nationalities or between races. . . . A child is a child, with as much right to an opportunity for Self-realization as you. To take a human life—at whatever age, or of any color—is to take a human life. . . . According to your notions, no one person is responsible for the deaths of these people. Yet they were destroyed. Seemingly, you expect collective arrangements such as "the army" or "the government" to bear your guilt.[10]

On the matter of guilt, the Conscience adds that

> there can be no distinction between those who do the shooting and those who aid the act—whether they aid it behind the lines by making the ammunition, or by submitting to the payment of taxes for war. Moreover, the guilt would appear to be

[10]Leonard F. Read, *Conscience on the Battlefield* (Irvington-on-Hudson, N.Y.: Foundation for Economic Education, 1951), pp. 8–11. It is indicative of the decay of the older libertarian movement and of FEE that Read's pamphlet was never included in FEE's *Essays on Liberty* and was allowed to disappear rather quickly from circulation.

> even greater on the part of those who resorted to the coercive power of government to get you to sacrifice your home, your fortune, your chance of Self-realization, your life—none of which sacrifices do they themselves appear willing to make.

In introducing his pamphlet, Read wrote: "War is liberty's greatest enemy, and the deadly foe of economic progress." Seconding that view was libertarian leader F.A. "Baldy" Harper, in a FEE pamphlet, "In Search of Peace," published in the same year. There Harper wrote:

> Charges of pacifism are likely to be hurled at anyone who in troubled times raises any question about the race into war. If pacifism means embracing the objective of peace, I am willing to accept the charge. If it means opposing all aggression against others, I am willing to accept the charge also. It is now urgent in the interest of liberty that many persons become "peacemongers . . ."
>
> So the nation goes to war, and while war is going on, the real enemy [the idea of slavery]—long ago forgotten and camouflaged by the processes of war—rides on to victory in both camps. . . . Further evidence that in war the attack is not leveled at the real enemy is the fact that we seem never to know what to do with "victory . . ." Are the "liberated peoples to be shot, or all put in prison camps, or what? Is the national boundary to be moved? Is there to be further destruction of the property of the defeated? Or what? . . . Nor can the ideas of [Karl Marx] be destroyed today by murder or suicide of their leading exponent, or of any thousands or millions of the devotees. . . . Least of all can the ideas of Karl Marx be destroyed by murdering innocent victims of the form of slavery he advocated, whether they be conscripts in armies or victims caught in the path of battle.[11]

Harper then added that Russia was supposed to be the enemy, because our enemy was communism.

---

[11]F.A. Harper, *In Search of Peace* (Irvington-on-Hudson, N.Y.: Foundation for Economic Education, 1951), pp. 3, 23–25; reprinted by the Institute for Humane Studies, 1971.

> But if it is necessary for us to embrace all these socialist-communist measures in order to fight a nation that has adopted them—because they have adopted these measures—why fight them? Why not join them in the first place and save all the bloodshed? . . . There is no sense in conjuring up in our minds a violent hatred against people who are the victims of communism in some foreign nation, when the same governmental shackles are making us servile to illiberal forces at home.

Dean Russell, another staff member at FEE, added to the anti-militarist barrage.

> Those who advocate the "temporary loss" of our freedom in order to preserve it permanently are advocating only one thing: the abolition of liberty. In order to fight a form of slavery abroad, they advocate a form of bondage at home! However good their intentions may be, these people are enemies of your freedom and my freedom; and I fear them far more than I fear any potential Russian threat to my liberty. These sincere but highly emotional patriots are clear and present threats to freedom; the Russians are still thousands of miles away.[12]

The Russians would only attack us, Russell pointed out, "for either of two reasons: fear of our intentions or retaliation to our acts." The Russians' fear would

> evaporate if we pulled our troops and military commitments back into the Western Hemisphere and kept them here. . . . As long as we keep troops on Russia's borders, the Russians can be expected to act somewhat as we would act if Russia were to station troops in Guatemala or Mexico—even if those countries wanted the Russians to come in!

[12]Dean Russell, "The Conscription Idea," *Ideas on Liberty* (May 1955): 42.

Dean Russell concluded his critique of American foreign policy:

> I can see no more logic in fighting Russia over Korea or Outer Mongolia, than in fighting England over Cyprus, or France over Morocco. . . . The historical facts of imperialism and spheres of influence are not sufficient reasons to justify the destruction of freedom within the United States by turning ourselves into a permanent garrison state and stationing conscripts all over the world. We are rapidly becoming a caricature of the thing we profess to hate.

My own reaction to the onset of the Korean War was impassioned and embittered, and I wrote a philippic to an uncomprehending liberal friend which I believe holds up all too well in the light of the years that followed:

> I come to bury Liberty, not to praise it; how could I praise it when the noble Brutus—Social Democracy—has come into full flower? . . . What had we under the regime of Liberty? More or less, we had freedom to say whatever we pleased, to work wherever we wanted, to save and invest capital, to travel wherever we pleased, we had peace. These things were all very well in their day, but now we have Social Democracy. . . . Social Democracy has the draft, so all of us can fight for lasting peace and democracy all over the world, rationing, price control, allocation . . . the labor draft, so we can all serve society at our best capacities, heavy taxes, inflationary finance, black markets . . . healthy "economic expansion." Best of all, we shall have permanent war. The trouble, as we all know, with the previous wars is that they ended so quickly. . . . But now it looks as if that mistake has been rectified. We can . . . proclaim as our objective the occupation of Russia for twenty years to really educate her people in the glorious principles of our own Social Democracy. And if we really want to battle for Democracy, let's try to occupy and educate China for a couple of generations. That should keep us busy for a while.
>
> In the last war, we were hampered by a few obstructionist, isolationist, antediluvians, who resisted such salutary steps as a draft of all labor and capital, and total planning for mobilization by benevolent politicians, economists, and sociologists. But under our permanent war setup, we can easily push

this program through. If anyone objects, we can accuse him of giving aid and comfort to the Commies. The Democrats have already accused the reactionary obstructionist [Senator] Jenner (R., Ind.) of "following the Stalinist line."

Yes, the obstructionists are licked. Social Democracy has little to fear from them. Whoever the genius was who thought up the permanent war idea, you've got to hand it to him. We can look forward to periods of National Unity, of a quintupling of the National Income, etc. There is a little fly in the ointment that some obstructionists may mention—the boys actually doing the fighting may have some objections. But we can correct that with a $300 billion "Truth" campaign headed, say, by Archibald MacLeish, so they will know what they are fighting for. And, we've got to impose equivalent sacrifices on the home front, so our boys will know that things are almost as tough at home. . . .

There you have it. The Outlines of the Brave New World of Democratic Socialism. Liberty is a cheap price to pay. I hope you'll like it.[13]

---

[13]The only response of my liberal friend was to wonder why I had written him a letter sounding like the statement of "some business organization."

10

The Postwar Renaissance IV: Swansong of the Old Right

In addition to being staunch opponents of war and militarism, the Old Right of the postwar period had a rugged and near-libertarian honesty in domestic affairs as well. When a nationwide railroad strike loomed, it was the liberal Harry Truman who proposed to draft the strikers into the army and force them to keep working, and it was Senator Taft who led the opposition to the move as slavery. The National Association of Manufacturers (NAM), in those days before big business-corporate liberalism had conquered it in the name of a "partnership of government and industry," took a firm *laissez-faire* line. Its staff economist, Noel Sargent, was a believer in the free market, and the dean of *laissez-faire* economics, Ludwig von Mises, was one of the NAM's consultants. In those days, NAM was largely small-business oriented, and indeed, various small businessmen's organizations formed the business base for the organized right. Indeed, it was in the high places of the NAM that Robert Welch learned the anti-Establishment views that were later to erupt into the John Birch Society.

But even in those early days, the handwriting was on the wall for the NAM as a *laissez-faire* organization. The first great turning point came in the spring of 1947, after a conservative Republican majority had captured both houses of Congress in a mass uprising of voters against the Fair Deal, and partially in reaction against the power of labor unionism. The NAM, since the inception of the Wagner Act, had been pledged, year in and year out, to outright repeal of the law, and therefore to a repeal of the special privileges that the Wagner

Act gave to union organizing. When the 80th Congress opened in the winter of 1946 the NAM, which now finally had its chance to succeed in Wagner repeal, shifted its stand in a dramatic battle, in which the corporate Big Business liberals defeated the old *laissez-fairists*, headed by B.E. Hutchinson of Chrysler, who was also a leading trustee of FEE. The NAM, on the point of a significant *laissez-faire* victory in labor relations, thus turned completely and called simply for extending the powers of the National Labor Relations Board (NLRB) to regulate unions as well as business—a notion which soon took shape in the Taft-Hartley Act. It was the Taft-Hartley Act that completed the Wagner Act process of taming as well as privileging industrial unionism, and bringing the new union movement into the cozy junior partnership with Big Business and Big Government that we know so well today. Once again, Taft, in opposition to the purists and "extreme" Rightists in Congress, played a compromising role.

One thing that the Old Right specialized in was anti-Establishment muckraking. The Hearst columns of Westbrook Pegler were a leading example.[1] But particularly delightful was the anti-Wall Street muckraking of the *Chicago Tribune* under Colonel McCormick. For the *Tribune* understood clearly and zeroed in on the Wall Street-Anglophile Establishment that ran and still runs this country, and was fearless in continuing exposés of this ruling elite. The old files of the *Chicago Tribune* are a rich source of information for the anti-Establishment historian.[2]

One example is a series of articles by William Fulton and others in the *Tribune*, from July 15–July 31, 1951, of what we might call

---

[1]Interestingly, every one of the delightful exposés of Franklin and Eleanor Roosevelt by Pegler, which caused such shock and horror among liberals at the time, has now turned out to be correct—with Pegler, of course, never receiving credit by historians for his pioneering journalism.

[2]For the only example that I know of an appreciative attitude toward right-wing muckraking by a New Left historian, see G. William Domhoff, *The Higher Circles: The Governing Class in America* (New York: Random House, 1970), pp. 281–308.

"Rhodes Scholar Revisionism," in which the journalists traced the Rhodes Scholar Anglophile influence in the foreign policymaking bodies of the U.S. government. The title for the series was "Rhodes' Goal: Return U.S. to British Empire." Named as Rhodes Scholars were such leading American "internationalists" as Dean Rusk, George McGhee, Stanley K. Hornbeck, W. Walton Butterworth, Prof. Bernadotte E. Schmitt, Ernest A. Gross (an Oxford student, though not strictly a Rhodes scholar), ditto Henry R. Luce, Clarence K. Streit, Frank Aydelotte, and many others, including tie-ins with the Council on Foreign Relations, the Carnegie and Rockefeller Foundations, and the *New York Times* and *Herald-Tribune*.

One of the most sophisticated pieces of right-wing muckraking in this era was undertaken by the Reece Committee of the House to investigate tax-exempt foundations during 1953–54. Staffed by such leading conservatives as attorney René Wormser (brother of Felix E. Wormser, Eisenhower's Secretary of Interior) and Norman Dodd, the Reece Committee zeroed in on alleged Communist and also liberal and socialist tie-ins with the large foundations: Rockefeller, Carnegie, Ford, etc. But, furthermore, the Committee attacked the large foundations for invariably sponsoring empirical and quantitatively oriented studies in the social sciences and thus leading these disciplines into a "scientistic" promotion of technocratic and spurious "value-freedom" to the neglect of the qualitative and the ethical. Here, the Reece Committee, following upon the searching critiques of liberal empiricism and scientism leveled by F.A. Hayek, and by the conservative University of Pennsylvania sociologist Albert H. Hobbs, hit an extremely important flaw in the new, postwar social science, but the committee's insights were buried in an avalanche of vituperation in the Establishment press. The foundations' man on the committee, obstructing its purposes and in quiet league with the Eisenhower White House, was Rep. Wayne Hays (D., Ohio), a Truman and later a Lyndon Johnson Democrat.[3]

[3]A valuable summary of the Committee's work can be found in a book by its general counsel, René A. Wormser, *Foundations: Their Power and Influence* (New York: Devin-Adair, 1958). Some of Wormser's section

Some of the statements of maverick, antiquantitative social scientists to the committee make fascinating reading in the light of the rediscovery by the New Left in recent years of a critical view of empiricist, pseudo "value-free" social science. Thus University of Pennsylvania sociologist James H.S. Bossard wrote to the Reece Committee:

> For some years, I have regarded with increasing apprehension the development of what I have called the comptometer school of research in social sciences. By this I mean the gathering of detailed social data and their manipulation by all the available statistical techniques. . . . My own interest lies more in the development of qualitative insights. This accords with my judgment of the nature of the life process, that it cannot be reduced to statistical formulas but that it is a richly diversified complex of relations.[4]

---

heads are instructive: "Politics in the Social Sciences," "The Exclusion of the Dissident," "Foundation-Fostered Scientism," "The 'Social Engineers' and the 'Fact-Finding Mania,'" "Mass Research-Integration and Conformity." Wormser reports that the foundations were able to force the committee to fire two particularly knowledgeable staff members early in the investigation. Both of these men were libertarian-oriented: my friend George B. DeHuszar, close to the *Chicago Tribune* people; and the Viennese economist Dr. Karl Ettinger, friend of Ludwig von Mises. Ettinger's uncompleted studies would have investigated patterns of giving in foundation support of colleges, as well as a survey of control of the learned journals as an instrument of power and their relationships with the foundations, and a study of the interlocks between foundations, research institutions, and government. For the full flavor of the Reece Committee, see the *Hearings Before the Special Committee to Investigate Tax Exempt Foundations and Comparable Organizations*, House of Representatives, 83rd Congress, 2nd session, Parts 1 and 2 (Washington, D.C.: U.S. Government Printing Office, 1954). For a conservative critique of scientism in that era, see Albert H. Hobbs, *Social Problems and Scientism* (Pittsburgh: Stackpole Co., 1953).

[4]*Hearings*, p. 1188.

In a typically hard-hitting letter, Harvard sociologist Pitirim A. Sorokin affirmed that foundations discriminate in favor of empirical research and "greatly discriminate against theoretical, historical, and other forms of nonempirical research," aided and abetted by discrimination on behalf of mathematical and mechanical models, "or other imitative varieties of so-called natural science sociology." The results of this social science have been in most cases "perfectly fruitless and almost sterile" or even in some cases, "rather destructive morally and mentally for this Nation."[5]

There was in the work of the Reece Committee, however, a grave inner contradiction, one that in the long run was probably more destructive of its work than all the sniping of Wayne Hays. This was the fact that the conservatives and quasi-libertarians on the committee were wielding the coercive arm of government—the congressional committee—to harass private foundations . . . and for what reason? Largely because the foundations had allegedly been advocating government control over private organizations! And the Reece Committee ended by advocating government restrictions on the private foundations; in short, the Committee called for further government controls over private institutions for the sin of advocating government controls over private institutions! The upshot was merely to launch the modern trend toward ever-tighter regulation of foundations, but not in any way to change their ideological or methodological drift.

Another fascinating piece of combined muckraking and analysis in this era was a large, sprawling book by *Chicago Tribune* reporter Frank Hughes, *Prejudice and the Press*.[6] The Hughes book was a lengthy attack on the corporate-liberal "Commission" on the Freedom of the Press, which had been largely financed by Henry Luce and was headed by Robert M. Hutchins.[7] The "Commission,"

---

[5]Ibid., p. 1191. Also see the remarks of Harvard sociologist Carle C. Zimmerman, in ibid., pp. 1193–94.

[6](New York: Devin-Adair, 1950).

[7]The private "commission" included such liberal intellectuals as Zechariah Chafee, Jr., William E. Hocking, Harold Lasswell, Reinhold

which had published its report in 1947, had called for a "free" press in the modern sense of being "responsible"; in contrast, Hughes countered with a ringing affirmation of the Bill of Rights and the "old-fashioned" American ideal of the freedom of the press. Hughes pointed out that the basic idea of modern liberals is

> to make the press "accountable" or "responsible" to society or the community, which . . . can only mean to government. . . . If liberty means anything at all, freedom of the press is freedom from the government.[8]

The great watershed, the single event that most marked the passing of the old isolationist Right, was the defeat of Senator Taft by Eisenhower in the Wall Street capture of the 1952 presidential nomination. With the Democrats vulnerable, 1952 was at last a chance for the Old Right to achieve dominance on the national scene. But the defeat of Taft in the outrageous Eisenhower theft of the nomination, coupled with the death of the great Senator the following year, ended the Old Right as a significant faction of the Republican Party. In effect, it also was to end my own identification with Republicanism and with the "extreme right" on the political spectrum.

I had not been active in the Young Republican Club since the disappointment of the Dewey nomination in 1948, but I was still a member, and Ronnie Hertz, a libertarian friend of mine, exercised some clout in the club as head of its midtown luncheon committee, to which we invited isolationist and libertarian speakers. I was not a Taft enthusiast on any absolute scale, because of his repeated compromises and "sellouts" in domestic and foreign affairs, and in the climactic meeting of the club that voted for the presidential endorsement, in which Taft won a sizable minority, Ronnie and I cast our two votes for Senator Everett Dirksen (R., Ill.). In that

---

Niebuhr, George Schuster, Robert Redfield, Charles E. Merriam, and Archibald MacLeish; and businessman Beardsley Ruml and counsel John Dickinson.

[8]Hughes, *Prejudice and the Press*, p. 5.

more innocent day, Dirksen had not yet won his stripes as the supreme political opportunist; instead, under the aegis of the *Chicago Tribune*, he then had a solidly "extremist" voting record, including one of the few votes cast against the draft. But in the momentous convention itself, I was of course for Taft and still more in opposition to the leftist—corporate liberal—Wall Street takeover, which conquered on the crest of an outrageous press campaign implying that Taft had "stolen" the Southern delegations. When Taft was cheated out of the nomination, I for one walked out of the Republican Party, never to return. In the election I supported Stevenson, largely as the only way to get the Wall Street incubus off the back of the Republican Party.

It is important to note that the later, 1960s Republican right wing, the Goldwater-Buckley Right, had no connection with the old Taft Right, even organizationally. Thus, Barry Goldwater was himself an Eisenhower delegate from Arizona; the conservative warmonger Senator General Pat Hurley, was an Eisenhower man from New Mexico; the two doyens of the China Lobby were anti-Taft: Representative Walter Judd (R., Minn.) being for Eisenhower and Senator William Knowland (R., Calif.) being a supporter of Governor Earl Warren, who was decisive in throwing his support to Ike on the Southern delegate question. Richard Nixon was also instrumental in the California deal, and both Nixon and Warren went on to their suitable rewards. And furthermore, the famous Southern delegation fight was scarcely what it seemed on the surface. The Taft delegations in the South were largely Negro, hence their name of "Black and Tan," and were led by the veteran black Republican Perry Howard of Mississippi, whereas the Eisenhower delegations, the representatives of the "progressive" white suburbanite businessmen of the Southern Republican future, were known quite properly as the Lilywhites.

Meanwhile, let us note the bitter but accurate portrayal of the Taft defeat by *Chicago Tribune* reporter Chesly Manly two years later, as an example also of the right-wing muckraking style:

> New York banks, connected with the country's great corporations by financial ties and interlocking directorates, exerted their powerful influence on the large uncommitted

> delegations for Eisenhower. They did it more subtly, but no less effectively, than in 1940 when they captured the Republican convention for Willkie. Having made enormous profits out of foreign aid and armaments orders, the bankers and corporation bosses understood each other perfectly. The Wall Street influence was most fruitful in the Pennsylvania delegation . . . and in that of Michigan. . . . Arthur Summerfield, Michigan's national committeeman and the largest Chevrolet dealer in the world, was rewarded for his delivery of the bulk of the Michigan delegation by appointment as Eisenhower's campaign manager and later as his Postmaster General. Charles E. Wilson, President of the General Motors Corporation, which had strong influence in the Michigan delegation, became Secretary of Defense. Winthrop W. Aldrich, head of the Chase National Bank and kinsman of the Rockefeller brothers, the front man for Wall Street, was in Chicago pulling wires for Eisenhower, and his labors paid off with an appointment as ambassador to Great Britain.[9]

With the election of Eisenhower, the old right wing of the Republican Party began to fade out of the picture. But Senator Taft had one final moment of glory. In the last speech on foreign policy delivered before his death, Taft attacked the foreign policy hegemony beginning to be exercised by Secretary of State John Foster Dulles,[10] the epitome of global warmongering and anti-Communism, the man who hailed from the top Wall Street law firm of Sullivan and Cromwell and was a long-time counsel for the Rockefeller interests. In this speech, delivered on May 26, 1953, Taft leveled at the Dulles policies the same criticism he had made against the similar policies of Harry Truman: the system of worldwide military alliances and aid was "the complete antithesis

---

[9]Chesly Manly, *The Twenty-Year Revolution: From Roosevelt to Eisenhower* (Chicago: Henry Regnery Company, 1954), pp. 20–21.

[10]The Dulles family stain on American foreign policy included John Foster's brother Allen, who headed the CIA, and his sister Eleanor, at the Asia desk of the State Department.

of the UN Charter," a threat to Russian and Chinese security, and furthermore valueless for the defense of the United States.

Taft in particular centered his fire on Dulles's nascent policy in Southeast Asia. He was especially concerned because the United States was increasing to 70 percent its support of the costs of the fight of the French puppet regime in Indo-China against the revolutionary forces of Ho Chi Minh. Taft feared—with great prescience!—that Dulles's policy, upon the inevitable defeat of French imperialism in Indo-China, would lead to its eventual replacement by American imperialism, and—to Taft the worst of all possibilities—the sending of American forces to Vietnam to fight the guerrillas.

Declared Taft:

> I have never felt that we should send American soldiers to the Continent of Asia, which, of course, included China proper and Indo-China, simply because we are so outnumbered in fighting a land war on the Continent of Asia that it would bring about complete exhaustion even if we were able to win. . . . So today, as since 1947 in Europe and 1950 in Asia, we are really trying to arm the world against Communist Russia, or at least furnish all the assistance which can be of use to them in opposing Communism.
>
> Is this policy of uniting the free world against Communism in time of peace going to be a practical long-term policy? I have always been a skeptic on the subject of the military practicability of NATO. . . . I have always felt that we should not attempt to fight Russia on the ground on the Continent of Europe any more than we should attempt to fight China on the Continent of Asia.[11]

In the months immediately following Taft's death, American support of the French armies and of its puppet government in

---

[11]Robert A. Taft, "United States Foreign Policy: Forget United Nations in Korea and Far East," *Vital Speeches* 19, no. 17 (June 15, 1953): 530–31. Also see Leonard P. Liggio, "Why the Futile Crusade?" *Left and Right* 1, no. 1 (Spring, 1965): 60–62.

Vietnam was greatly increased by Dulles, but while Dulles and Nixon urged American bombing of Ho Chi Minh's forces, Eisenhower himself, who had been greatly influenced by his brief but deep association with Taft during and after the 1952 campaign, listened to such Taft supporters in his cabinet as George Humphrey and decided not to use American forces directly in Vietnam without the prior consent of Congress. By following this Taftian principle, the Eisenhower administration allowed the Great Debate in the Senate, as well as the opposition of Great Britain, to block it from an immediate Vietnam adventure. The ex-isolationist Alexander Wiley (R., Wis.) summed up the feelings of the majority of Senate Republicans when he declared: "If war comes under this administration, it could well be the end of the Republican Party." And Senator Lyndon B. Johnson (D., Tex.) summed up the view of the Democrats by saying that he was opposed to "sending American GIs into the mud and muck of Indochina on a blood-letting spree to perpetuate colonialism and white man's exploitation in Asia."[12]

As a result of these pressures, and in defiance of Dulles, Nixon, and the Pentagon, President Eisenhower moved toward the Geneva Agreement of 1954; all-out American intervention in Vietnam was mercifully postponed, though unfortunately not permanently abandoned. In death, Senator Robert Taft's influence on American foreign policy was greater, at least for the moment, than it had ever been in life.

---

[12]Bernard B. Fall, *The Two Viet-Nams* (New York: Frederick A. Praeger, 1963), pp. 227–28. Also see Liggio, "Why the Futile Crusade?" p. 62.

11

Decline of the Old Right

After the death of Taft and as the Eisenhower foreign policy began to take on the frozen Dullesian lineaments of permanent mass armament and the threat of "massive nuclear retaliation" throughout the globe, I began to notice isolationist sentiment starting to fade away, even among old libertarian and isolationist compatriots who should have known better. Old friends who used to scoff at the "Russian threat" and had declared The Enemy to be Washington, D.C. now began to mutter about the "international Communist conspiracy." I noticed that young libertarians coming into the ranks were increasingly infected with the Cold War mentality and had never even heard of the isolationist alternative. Young libertarians wondered how it was that I upheld a "Communist foreign policy."

In this emerging atmosphere, novelist Louis Bromfield's non-fiction work of 1954, *A New Pattern for a Tired World*,[1] a hard-hitting tract on behalf of free-market capitalism and a peaceful foreign policy, began to seem anachronistic and had almost no impact on the right wing of the day.

Bromfield charged:

> Aside from the tragic drain on our youth, whether drafted for two of the best years of their lives or maimed or killed or imprisoned, the grandiose "containment" policy means an immense and constant drain in terms of money. . . .

---

[1](New York: Harper and Bros., 1954).

And further:

> One of the great failures of our foreign policy throughout the world arises from the fact that we have permitted ourselves to be identified everywhere with the old, doomed and rotting colonial-imperialist small European nations which once imposed upon so much of the world the pattern of exploitation and economic and political domination. This fact lies at the core of our failure to win the support and trust of the once-exploited nations and peoples who are now in rebellion and revolution in all parts of the world but especially in Asia. We have not given these peoples a real choice between the practices of Russian Communist imperialism or Communism and those of a truly democratic world in which individualism, American capitalism and free enterprise are the very pillars of independence, solid economics, liberty and good living standards. We have appeared to these peoples themselves . . . in the role of colonial imperialists . . . and of supporters in almost every case of the rotting old European empires. . . .
>
> None of these rebellious, awakening peoples will, in their hearts or even superficially, trust us or cooperate in any way so long as we remain identified with the economic colonial system of Europe; which represents, even in its capitalist pattern, the last remnants of feudalism. . . . We cannot appear to these Asiatic peoples in the role of friend and benefactor while we are at the same time financing, attempting to restore to power and even providing arms to the very forces of the dying colonial empires, against which they are in rebellion.
>
> This is exactly what we are doing in Indo-China and in Hong Kong and elsewhere in the world under a confused policy based upon the doomed past rather than upon the inevitable dynamic pattern of the future. We leave these awakening peoples with no choice but to turn to Russian and Communist comfort and promises of Utopia. We make it possible everywhere . . . for the Communists . . . to create the impression that what in fact is merely an intense assertion of nationalism is really a Communist liberation, planned and carried out by Communist influence. . . .
>
> We are playing the politics of a vanished world, blindly and stupidly attempting to surround and contain what can not be contained, blocking the free exchange of goods and

> keeping the world in a constant uproar by making alliances and setting up military installations everywhere. It is an antique pattern of power politics.[2]

Again on Asia:

> The battle in Indo-China engages . . . countless Indo-Chinese . . . who hate French domination. . . . Yet there are even those, principally in armed forces of the U.S., who would, if they dared, advocate drafting American boys from Ohio, Iowa, Kansas and elsewhere and sending them into this struggle where they or the nation itself have no proper place and where our intervention can only serve to do us tragic harm in the long run. . . .
>
> [Korea] may well prove to be not the martyred heroic nation which the sentimental have made of her, but merely the albatross around our neck which can carry us deeper and deeper into tragic complications and future wars. Because we have no real reason to be in Korea, unless, as every Asiatic suspects, for reasons of power and exploitation. To say that a country so remote and insignificant as Korea is our first line of defense is to say that every nation in every part of the world is also our "first line of defense"—a conception which is obviously fantastic and grotesque to the borders of megalomania. . . .
>
> Our permanent occupation of Korea in order to maintain her economic and political independence artificially is an act against the whole trend of world revolution and the irresistible forces of our times. . . . We must stay in Korea indefinitely and eventually retire and accept defeat or involve ourselves and the world in a war which may well be for us and will be certainly for all Europe the end of the road. . . . The Korean situation . . . will not be settled until we withdraw entirely from an area in which we have no right to be and leave the peoples of that area to work out their own problems.[3]

---

[2]Louis Bromfield, *A New Pattern for a Tired World* (New York: Harper and Bros., 1954), pp. 49–55.

[3]Ibid., pp. 60–63.

Bromfield concluded that the whole of our foreign policy was not "worth the torture or the life of one unwilling conscript, even if it were not the most dangerous and destructive of policies to the peace and welfare of the world."[4]

In this period of slippage of devotion to peace, in a right wing on which the Bromfield book made little impact, I determined to try to reaffirm the older foreign policy tradition in the conservative-libertarian movement. In April 1954, William Johnson put together an all-isolationist, all-peace issue of *Faith and Freedom* that was one of the last intellectual gasps of the isolationist-libertarian Right. The issue included an article by Garet Garrett, "The Suicidal Impulse," which continued his analysis of "The Rise of Empire." Garrett declared that the American Empire had built up "the most terrible killing machine mankind had ever known," that we were brandishing our "immense stock of atomic bombs," that there were American troops and air bases throughout the globe, and that there was "from time to time a statement from an eminent American military person saying the American Air Force is prepared to drop bombs in Russia with the greatest of ease, on targets already selected." Garrett concluded that the "allure of world leadership weaves a fatal spell. The idea of imposing universal peace on the world by force is a barbarian fantasy."[5]

Also included in the *Faith and Freedom* issue was Ernest T. Weir, the right-wing union-busting industrialist of the 1930s, World War II isolationist, and head of the National Steel Corporation of Pittsburgh. Weir, the Cyrus Eaton of the 1950s, had been stumping the country and publishing pamphlets calling for a negotiated peace with the Soviet Union and Communist China and an end to the Cold War. In his article, "Leaving Emotions Out of Foreign Policy," Weir declared that

> we have to accept the fact that it is not the mission of the United States to go charging about the world to free it from

---

[4]Ibid., p. 75.

[5]Garet Garrett, "The Suicidal Impulse," *Faith and Freedom* 5, no. 8 (April 1954): 6.

> bad nations and bad systems of government. We must reconcile ourselves to the fact that there will always be bad nations and bad systems and that our task is to contrive some basis other than warfare on which we can live in the world.[6]

My own contribution to the issue was "The Real Aggressor," under the *nom de plume* of "Aubrey Herbert," in which I tried to establish a libertarian basis for an isolationist and peaceful foreign policy, and called for peaceful coexistence, joint disarmament, withdrawal from NATO and the UN, and recognition of Communist China, as well as free trade with all countries.

For our pains, both Mr. Weir and I were red-baited in the Social Democratic *New Leader* by William Henry Chamberlin. The fact of Chamberlin's growing influence on the intellectual Right was symptomatic of its accelerating decay. A former Communist fellow-traveler in the 1930s, Chamberlin seemed able to shift his principles at will, writing assiduously for both the *Wall Street Journal* and the *New Leader*, supporting free-market economics in the former publication and statism in the latter. He was also capable of writing a book[7] praising isolationism and the Munich pact for World War II, while at the same time denouncing present-day isolationists and opponents of the Cold War as "appeasers" and proponents of "another Munich." But in one sense this new Chamberlin was consistent; for he was one of that growing legion of ex-Communist and ex-fellow traveler journalists who spearheaded the ideological front for the Cold War and the world anti-Communist crusade. In his article "Appeasement on the Right,"[8] Chamberlin charged that Weir's article "could have appeared in the *Nation*, perhaps even in *Masses and Mainstream*"; as

---

[6]Ernest T. Weir, "Leaving Emotions Out of Our Foreign Policy," ibid., p. 8.

[7]William Henry Chamberlin, *America's Second Crusade* (Chicago: Henry Regnery, 1950).

[8]William Henry Chamberlin, "Appeasement on the Right," *New Leader* (May 17, 1954).

for my article, I had laid "down a blueprint for America policy tailor-made to the specifications of the Kremlin."

It was the first time that I had ever been red-baited, though it was not to be the last, and to a professed "extreme right winger" this charge was something of a shock. When I replied in the *New Leader* and noted that Chamberlin himself had hailed appeasement and Munich a short while before, Chamberlin responded in characteristic fashion: that Ernest Weir had been recently hailed in the Warsaw *Trybuna Ludu*, and that perhaps I would soon "receive [my] appropriate recognition from the same or a similar source."[9]

Soon afterward, I signed on to replace Chodorov as monthly Washington columnist of *Faith and Freedom*, and month in and month out, until the end of 1956, I hammered away at the statism of the Eisenhower administration. Troubled at the growing adherence to militarism and the Cold War on the right wing, I particularly blasted away at these trends. While calling for withdrawal from the United Nations, I urged that it recognize reality and admit China to membership; calling for neutralism and isolationism, I expressed the hope for neutralism abroad and a neutralist and peacefully reunified Germany; attacking permanent expansion of the United States beyond our shores, I called for granting Hawaii, Alaska, and Puerto Rico their independence instead of incorporating them as permanent states. In early 1956, I attacked the Eisenhower administration for torpedoing the second Geneva conference and its hopes for détente and disarmament: first, by presenting a demand for German reunification under NATO as

---

[9]Ibid., p. 21; letter from Aubrey Herbert and reply by Chamberlin, ibid., June 21, 1954, p. 29. As far as I know, the Polish accolade never came. As for the demoralized and bleeding domestic Left, one of the few pieces of recognition of the anti-imperialist Right was in the *New York Compass* of January 2, 1952, seconded by the *National Guardian* of January 9, 1953, both of which praised an excellent article by Garet Garrett in the *Wall Street Journal*. Garrett had attacked the bipartisan imperialist foreign policy and denounced all the presidential candidates, including Taft, for supporting it.

our prime demand at the conference; and second, by withdrawing our longstanding demand for simultaneous disarmament *and* inspection as soon as the Russians had agreed to our own position, and later substituting instead Ike's demagogic proposal for "open skies." A few months later, I sharply criticized the Right for springing to the defense of the Marine drill instructor who brutally ordered six men to watery graves in a senseless death march at Parris Island. How is it, I asked, that only the left-liberals had risen to champion freedom against brutality and militarism?

My most severe tangle with the pro-war Right came in a series of debates in early 1955 on whether or not to fight for Formosa, a question which loomed large in that year.

In my March column I called for withdrawal from Formosa, attacked the manic logic which demanded an endless series of bases to "protect our previous bases," and asked how *we* would feel if the Chinese were occupying and fortifying an island three miles off *our* coast? Furthermore, I hailed the call for peace recently delivered by the hero of the war right, Douglas MacArthur, and also praised Rep. Eugene R. Siler (R., Ky.) for picking up the old isolationist baton and voting against the blank-check congressional resolution of January 29 on Formosa because he had promised his constituents that he would never help to "engage their boys in war on foreign soil."

This article precipitated a debate with a fellow columnist on *Faith and Freedom*, William S. Schlamm, another leader of the new trends on the right wing, and formerly book review editor of the then-major intellectual right-wing magazine, the *Freeman*. Schlamm was typical of the New Rightist: formerly a leading German Communist and editor of *Die Rote Fahne*, Schlamm was now dedicating his career to whipping up enthusiasm for the crushing of his old comrades, at home and abroad. In his zeal for the world anti-Communist crusade, I could never—and still cannot—detect one iota of devotion to freedom in Schlamm's worldview. What was he doing on *Faith and Freedom* to begin with? When *National Review* was founded in late 1955, Schlamm became its book review editor and, for a while, its chief theoretician; later he was to return to Germany and gain a large popular following for an ultra-hard-line foreign policy against the East.

Schlamm and I had a series of two debates—"Fight for Formosa—or Not?"—in the May and June issues of *Faith and Freedom.* I accused him of advocating preventive war, and reminded our readers that we had not been attacked by either Russia or China, and that a world war would mean the total destruction of civilization. And why, I asked, as I had before in those columns, do the pro-war conservatives, supposedly dedicated to the superiority of capitalism over Communism, by thirsting for an immediate showdown, implicitly grant that time is on the side of the Communist system? I then reaffirmed that surely any libertarian must hold "the enemy" to be not Russian Communism but any invasion of our liberty by the State; to give up our freedom in order to "preserve" it is only succumbing to the Orwellian dialectic that "freedom is slavery." As for Schlamm's position that we had already been "attacked" by Communism, I pointed out the crucial distinction between *military* and "ideological" attack, a distinction to which the libertarian, with his entire philosophy resting on the difference between violent aggression and nonviolent persuasion, should be particularly attuned. My puzzlement should have been solved by realizing that Mr. Schlamm was the furthest thing from a "libertarian." I also called for realistic negotiations with the Communist world, which would result in mutual atomic and bacteriological disarmament.

More important in trying to stem the efforts of the war crowd to take over the Right was the redoubtable Frank Chodorov. It turned out to be a tragedy for the libertarian cause that Frank had liquidated his magnificent *analysis* in the early 1950s and merged it into *Human Events,* where he then served as an associate editor. Frank was also my predecessor as Washington columnist of *Faith and Freedom.* In the summer of 1954, Frank took up the editorship of the *Freeman,* the leading organ of the intellectual Right, previously a weekly and by this time reduced to a monthly issued by the Foundation for Economic Education. In his September *Freeman* editorial ("The Return of 1940?") Chodorov proclaimed that the old isolationist-interventionist split among conservatives and libertarians was once again coming into play. "Already the libertarians are debating among themselves on the need of putting off the struggle for freedom until after the threat of communism, Moscow style, shall have been removed, even by war." Frank pointed out the consequences of our entry into World War II: a massive debt burden, a gigantic tax structure, a permanent incubus of conscription, an enormous federal bureaucracy, the loss of our sense of personal freedom and independence. "All this," Frank concluded,

> the "isolationists" of 1940 foresaw. Not because they were endowed with any gift of prevision, but because they knew history and would not deny its lesson: that during war the State acquires power at the expense of freedom, and that because of its insatiable lust for power the State is incapable of giving up any of it. The State never abdicates.[10]

Any further war would be infinitely worse, and perhaps destroy the world in the process.

Chodorov's editorial drew a rebuttal from the indefatigable Willi Schlamm, and the two debated the war question in the pages of the November 1954 *Freeman*. Chodorov's rebuttal, "A War to Communize America," was his last great reaffirmation of the isolationist Old Right position. Chodorov began,

> We are again being told to be afraid. As it was before the two world wars so it is now; politicians talk in frightening terms, journalists invent scare-lines, and even next-door neighbors are taking up the cry: the enemy is at the city gates; we must gird for battle. In case you don't know, the enemy this time is the U.S.S.R.[11]

Chodorov centered on the question of conscription, since "to fight a war with Russia on foreign soil," the interventionists conceded, required this form of slavery. "I don't think a single division could

---

[10]Frank Chodorov, "The Return of 1940?" *Freeman* (September 1954): 81.

[11]Frank Chodorov, "A War to Communize America," *Freeman* (November 1954): 171.

have been raised by the volunteer system for the Korean adventure." And if the American people do not want to fight in such wars, by what right are they to be "compelled to fight them?" And: "We are told that we must fear the Russians. I am more afraid of those who, like their forebears, would compel us against our will to fight the Russians. They have the dictator complex."[12] Chodorov then reiterated that any further war would end whatever liberty we had, that slavery to an American master was no better than slavery to some foreign master: "Why go to war for [the] privilege" of choosing one or the other? As for ourselves being invaded, there was no real possibility of such a thing happening. The only thing we had to fear in the current situation was "the hysteria of fear" itself. The only way to remove this fear on both sides, Chodorov concluded, was for us to "abandon our global military commitments" and return home.

As for the alleged Russian threat to Western Europe if we should withdraw, "it would be hard on the Europeans if they fell into Soviet hands; but not any worse than if we precipitated a war in which their homes became the battlefield."[13] And if these countries do, in fact, desire communism, then "our presence in Europe is an impertinent interference with the internal affairs of these countries; let them go communist if they want to."[14]

Unfortunately, shortly afterward Chodorov was ousted as editor; a man of stubborn independence and integrity, Chodorov would not submit to any form of mental castration. With Chodorov gone, Leonard Read could return to his long-standing policy of never engaging in direct political or ideological controversy, and the *Freeman* proceeded to sink into the slough of innocuous desuetude in which it remains today. Chodorov was now deprived of a libertarian outlet, his great voice was stilled; and this loss was made final by the tragic illness that struck in 1961 and in which Frank spent the last years of his life. Aggravating the

---

[12]Ibid., p. 172.

[13]Ibid., p. 174.

[14]Ibid., p. 173

tragedy was his ideological betrayal by close friends such as young William F. Buckley, whom Frank had discovered as a writer while editing *Human Events* (and who in a recent "Firing Line" exchange with Karl Hess dared to bring up the name of the dead Chodorov as a libertarian sanction for his own pro-war stance). Even more poignant is the history of the Intercollegiate Society of Individualists, which Frank had founded in 1952 as a "fifty-year project" to win the college campuses away from statism and toward individualism. In 1956, ISI left FEE's offices to take up headquarters in Philadelphia. Frank's selection to succeed him as head of ISI, E. Victor Milione, has since taken ISI squarely into the traditionalist-conservative camp, even to the extent—at about the time of Frank's death in late 1966—of changing the name of Chodorov's brainchild to the "Intercollegiate Studies Institute." It seems that the name "individualist" was upsetting conservative businessmen, to whom it conjured up visions of the rebels of the New Left. Oh, liberty! What crimes are committed in thy name![15]

Another grave blow to isolationism and the Old Right was the loss of *Human Events*. From the beginning, the three owners of *Human Events* had been Felix Morley, the theoretician; Frank Hanighen, the journalist; and Henry Regnery, the financial supporter. Before and during World War II, all had been isolationists, but after the war Hanighen, followed by Regnery, began to jump on the anti-Communist and pro-interventionist bandwagon, much to the resistance of Morley. Morley, who in his autobiography paid high tribute to the influence of Nock, scoffed at his colleagues' emphasis on the Hiss case. Once Franklin Roosevelt, guided by Harry Hopkins, had brought about a "Communist victory,"

---

[15]The idea of the name change originated in the fall of 1960 with Bill Buckley, but Chodorov never accepted the change. It took until near the point of Chodorov's death that Milione was willing to make the break, and thereby symbolize another takeover by the Buckleyite New Right. George H. Nash, *The Conservative Intellectual Movement in America Since 1945* (New York: Basic Books, 1976), p. 390.

declared Morley, "it seemed silly to bother about the hole-and-corner machinations of a few fellow-travelers as accused communist turncoats." In addition to ideology, Hanighen was particularly motivated by moolah: Hanighen

> believed that the Hiss case would prove sensational, as indeed it did, and that we could greatly increase our circulation by exploiting it, as also Senator McCarthy's sweeping charges. He was probably right, since after I left it the little publication grew rapidly by climbing aboard the anti-Communist bandwagon.[16]

Finally, the split came in February 1950, over Hanighen's insistence that *Human Events* go all-out in support of American intervention in behalf of Chiang Kai-shek's regime now holed up in Taiwan. Regnery sided with Hanighen, and so Morley was bought out by his partners. Looking back on this forced separation Morley concluded:

> In retrospect I see this episode as symptomatic of that which has come to divide the conservative movement in the United States. Frank and Henry, in their separate ways, moved on to associate with the far Right in the Republican Party. My position remained essentially "Libertarian," though it is with great reluctance that I yield the old terminology of "liberal" to the socialists. I was, and continue to be, strongly opposed to centralization of political power, thinking that this process will eventually destroy our federal republic, if it has not already done so. The vestment of power in HEW [the Department of Health, Education and Welfare] is demonstrably bad, but its concentration in the Pentagon and CIA is worse because the authority is often concealed and covertly

[16]Felix Morley, *For the Record* (South Bend, Ind.: Regnery Gateway, 1979), p. 430. In a rather sharper and less mellow account of the break written for a 30th-anniversary celebration of *Human Events*, Morley wrote that Hanighen was beginning to consider him "soft on Communism." Felix Morley, "The Early Days of *Human Events*," *Human Events* (April 27, 1974): 26, 28, 31. Cited in Nash, *Conservative Intellectual Movement*, pp. 124–25.

> exercised. Failure to check either extreme means continuous deficit financing and consequent inflation which in time can be fatal to the free enterprise system.[17]

Morley, a friend of Bob Taft, had been slated for a high appointment in the State Department if Taft had become President in 1953; but it was not to be.

But by the mid-1950s the battle for Old Right isolationism had not yet been completely lost. Thus, at the end of 1955, For America, a leading right-wing political action group headed by Notre Dame Law School Dean Clarence Manion, issued its political platform. Two of its major foreign policy planks were "Abolish Conscription" and "Enter No Foreign Wars unless the safety of the United States is directly threatened." Not a word about liberating Communist countries, or about stopping Communism all over the world. As for our small libertarian group, right-wing anarchists Robert LeFevre and Thaddeus Ashby were able to gain control, for a short but glorious time, of the right-wing Congress of Freedom, headed by Washingtonian Arnold Kruckman. On April 24, 1954, LeFevre and Ashby managed to push through the Congress a libertarian platform, specifically calling for the abolition of conscription, the "severing our entangling alliance with foreign nations," and the abolition of all foreign aid. The platform declared: "We decry the war we have lost in Korea and we will oppose American intervention in the war in Indochina." More orthodox rightists, however, managed to regain control of the Congress the following year.

The last great political gasp of the isolationist Right came in the fight for the Bricker Amendment, the major foreign-policy plan of the conservative Republicans during the first Eisenhower term. Senator John W. Bricker (R., Ohio) had been the ill-fated right-wing candidate for president in 1948, and was Taft's natural

---

[17]Morley, *For the Record*, p. 437. Morley pays tribute to the fact that Regnery, despite these criticisms, was happy to publish his book.

successor after the death of his fellow Ohioan. The Bricker Amendment to the Constitution was designed to prevent the threat of international treaties and executive agreements becoming the supreme law of the land and overriding previous internal law or provisions of the Constitution. It provided that no treaty or executive agreement conflicting with, or not made in pursuance of, the Constitution, shall have any force; and that no such treaty or executive agreement shall become effective as internal law except by domestic legislation that would have been valid in the absence of the agreement. Favoring the Amendment were a battery of right-wing groups: veterans and patriotic organizations, the American Farm Bureau Federation, the Chamber of Commerce, Pro America, the National Small Business Association, the Conference of Small Business Organizations, Merwin K. Hart's National Economic Council, the Committee for Constitutional Government, Rev. Fifield's Freedom Clubs, Inc., and large chunks of the American Bar Association. The major opponent of the Amendment was the Eisenhower administration, in particular Secretary of State Dulles and Attorney General Herbert Brownell, ably seconded by the forces of organized liberalism: the Americans for Democratic Action, the AFL, B'nai B'rith, the American Jewish Congress, the American Association for the United Nations, and the United World Federalists.

The climactic vote on the Bricker Amendment came in the U.S. Senate in February 1954, the Amendment going down to a severe defeat. While the overwhelming majority of right-wing Republicans voted for the Amendment, there were some significant defections, including William Knowland and Alexander Wiley (R., Wis.), a former isolationist who was playing the iniquitous "Vandenberg role" as Chairman of the Foreign Relations Committee in what might well have been the last Republican-controlled Senate.[18]

---

[18]On the Bricker Amendment struggle, see Frank E. Holman, *Story of the "Bricker" Amendment (The First Phase)* (New York: Committee for Constitutional Government, 1954). Holman, a past president of the American Bar Association, was a leader in the forces for the amendment. Included as appendices to the book were pro-Bricker

It is indicative of the later decline of the Old Right that the Bricker Amendment was to race away and disappear totally in right-wing councils, never to be heard from again. In particular, the New Right, which began to emerge in force after 1955, was able to bury the Bricker Amendment, as well as the isolationist sentiment that it embodied, in some form of Orwellian "memory hole."

If the Bricker Amendment was the last isolationist pressure campaign of the Old Right, the third-party ticket of 1956 was its last direct political embodiment. I had been yearning for an Old Right third party ever since the disgraceful Republican convention of 1952, and some Taftites tried to launch a Constitution Party, nominating Douglas MacArthur that very fall, only to lament that there was not enough time, and that 1956 would be the Year. Third-party discussions and movements by disgruntled Old Rightists began in late 1955, and numerous conservative, Constitution, and "New" Parties sprang up in various states. But there was precious little organization or money or political savvy in these attempts, and none of the top right-wing leaders endorsed their efforts.

I myself was involved in two third-party attempts in New York, a minuscule Constitution Party and a larger Independent Party, headed by an elderly man named Dan Sawyer. I vividly remember a good-sized rally held by the Independents in early 1956. One featured speaker was Kent Courtney of New Orleans, who with his wife, Phoebe, was the main founder of the new party. A particular feature was a colorful old gent, whose name escapes me, looking like a stereotyped Kentucky colonel, who limped his way to the stand. The Colonel, for such I believe he was, though from Texas, proclaimed that he was an unsung founder of the science of public opinion polling, and that he had been President Coolidge's opinion poll adviser. (And had Hoover only listened to him! . . .) At any rate, the Colonel assured us, from the very depths of his public opinion know-how, that *any* Democrat was certain to defeat Eisenhower in the 1956 election. Such was the acumen of the third-party

---

Amendment statements by the veteran individualist and isolationist Samuel Pettingill, Clarence Manion, Garet Garrett, and Frank Chodorov.

leadership. Unsurprisingly, the Independent Party of New York held no further meetings.

The Constitution Party of New York was even shorter lived. Again, I attended only one "mass" meeting, presided over by a young lawyer named Ed Scharfenberger in a tiny Manhattan restaurant. Scharfenberger gave me to understand that I could help write the platform of the party, but something told me that the party was not long for this world. The Constitution Party's great talking point was its connection with a mini-network of Constitution groups headed by the party in Texas, which actually got on the ballot and ran some candidates.

My own personal candidate for president in 1956 was Governor Bracken Lee of Utah, who was certainly the closest thing to a libertarian in political life. There were indeed few other governors who advocated repeal of the income tax, sold state colleges to private enterprise, refused Federal grants-in-aid for highways, denounced social security, urged withdrawal from the UN, or proclaimed foreign aid to be unconstitutional.

In fact, a third party did get underway, but once again it began very late, in mid-September of the election year, and so could get on the ballot in only a few states. The New Party, in a States' Rights Convention, nominated T. Coleman Andrews of Virginia for president, and former Representative Thomas H. Werdel (R., Calif.) for vice president. Andrews had made himself an antitax hero by serving for several years as Eisenhower's Commissioner of Internal Revenue, and then resigning to stump the country for repeal of the Sixteenth (income tax) Amendment. I firmly supported the Andrews-Werdel ticket, not the least of whose charms was the absence of any call for a worldwide anti-Communist crusade. The Bricker Amendment, opposition to foreign aid, and withdrawal from the UN was the extent of their foreign affairs program, and the same in fact could be said about the Constitution parties. Andrews-Werdel reached their peak in Virginia and Louisiana, where they polled about 7 percent of the vote, carrying one county—Prince Edward in Virginia—while J. Bracken Lee collected over 100,000 votes in Utah in an independent race for president in his home state.

While I supported Andrews-Werdel, I made clear to my *Faith and Freedom* readers that between the two major candidates I favored Adlai Stevenson. The major motive was not, as in 1952, to punish the left Republicans for taking over the party. Presaging my later political career, my major reason was the decidedly more pro-peace stand that Stevenson was taking: specifically in his call for abolition of testing of H-bombs as well as his suggestion that we abolish the draft. This was enough to push me in a Stevensonian direction.

Soon after the election, Bill Johnson, who had always commended my columns, flew East to inform me that I was being dumped as Washington columnist. Why? Because his Protestant minister readership had come to the conclusion that I was a "Communist." Red-baiting again, and this time from "libertarians"! I protested that, month in and month out, I had consistently attacked government and defended the individual; how could this possibly be "Communist"? The lines were tightening. *Faith and Freedom* itself collapsed shortly thereafter (*not*, I must hasten to add, because of my dismissal). Bill Johnson went on to join Dick Cornuelle in the Volker Fund operation.

The demise of *Faith and Freedom*, and of its controlling organization, Spiritual Mobilization (SM), was symptomatic of the grievous decline of the libertarian wing of the Old Right in the latter half of the 1950s. In the midst of libertarianism's—and the Old Right's—gravest crisis since World War II, Spiritual Mobilization, instead of providing leadership in these stormy times, turned toward what can only be called neo-Buddhist mystical gabble. In the mid-1950s, the Reverend Fifield had turned over day-to-day operation of SM to Jim Ingebretsen, a libertarian and old friend of Leonard Read who had been an official with the Chamber of Commerce. No sooner did he assume the reins of SM, however, than he—and the rest of the influential SM group—fell under the charismatic influence of the gnomic English neo-Buddhist mystic, Gerald Heard. Heard, who liked to think of his murky lucubrations as the requirements of "science," had already converted Aldous Huxley and Christopher Isherwood to Heardian mysticism (it was Heard who had provided the model for the guru who converted Huxley's sophisticated hero to mysticism in *Eyeless in Gaza*). Heard had set up shop in a retreat provided by a businessman patron in an estate called Idyllwild in the Los Angeles area; and there he organized retreats for all the once-active libertarian Old Right businessmen. In particular, Heard, blathering about the "Growing Edge" and the paranormal, organized mystical sessions which included experiments in hallucinogenic "mad mushrooms" and even LSD. It is fascinating that Heard and his crew were proto-Timothy Leary types—an incongruous leap into a genteel but highly debilitating form of right-wing "counter-culture." One thing that plunging into this nonsense accomplished, of course, was to convince the participants that liberty, statism, economics, politics, and even ethics were not really important; that the only thing that really counted was advances in personal spiritual "awareness."

Even though presumably not designed for that purpose, this was a beautiful way to destroy an active ideological movement. All the participants became tainted in one way or another. Thaddeus Ashby, who had become assistant editor of *Faith and Freedom*, influenced Johnson, and Gerald Heard obtained a regular column there, every month issuing incomprehensible Confucius-like pronouncements. (A typical column began: "People ask me, Mr. Heard, will there be war? And I answer: 'Have you read Maeterlinck's *The Life of the Bee*'?"—I am sure a most useful answer to the burning foreign policy question.) Ashby ended up dropping out of libertarian ideology altogether, and pursuing the mad mushroom in Mexico and the bizarre path of Tantric Yoga. Bill Mullendore's enthusiasm for liberty weakened. And Ingebretsen was so influenced as to go virtually on permanent retreat. Business contributions fell off drastically, despite a last-minute desperate attempt to transform *Faith and Freedom* into an exclusively antiunion organ, and the Rev. Fifield, who had run SM since the 1930s, resigned in 1959, thus sounding the death knell for a once active and important organization.[19]

---

[19]For an illuminating discussion of the mysticism that laid Spiritual Mobilization low in the late 1950s, see Eckard Vance Toy, Jr., "Ideology and Conflict in American Ultraconservatism, 1945–1960" (Ph.D. diss., University of Oregon, 1965), pp. 156–90.

Even Leonard Read was affected, and Read's flirtation on the fringes of the Growing Edge group could only accelerate the steady deterioration of FEE. Leonard had always had a mystical streak; thus, he treated every newcomer to FEE to a one-hour monologue to the effect that "scientists tell me that if you could blow up an atom to the size of this room, and then step inside it, you would hear beautiful music." (I forbore to ask him whether it would be Bach or Beethoven.) Apparently, this nonsense went over well with many FEE devotees. It, of course, could not go over at all with Frank Chodorov, a down-to-earth type who enjoyed discussing real ideas and issues. It's no wonder that Chodorov lasted for such a short time in such an intellectually stultifying atmosphere.

In the meanwhile, *libertarian social life* in New York City had been a lowly business. There were no young libertarians in New York after Dick Cornuelle moved West, and what few there were—who included no anarchists—clustered around the Mises Seminar at New York University. A path out of the wilderness came in late 1953, when I met at the seminar a brilliant group of young and budding libertarians; most were then seniors in high school, and one, Leonard Liggio, was a sophomore at Georgetown. Some of this group had formed a Cobden Club at the Bronx High School of Science and the group as a whole had met as activists in the Youth for Taft campaign in 1952. The conversion of this group to anarchism was a simple matter of libertarian logic, and we all became fast friends, forming ourselves into a highly informal group called the Circle Bastiat, after the nineteenth-century French *laissez-faire* economist. We had endless discussions of libertarian political theory and current events, we sang and composed songs, joked about how we would be treated by "future historians," toasted the day of future victory, and played board games until the wee hours. Those were truly joyous times.

When I first met them, the Circle had, after the Taft defeat, formed the libertarian wing of a conservative-libertarian coalition that had constituted the Students for America; in fact the Circle kids totally controlled the Eastern branch of the SFA, while its president, Bob Munger, a conservative with rightist political connections, controlled the West. Unfortunately, however, only Munger had access to the financing, and when he was drafted shortly thereafter, SFA fell apart. From then on, we continued throughout the 1950s as an isolated though rollicking group in New York.

By the mid-1950s, the Old Right was demoralized politically with Taft dead, the Bricker Amendment defeated, and Eisenhower Republicanism triumphant, while intellectually the fading of the Old Right left a vacuum: the *Freeman* was to all intents and purposes finished, FEE was declining, Chodorov was incapacitated, Garrett dead, and Felix Morley, for persistent isolationism, was ousted from the *Human Events* that he had helped to found. *Faith and Freedom* and Spiritual Mobilization were likewise dead.

Finally, the death of Colonel McCormick in April 1955 deprived isolationism and its Middle-Western base of its most important and dedicated voice, as the publisher molding the *Chicago Tribune*. There were by now literally no libertarian or isolationist publishing outlets available. The time was ripe for the filling of the vacuum, for the seizure of this lost continent and lost army, and for their mobilization by a man and a group that could supply intelligence, glibness, erudition, money, and political knowhow to capture the right wing for a very different cause and for a very different drummer. The time had come for Bill Buckley and *National Review*.

12

NATIONAL REVIEW AND THE TRIUMPH OF THE NEW RIGHT

Garet Garrett had called the shots: in referring to the triumph of the New Deal and then of American Empire, he had summed up the strategy: "revolution within the form." The New Right did not bother, would not rouse possible resistance, by directing a frontal assault on the old idols: on the dead Senator Taft, on the Bricker Amendment, or on the old ideals of individualism and liberty. Instead, they ignored some, dropped others, and claimed to come to fulfill the general ideals of individualism in a new and superior "fusion" of liberty and ordered tradition.

How, specifically, was the deed done? For one thing, by hitting us at our most vulnerable point: the blight of anti-Communism. For red-baiting came easily to all of us, even the most libertarian. In the first place, there were the terrible memories of World War II: the way in which the Communist Party had gleefully adopted the mantle of war patriots, of "twentieth-century Americanism," and had unashamedly smeared all opponents of war as agents of Hitler. Conservative and former liberal isolationists could scarcely forget and forgive; and hence, when the Cold War began, when the "great patriotic coalition" of the U.S. and Russia fell apart, it was difficult for the Old Right to resist the temptation to avenge themselves, to turn the agents-of-a-foreign-power smear back upon their old tormentors. Furthermore, blinded by hatred of Russia as an interventionist power, we mistakenly believed that repudiation of the fruits of the Russian alliance, including Teheran and Yalta, was in itself a repudiation of World War II. We unfortunately did not realize—as later New Left historians were to point out—that the Cold War and the intervention into World War II were part and parcel of the same development: that one was the inevitable outgrowth of the other, and that both were an integral part of American imperialism rampant.

But the problem was still deeper than that. For our main problem was our simplistic view of the ideological-political spectrum. We all assumed that there were two poles: a "left" pole of Communism, socialism, and total government; and a "right" pole of libertarianism and individualist anarchism. Left of center were the liberals and Social Democrats; right of center were the conservatives. From that simplistic spectrum we concluded, first, that conservatives, no matter how divergent, were our "natural" allies, and second, that there was little real difference between liberals and Communists. Why not then fuzz the truth just a bit, and use the anti-Communist bludgeon to hit at the liberals, especially since the liberals had become entrenched in power and were running the country? There was a temptation that few of us could resist.

What we didn't fully realize at the time was that the Communists and socialists had not invented statism or Leviathan government, that the latter had been around for centuries, and that the current developing Liberal-conservative consensus and in particular the triumph of Liberalism was a reversion to the old despotic *ancien régime*. This *ancien régime* was the Old Order against which the libertarian and *laissez-faire* movements of the eighteenth and nineteenth centuries had emerged as a revolutionary opposition: an opposition on behalf of economic freedom and individual liberty. Jefferson, Cobden, and Thoreau as our forbears were ancestors in more ways than one; for both we and they were battling against a mercantilist statism that established bureaucratic despotism and corporate monopolies at home and waged imperial wars abroad. But if socialism and liberalism are reversions to the Old European Conservatism, then it becomes clear that it is statist conservatism—now joined by liberalism and social democracy—that is still, and not simply in 1800, the major enemy of liberty. And if liberals and Communists sound alike, this does not mean, as we thought then, that Liberals had somehow become crypto-Communists; on the contrary, it was a sign that Communists had become Liberals!

But for us this analysis—to be developed by Leonard Liggio—was still far in the future. During the 1940s and '50s we merrily engaged in red-baiting. My own position was characteristically libertarian: I distinguished between "compulsory" red-baiting, using the power of the State to repress Communists and leftists, which I deplored, and "voluntary" red-baiting by private organizations and groups, which I supported. The former included the Smith Act prosecutions, the McCarran Act, and the inquisitions of HUAC. Another of my blind spots is that I did not realize the virtual impossibility of keeping domestic and foreign red-baiting strictly separate; it was psychologically and politically impossible to persecute or harass Communists or leftists at home, while at the same time pursuing a policy of peace, neutrality, and friendship with Communist countries overseas. And the global anti-Communist crusaders knew this truth all too well.

From early in the postwar period, the major carriers of the anti-Communist contagion were the ex-Communist and ex-leftist intellectuals. In a climate of growing disillusion with the fatuous propaganda of World War II, the ex-Communists hit the intellectual and political worlds like a bombshell, more and more forming the spearhead of the anti-Communist crusade, domestic and foreign. Sophisticated, worldly, veteran polemicists, they had been there: to naive and breathless Americans, the ex-leftists were like travelers from an unknown and therefore terrifying land, returning with authentic tales of horror and warning. Since they, with their special knowledge, knew, and since they raised the terrible warnings, who were we to deny that truth? The fact that "ex-es" throughout history have tried frantically to expiate their guilt and their fear of having wasted their lives by attempting to denigrate and exterminate their former love—that fact was lost on us as well as on most of America.

From the very end of the war, the "ex-es" were everywhere on the Right, whipping up fear, pointing the finger, eager to persecute or exterminate any Communists they could find, at home and abroad. Several older generation "ex-es" from the prewar era were prominent. One was George E. Sokolsky, columnist for the *New York Sun*, who had been a Communist in the early 1920s. Particularly prominent on the Right was Dr. J.B. Matthews, foremost Communist fellow-traveler of the early 1930s, who by the end of that decade was chief investigator for the Dies Committee; Matthews was to make a fortune out of his famous "card files," a mammoth collection of "Communist front" names which he would use to sell his services as finger-man for industries and organizations; pleasant and erudite, Matthews had been converted from socialism partly by reading Mises's *Socialism*. But the first libertarian-red-baiting marriage was effected shortly after the end of the war by the veteran red-baiter Isaac Don Levine, who founded a little-known monthly called *Plain Talk*, which featured a curious mixture of libertarian political philosophy and ferocious exposés of alleged "Reds" in America. It was particularly curious because Don Levine has never, before or since that short-lived venture, ever exhibited any interest in freedom or libertarianism. When *Plain Talk* folded Don Levine moved to West Germany to play in the *revanchist* politics of East European *emigré* groups.

Plain Talk disappeared after several years to make way for the weekly *Freeman* in 1950, a far more ambitious and better-financed venture which, however, never achieved anything like the influence or readership of the later *National Review*. Again, this was a libertarian-conservative-red-baiting coalition venture. Coeditors were two veteran writers and journalists: Henry Hazlitt, a *laissez-faire* economist but never an isolationist; and John Chamberlain, a man of libertarian instincts and a former isolationist, but an ex-leftist deeply scarred by a Communist cell which had been nasty to him in *Time* magazine.[1] And so the isolationist cause was never well represented in the *Freeman*; furthermore, Willi Schlamm later

[1]Don Levine had been slated to be a coeditor, but was booted out before the venture began because he had angered financial backers of the *Freeman* by attacking Merwin K. Hart in *Plain Talk* as being "anti-Semitic" (read: anti-Zionist).

came in as book editor, and Chamberlain brought in the profoundly antilibertarian Forrest Davis to be a third coeditor. Davis, along with Ernest K. Lindley, had written the official Roosevelt administration apologia for Pearl Harbor, and then moved on to become a ghostwriter for Joe McCarthy.[2]

It was, in fact, McCarthy and "McCarthyism" that provided the main catalyst for transforming the mass base of the right wing from isolationism and quasi-libertarianism to simple anti-Communism. Before McCarthy launched his famous crusade in February 1950, he had not been particularly associated with the right wing of the Republican Party; on the contrary, his record was more nearly liberal and centrist, statist rather than libertarian. It should be remembered that red-baiting and anti-Communist witch-hunting was launched by the liberals and, even after McCarthy arose, it was the liberals who were the most effective at this game. It was, after all, the liberal Roosevelt administration that passed the Smith Act, which was then used against Trotskyites and isolationists during World War II and against the Communists after the war; it was the liberal Truman administration that prosecuted Alger Hiss and the Rosenbergs—and that launched the Cold War; it was the eminently liberal Hubert Humphrey who put through a clause in the McCarran Act of 1950 threatening concentration camps for "subversives."

In fact, New Left historians Steinke and Weinstein have shown that McCarthy himself learned his red-baiting from none other than the saintly Social Democratic figure Norman Thomas. During the 1946 campaign, McCarthy first ran for the Senate against the great isolationist leader Robert LaFollette, Jr. While McCarthy did a little red-baiting of the still-consistent isolationist LaFollette in the primary, McCarthy was then a standard internationalist, or Vandenberg, Republican, with indeed a few maverick

[2]His most famous ghostwritten piece was McCarthy's famous attack on the record of General George Marshall—an attack, significantly, which began during World War II, thus deliberately ignoring Marshall's black record on Pearl Harbor.

endorsements of the idea of negotiating peace with the Soviet Union. Then, on August 26, 1946, Norman Thomas, speaking at an annual picnic of the Wisconsin Socialist Party, red-baited the Democratic Senatorial candidate, Howard J. McMurray. Thomas in particular accused McMurray of being endorsed by the *Daily Worker*, an accusation that McCarthy picked up eagerly a few weeks later. McCarthy had gotten the bit in his teeth; he had learned how from a veteran of the internecine struggles on the Left.[3]

McCarthy's crusade effectively transformed the mass base of the right wing by bringing into the movement a mass of urban Catholics from the Eastern seaboard. Before McCarthy, the rank-and-file of the right wing was the small-town, isolationist Middle West, the typical readers of the old *Chicago Tribune*. In contrast to the old base, the interest of the new urban Catholic constituency in individual liberty was, if anything, negative; one might say that their main political interest was in stamping out blasphemy and pornography at home and in killing Communists at home and abroad. In a sense, the subsequent emergence of Bill Buckley and his highly Catholic-ish *National Review* reflected this mass influx and transformation. It is surely no accident that Buckley's first emergence on the political scene was to coauthor (with his brother-in-law, L. Brent Bozell, a convert to Catholicism), the leading pro-McCarthy work, *McCarthy and His Enemies* (1954). To the McCarthy banner also flocked the increasingly powerful gaggle of ex-Communists and ex-leftists: notably, George Sokolsky, a leading McCarthy adviser, and J.B. Matthews, who was chief investigator for McCarthy until he stepped on too many toes by denouncing the supposedly massive "infiltration" of the Protestant clergy by the Communist Party.

---

[3]On this instructive episode, see John Steinke and James Weinstein, "McCarthy and the Liberals," in *For a New America: Essays in History and Politics from Studies on the Left, 1959–1967*, James Weinstein and David Eakins, eds. (New York: Random House, 1970), pp. 180–93.

Not seeing this transformation process at work at the time, I myself was a McCarthy enthusiast. There were two basic reasons. One was that while McCarthy was employing the weapon of a governmental committee, the great bulk of his victims were not private citizens but government officials: bureaucrats and Army officers. Most of McCarthy's red-baiting was therefore "voluntary" rather than "compulsory," since the persons being attacked were, as government officials, fair game from the libertarian point of view. Besides, day in and day out, such Establishment organs as the *New York Times* kept telling us that McCarthy was "tearing down the morale of the executive branch"; what more could a libertarian hope for? And "tearing down the morale of the Army" to boot! What balm for an antimilitarist!

Recently, I had occasion to see once again, after all these years, Emile D'Antonio's film of the McCarthy censure hearings, *Point of Order*. Seeing it with an old-time member of the Circle who had also abandoned the right wing long since, we were curious about how we would react; for neither of us had really rethought the long-dead McCarthy episode. Within minutes, we found ourselves cheering once again, though in a rather different way, for that determined symbol of the witch-hunt. For the film began with McCarthy pointing as his basic premise to some crazed map of the United States with the "international Communist conspiracy" moving in a series of coordinated arrows against the United States. (It was for all the world like some '50s issue of the Harvard *Lampoon*, satirizing an absurd military "menace.") But the crucial point is that McCarthy's Army and Senatorial adversaries never contested this absurd axiom; and once given the axiom, McCarthy's relentless logic was impeccable. As Steinke and Weinstein point out, McCarthy did not invent witch-hunting and red-baiting. "Nor, as many liberals complain, did he abuse or misuse an otherwise useful tool; he simply carried it to its logical conclusion." Indeed, he took the liberals' own creation and turned it against them, and against the swollen Leviathan Army officials as well; and to see them get at least a measure of comeuppance, to see the liberals and centrists hoisted on their own petard, was sweet indeed. In the words of Steinke and Weinstein, McCarthy

> rode the monster too hard, turning it against its creators, and they, realizing finally that their creation was out of control, attempted in flaccid defense to turn it back upon him.[4]

As a bit of personal corroboration, I fully remember the reaction of a close acquaintance, an old Russian Menshevik, a member of the Russian Social Democratic Federation and veteran anti-Communist, when McCarthy's movement began. He was positively gleeful, and ardently supported the McCarthy crusade; it was only later, when he "went too far" that the old Menshevik felt that McCarthy had to be dumped.

But there was another reason for my own fascination with the McCarthy phenomenon: his populism. For the '50s was an era when liberalism—now accurately termed "corporate liberalism"—had triumphed, and seemed to be permanently in the saddle. Having now gained the seats of power, the liberals had given up their radical veneer of the '30s and were now settling down to the cozy enjoyment of their power and perquisites. It was a comfortable alliance of Wall Street, Big Business, Big Government, Big Unions, and liberal Ivy League intellectuals; it seemed to me that while in the long run this unholy alliance could only be overthrown by educating a new generation of intellectuals, that in the short run the only hope to dislodge this new ruling elite was a populist short-circuit. In sum, that there was a vital need to appeal directly to the masses, emotionally, even demagogically, *over the heads* of the Establishment: of the Ivy League, the mass media, the liberal intellectuals, of the Republican-Democrat political party structure. This appeal could be done—especially in that period of no organized opposition whatever—only by a charismatic leader, a leader who could make a direct appeal to the masses and thereby undercut the ruling and opinion-molding elite; in sum, by a populist short-circuit. It seemed to me that this was what McCarthy was trying to do; and that it was largely this appeal, the open-ended sense that there was no audacity of which McCarthy was not

---

[4]Ibid., p. 180.

capable, that frightened the liberals, who, from their opposite side of the fence, also saw that the only danger to their rule was in just such a whipping up of populist emotions.[5]

My own quip at the time, which roughly summed up this position, was that in contrast to the liberals, who approved of McCarthy's "ends" (ouster of Communists from offices and jobs) but disapproved of his radical and demagogic means, I myself approved his means (radical assault on the nation's power structure) but not necessarily his ends.

It is surely no accident that, with their power consolidated and a populist appeal their only fear, the liberal intellectuals began to push hard for their proclamation of the "end of ideology." Hence their claim that ideology and hard-nosed doctrines were no longer valuable or viable, and their ardent celebration of the newfound American consensus. With such enemies and for such reasons, it was hard for me not to be a "McCarthyite."

The leading expression of this celebration of consensus combined with the newfound fear of ideology and populism was Daniel Bell's collection, *The New American Right* (1955). This collection was also significant in drawing together ex-radicals (Bell, Seymour Martin Lipset, Richard Hofstadter, Nathan Glazer) along with an antipopulist liberal "conservative" (Peter Viereck), into this pro-elitist and antipopulist consensus. Also noteworthy is the book's dedication to S.M. Levitas, executive editor of the Social Democratic *New Leader*, the publication that bound "responsible" red-baiters and liberals into the postwar Cold War consensus.[6]

---

[5]It is precisely this sort of analysis that has made many astute members of the New Left in a sense sympathetic to the George Wallace movement of recent years. For while the Wallaceite *program* may be questionable, his *analysis* of the Establishment and his tapping of middle-class sentiment against the ruling elite that oppresses them earns from the New Left a considerable amount of sympathy.

[6]Daniel Bell, ed., *The New American Right* (New York: Criterion Books, 1955). The book was updated eight years later, with new chapters

The peak of my populist and McCarthyite activities came during the height of the McCarthy turmoil, in the furor over the activities of Roy Cohn and S. David Schine. It was shortly after the founding of the Circle Bastiat, and the kids of the Circle, in their capacity as leaders of the still-functioning Students for America, were invited to address a massive testimonial dinner given for Roy Cohn upon his forced ouster from the McCarthy Committee at the Hotel Astor in New York on July 26, 1954. Major speakers were such McCarthyite leaders as Godfrey P. Schmidt, Colonel Archibald Roosevelt, George Sokolsky, Alfred Kohlberg, Bill Buckley, and Rabbi Benjamin Schultz. But the speech which drew the most applause, and which gained a considerable amount of notoriety, was the brief address given by one of our Circle members (George Reisman), which I had written. The speech asked why the intensity of the hatred against Cohn and McCarthy by the liberal intellectuals; and it answered that a threat against Communists in government was also felt to be a threat against the "Socialists and New Dealers, who have been running our political life for the last twenty-one years, and are still running it!" The speech concluded in a rousing populist appeal that

> As the *Chicago Tribune* aptly put it, the Case of Roy Cohn is the American Dreyfus Case. As Dreyfus was redeemed, so will Roy Cohn when the American people have taken back their government from the criminal alliance of Communists, Socialists, New Dealers, and Eisenhower-Dewey Republicans.

Rabbi Schultz, presiding at the dinner, warily referred to the tumultuous applause for the Reisman speech as a "runaway grand jury," and the applause and the speech were mentioned in the

added from the perspective of the early 1960s. Daniel Bell, ed., *The New American Right: Expanded and Updated* (Garden City, N.Y.: Doubleday Anchor, 1963). From a later perspective, it is clear that this was a proto-neoconservative book, Bell, Glazer, and Lipset becoming prominent neocons in the 1970s and 1980s.

accounts of the *New York Journal-American*, the *New York Herald-Tribune*, Jack Lait's column in the *New York Mirror*, the *New York World-Telegram and Sun*, Murray Kempton's column in the *New York Post*, and *Time* magazine. Particularly upset was the veteran liberal and "extremist-baiting" radio commentator, George Hamilton Combs. Combs warned that "the resemblance between this crowd and their opposite members of the extreme left is startlingly close. This was a rightist version of the Henry Wallace convention crowd, the Progressive Party convention of '48."

Particularly interesting is the fact that the by-now-notorious concluding lines of the speech became enshrined in Peter Viereck's contribution to the Daniel Bell book, "The Revolt Against the Elite." Viereck saw the Reisman phraseology as a dangerous "outburst of direct democracy" which "comes straight from the leftist rhetoric of the old Populists and Progressives, a rhetoric forever urging the People to take back 'their' government from the conspiring Powers That Be." Precisely. Viereck also explained that he meant by "direct democracy," "our mob tradition of Tom Paine, Jacobinism, and the Midwestern Populist parties," which "is government by referendum and mass petition, such as the McCarthyite Committee of Ten Million." Being "immediate and hotheaded," direct democracy "facilitates revolution, demagogy, and Robespierrian thought control"—in contrast, I suppose, to the quieter but more pervasive elitist "thought control" of corporate liberalism.[7]

Since I failed to understand the interplay of domestic and foreign red-baiting that was at work in the McCarthy movement, I was bewildered when McCarthy, after his outrageous censure by the Senate in late 1954, turned to whooping it up for war on behalf of Chiang Kai-shek in Asia. Why this turnabout? It was clear that the New Right forces behind McCarthy were now convinced that domestic red-baiting, angering as it did the Center-Right establishment, had become counterproductive, and that from now on

---

[7]Peter Viereck, "Revolt Against the Elite," in *New American Right*, Bell, ed., pp. 97–98, 116.

the full stress must be on pushing for war against Communism abroad. In retrospect it is clear that a major force for this turn was the sinister figure of the millionaire Far Eastern importer, Alfred Kohlberg, a major backer of McCarthy who supplied him with much of his material, and boasted of his position as Dean of the powerful "China Lobby" on behalf of Chiang Kai-shek. While a failure in the short run, the McCarthy movement had done its work of shifting the entire focus of the right wing from libertarian, antistatist, and isolationist concerns to a focus and concentration upon the alleged Communist "menace." A diversion from domestic to foreign affairs would not only consolidate the right wing; it would also draw no real opposition from liberals and internationalist Republicans who had, after all, begun the Cold War in the first place.

The short-run collapse of the McCarthy movement was clearly due, furthermore, to the lack of any sort of McCarthyite *organization*. There were leaders, there was press support, there was a large mass base, but there were no channels of organization, no intermediary links, either in journals of opinion or of more direct popular organizations, between the leaders and the base. In late 1955, William F. Buckley and his newly formed weekly, *National Review*, set out to remedy that lack.

In 1951, when Bill Buckley first burst upon the scene with his *God and Man at Yale*, he liked to refer to himself as a "libertarian" or even at times as an "anarchist"; for in those early days Buckley's major ideological mentor was Frank Chodorov rather than, as it would soon become, the notorious Whittaker Chambers. But even in those early "libertarian" days, there was one clinker that made his libertarianism only phony rhetoric: the global anti-Communist crusade. Thus, take one of Buckley's early efforts, "A Young Republican's View," published in *Commonweal*, January 25, 1952. Buckley began the article in unexceptionable libertarian fashion, affirming that the enemy is the State, and endorsing the view of Herbert Spencer that the State is "begotten of aggression and by aggression." Buckley also contributed excellent quotations from such leading individualists of the past as H.L. Mencken and Albert Jay Nock, and criticized the Republican Party for offering no real alternative to the burgeoning of statism. But then in the remainder of the article he gave the case away, for there loomed the alleged Soviet menace, and all libertarian principles had to go by the board for the duration. Thus, Buckley declared that the "thus far invincible aggressiveness of the Soviet Union" imminently threatens American security, and that therefore "we have to accept Big Government for the duration—for neither an offensive nor a defensive war can be waged . . . except through the instrument of a totalitarian bureaucracy within our shores." In short, a totalitarian bureaucracy must be accepted so long as the Soviet Union exists (presumably for its alleged threat of imposing upon us a totalitarian bureaucracy?). In consequence, Buckley concluded that we must all support "the extensive and productive tax laws that are needed to support a vigorous anti-Communist foreign policy," as well as "large armies and air forces, atomic energy, central intelligence, war production boards and the attendant centralization of power in Washington—even with Truman at the reins of it all."[8] Thus, even at his most libertarian, even before Buckley came to accept Big Government and morality laws as ends in themselves, the pretended *National Review* "fusion" between liberty and order, between individualism and anti-Communism, was a phony—the individualist and libertarian part of the fusion was strictly rhetorical, to be saved for abstract theorizing and after-dinner discourse. The guts of the New Conservatism was the mobilization of Big Government for the worldwide crusade against Communism.

And so, when *National Review* was founded with much expertise and financing in late 1955, the magazine was a coming together to direct the newly transformed right wing on the part of two groups: all the veteran ex-Communist journalists and intellectuals, and the new group of younger Catholics whose major goal was anti-Communism. Thus, the central and guiding theme for both groups in this Unholy Coalition was the extirpation of Communism, at home and particularly abroad. Prominent on the new magazine were

---

[8]William F. Buckley, Jr., "A Young Republican's View," *Commonweal* 55, no. 16 (January 25, 1952): 391–93.

leading ex-leftists: James Burnham, former Trotskyite; Frank S. Meyer, formerly on the national committee of the Communist Party and head of its Chicago training school; ex-German Communist leader William S. Schlamm; Dr. J.B. Matthews; ex-leftist Max Eastman; ex-Communist Ralph DeToledano; former leading German Communist theoretician Professor Karl Wittfogel; John Chamberlain, a leading leftist intellectual of the thirties; ex-fellow traveler Eugene Lyons; ex-Communist Will Herberg; former Communist spy Whittaker Chambers; and a whole slew of others.

The Catholic wing consisted of two parts. One was a charming but ineffectual group of older European or European-oriented monarchists and authoritarians: e.g., the erudite Austrian Erik von Kuehnelt-Leddihn; the poet Roy Campbell; the pro-Spanish Carlist Frederick Wilhelmsen; and the Englishman Sir Arnold Lunn. I remember one night a heated discussion at a conservative gathering about the respective merits of the Habsburgs, the Stuarts, the Bourbons, the Carlists, the Crown of St. Stephen, and the Crown of St. Wenceslas; and which monarchy should be restored first. Whatever the merits of the monarchist position, this was not an argument relevant to the American tradition, let alone the American cultural and political scene of the day. In retrospect, did Buckley keep this group around as exotic trimming, as an intellectual counterpart to his own social jet set?

The other wing of younger Catholics was far more important for the purposes of the new magazine. These were the younger American anti-Communists, most prominently the various members of the Buckley family (who in closeness and lifestyle has seemed a right-wing version of the Kennedys), which included at first Buckley's brother-in-law and college roommate, L. Brent Bozell; and Buckley's then favorite disciple later turned leftist, Garry Wills. Rounding out the Catholic aura at *National Review* was the fact that two of its leading editors became Catholic converts: Frank Meyer and political scientist Willmoore Kendall. It was the essence of *National Review* as an anti-Communist organ that accounted for its being a coalition of ex-Stalinists and Trotskyites and younger Catholics, and led observers to remark on the curious absence of American Protestants (who had of course been the staple of the Old Right) from the heart of the Buckleyite New Right.[9]

In this formidable but profoundly statist grouping, interest in individual liberty was minimal or negative, being largely confined to some of the book reviews by John Chamberlain and to whatever time Frank Meyer could manage to take off from advocacy of all-out war against the Soviet bloc. Interest in free-market economics was minimal and largely rhetorical, confined to occasional pieces by Henry Hazlitt, who for his part had never been an isolationist and who endorsed the hard-line foreign policy of the magazine.

In the light of hindsight, we should now ask whether or not a major objective of *National Review* from its inception was to transform the right wing from an isolationist to global warmongering anti-Communist movement; and, particularly, whether or not the entire effort was in essence a CIA operation. We now know that Bill Buckley, for the two years prior to establishing *National Review*, was admittedly a CIA agent in Mexico City, and that the sinister E. Howard Hunt was his control. His sister Priscilla, who became managing editor of *National Review*, was also in the CIA; and other editors James Burnham and Willmoore Kendall had at least been recipients of CIA largesse in the anti-Communist Congress for Cultural Freedom. In addition, Burnham has been identified by two reliable sources as a consultant for the CIA in the years after World War II.[10] Moreover, Garry Wills relates in his memoirs of the conservative movement that Frank Meyer, to whom he was close at the time, was convinced that the magazine was a CIA operation. With his Leninist-trained nose for intrigue, Meyer must be considered an important witness.

---

[9]Thus, see George H. Nash, *The Conservative Intellectual Movement in America Since 1945* (New York: Basic Books, 1976), p. 127; and Samuel Francis, "Beautiful Losers: the Failure of American Conservatism," *Chronicles* (May 1991): 16.

[10]See Nash, *Conservative Intellectual Movement*, p. 372.

Furthermore, it was a standard practice in the CIA, at least in those early years, that no one ever resigned from the CIA. A friend of mine who joined the Agency in the early 1950s told me that if, before the age of retirement, he was mentioned as having left the CIA for another job, that I was to disregard it, since it would only be a cover for continuing Agency work. On that testimony, the case for *NR* being a CIA operation becomes even stronger. Also suggestive is the fact that a character even more sinister than E. Howard Hunt, William J. Casey, appears at key moments of the establishment of the New over the Old Right. It was Casey who, as attorney, presided over the incorporation of *National Review* and had arranged the details of the ouster of Felix Morley from *Human Events*.

At any rate, in retrospect, it is clear that libertarians and Old Rightists, including myself, had made a great mistake in endorsing domestic red-baiting, a red-baiting that proved to be the major entering wedge for the complete transformation of the original right wing. We should have listened more carefully to Frank Chodorov, and to his splendidly libertarian stand on domestic red-baiting: "How to get rid of the communists in the government? Easy. Just abolish the jobs."[11] It was the jobs and their functioning that was the important thing, not the quality of the people who happened to fill them. More fully, Chodorov wrote:

> And now we come to the spy-hunt—which is, in reality, a heresy trial. What is it that perturbs the inquisitors? They do not ask the suspects: Do you believe in Power? Do you adhere to the idea that the individual exists for the glory of the State? . . . Are you against taxes, or would you raise them until they absorbed the entire output of the country? . . . Are you opposed to the principle of conscription? Do you favor more "social gains" under the aegis of an enlarged bureaucracy? Or, would you advocate dismantling of the public trough at which these bureaucrats feed? In short, do you deny Power?

---

[11]Frank Chodorov, "Trailing the Trend," *analysis* 6, no. 6 (April 1950): 3. Quoted in Hamilton, "Introduction," p. 25.

> Such questions might prove embarrassing, to the investigators. The answers might bring out a similarity between their ideas and purposes and those of the suspected. They too worship Power. Under the circumstances, they limit themselves to one question: Are you a member of the Communist Party? And this turns out to mean, have you aligned yourselves with the Moscow branch of the church?
>
> Power-worship is presently sectarianized along nationalistic lines. . . . Each nation guards its orthodoxy. . . . Where Power is attainable, the contest between rival sects is unavoidable. . . . War is the apotheosis of Power, the ultimate expression of the faith and solidarization of its achievement.[12]

And Frank had also written:

> The case against the communists involves a principle of transcending importance. It is the right to be wrong. Heterodoxy is a necessary condition of a free society. . . . The right to make a choice . . . is important to me, for the freedom of selection is necessary to my sense of personality; it is important to society, because only from the juxtaposition of ideas can we hope to approach the ideal of truth.
>
> Whenever I choose an idea or label it "right," I imply the prerogative of another to reject that idea and label it "wrong." To invalidate his right is to invalidate mine. That is, I must brook error if I would preserve my freedom of thought. . . . If men are punished for espousing communism, shall we stop there? Once we deny the right to be wrong, we put a vise on the human mind and put the temptation to turn the handle into the hands of ruthlessness.[13]

While anti-Communism was the central root of the decay of the Old Right and the replacement by its statist opposite in

---

[12]Frank Chodorov, "The Spy-Hunt," *analysis* 4, no. 11 (September 1948): 1–2. Reprinted in Chodorov, *Out of Step* (New York: Devin-Adair, 1962), pp. 181–83.

[13]Frank Chodorov, "How to Curb the Commies," *analysis* 5, no. 7 (May 1949): 2.

National Review, there was another important force in transforming the American right wing, especially in vitiating its "domestic" libertarianism and even its rhetorical devotion to individual liberty. This was the sudden emergence of Russell Kirk as the leader of the New Conservatism, with the publication of his book *The Conservative Mind* in 1953. Kirk, who became a regular columnist of *National Review* as soon as it was founded, created a sensation with his book and quickly became adopted as the conservative darling of the "vital center." In fact, before Buckley became prominent as the leading conservative spokesman of the media, Russell Kirk was the most prominent conservative. After the appearance of his book, Kirk began to make speeches around the country, often in a friendly "vital center" tandem with Arthur Schlesinger, Jr.

For Kirk was far more acceptable to "vital center" corporate liberalism than was the Old Right. Scorning any trait of individualism or rigorous free-market economics, Kirk was instead quite close to the Conservatism of Peter Viereck; to Kirk, Big Government and domestic statism were perfectly acceptable, provided that they were steeped in some sort of Burkean tradition and enjoyed a Christian framework. Indeed, it was clear that Kirk's ideal society was an ordered English squirearchy, ruled by the Anglican Church and Tory landlords in happy tandem.[14] Here there was no fiery individualism, no trace of populism or radicalism to upset the ruling classes or the liberal intellectual Establishment. *Here* at last was a Rightist with whom liberals, while not exactly agreeing, could engage in a cozy dialogue.

It was Kirk, in fact, who brought the words "Conservatism" and "New Conservatism" into general acceptance on the right wing. Before that, knowledgeable libertarians had hated the word, and with good reason; for weren't the conservatives the ancient enemy, the eighteenth- and nineteenth-century Tory and reactionary suppressors of individual liberty, the ancient champions of the Old Order of Throne-and-Altar against which the eighteenth- and

---

[14]Kirk, too, was to follow other *National Review* leaders into Catholicism a decade later.

nineteenth-century liberals had fought so valiantly? And so the older classical-liberals and individualists resisted the term bitterly: Ludwig von Mises, a classical liberal, scorned the term; F.A. Hayek insisted on calling himself an "Old Whig"; and when Frank Chodorov was called a "conservative" in the pages of *National Review*, he wrote an outraged letter declaring, "As for me, I will punch anyone who calls me a conservative in the nose. I am a radical."[15] Before Russell Kirk, the word "conservative," being redolent of reaction and the Old Order, was a Left smear-word applied to the right wing; it was only after Kirk that the right wing, including the new *National Review*, rushed to embrace this previously hated term.

The Kirkian influence was soon evident in right-wing youth meetings. I remember one gathering when, to my dismay, one Gridley Wright, an aristocratic leader of Yale campus conservatism, declared that the true ideological struggle of our day, between left and right, had nothing to do with free-market economics or with individual liberty versus statism. The true struggle, he declared, was Christianity versus atheism, and good manners versus boorishness and materialistic greed: the materialist greed, for example, of the starving peoples of India who were trying to earn an income, a bit of subsistence. It was easy, of course, for a wealthy Yale man whose father owned a large chunk of Montana to decry the "materialistic greed" of the poor; was *this* what the right wing was coming to?

Russell Kirk also succeeded in altering our historical pantheon of heroes. Mencken, Nock, Thoreau, Jefferson, Paine, and Garrison were condemned as rationalists, atheists, or anarchists, and were replaced by such reactionaries and antilibertarians as Burke, Metternich, De Maistre, or Alexander Hamilton.[16]

---

[15]Letter to *National Review* 2, no. 20 (October 6, 1956): 23. Cited in Hamilton, "Introduction," p. 29.

[16]Kirk himself never equaled the success of *The Conservative Mind*. His later columns in *National Review* were largely confined to attacks upon

With its formidable array of anti-Communists and Catholic traditionalists, *National Review* quickly took over the lead and direction of the New Right, which it rapidly remolded in its own image. The "official" line of *National Review* was what came to be called "fusionist," whose leading practitioners were Meyer and Buckley; "fusionism" stressed the dominance of anti-Communism and Christian order, to be sure, but retained some libertarian rhetoric in a subordinate rank. The importance of the libertarian and Old Right rhetoric was largely political; for it would have been difficult for *National Review* to lead a conservative political revival in this country in the garb of monarchy and Inquisition. Without fusionism, the transformation of the right wing could not have taken place within the form, and might have alienated much of the right-wing mass base. Many of the other *National Review* intellectuals were, in contrast, impatient with any concessions to liberty. These included Kirk's Tory traditionalism; the various wings of monarchists; and Willmoore Kendall's open call for suppression of freedom of speech. The great thrust of Kendall, a *National Review* editor for many years, was his view that it is the right and duty of the "majority" of the community—as embodied, say, in Congress—to suppress any individual who disturbs that community with radical doctrines. Socrates, opined Kendall, not only *should* have been killed by the Greek community, but it was their bounden moral *duty* to kill him.

Kendall, incidentally, was symptomatic of the change in attitude toward the Supreme Court from Old Right to New. One of the major doctrines of the Old Right was the defense of the Supreme Court's role in outlawing congressional and executive incursions against individual liberty; but *now* the New Right, as typified by Kendall, bitterly attacked the Supreme Court day in and day out, and for what? Precisely for presuming to defend the liberty of the individual against the incursions of Congress and the Executive.

---

the follies of progressive education. To be fair, Nash's work reveals that Kirk was really an isolationist Old Rightist during World War II; his shift to the New Conservatism in the early 1950s remains something of a mystery. Nash, *Conservative Intellectual Movement*, pp. 70–76.

Thus, the Old Right had always bitterly attacked the judicial doctrines of Felix Frankfurter, who was considered a left-wing monster for undercutting the activist role of the Supreme Court in declaring various extensions of government power to be unconstitutional; but now Kendall and *National Review* were leading the Right in hailing Frankfurter precisely for this permissive placing of the judicial imprimatur on almost any action of the federal government. By staying in the same place, Felix Frankfurter had shifted from being a villain to a hero of the newly transformed Right, while it was now such libertarian activists as Justices Black and Douglas who received the abuse of the right wing. It was getting to be an ever weirder right-wing world that I was inhabiting. It was indeed the venerable Alexander Bickel, a disciple of Frankfurter's at Yale Law School, who converted young professor Robert Bork from a libertarian to a majoritarian jurist.

At the opposite pole from the Catholic ultras, but at one with them in being opposed to liberty and individualism, was James Burnham, who since the inception of *National Review* has been its cold, hard-nosed, amoral political strategist and resident Machiavellian. Burnham, whose *National Review* column was entitled "The Third World War," was the magazine's leading power and global anti-Communist strategist. In a lifetime of political writing, James Burnham has shown only one fleeting bit of positive interest in individual liberty: and that was a call in *National Review* for the legalization of firecrackers!

On the more directly political front, *National Review* obviously needed a "fusionist" for its political tactician, for the direct guidance of conservatism as a political movement. It found that tactician in its publisher, the former Deweyite Young Republican Bill Rusher. A brilliant political organizer, Rusher was able, by the late 1950s, to take over control of the College Young Republicans, and then the National Young Republican Federation.

Heading a group called the "Syndicate," Rusher has managed to control the national Young Republications ever since. In 1959, *National Review* organized the founding of the Young Americans for Freedom at Bill Buckley's estate at Sharon, Connecticut. Young Americans for Freedom soon grew to many thousand strong, and became in effect the collegiate youth-activist arm of the *National Review* political complex. Unfortunately, the bulk of young libertarians at the time stayed solidly in the conservative movement; heedless of the foreign policy betrayal of the Old Right, these young libertarians and semi-libertarians well served the purposes of *National Review* by lending the patina of libertarian rhetoric to such ventures as Young Americans for Freedom. Thus, Young Americans for Freedom's founding Sharon Statement was its only even remotely close approach to libertarianism; its actual activities have always been confined to anticommunism, including the attempted interdiction of trade with the Communist countries—and lately were expanded to attempting legal suppression of left-wing student rebellions. But the libertarian veneer was supplied not only by the title and by parts of the Sharon Statement, but also by the fact that Young Americans for Freedom's first president, Robert M. Schuchman, was a libertarian anti-Communist who had once been close to the old Circle Bastiat. More typical of the mass base of conservative youth was the considerable contingent at Sharon who objected to the title of the new organization, because, they said, "Freedom is a left-wing word." It would have been far more candid, though less politically astute, if the noble word *freedom* had been left out of Young Americans for Freedom's title.

By the late 1950s, Barry Goldwater had been decided upon as the political leader of the New Right, and it was Rusher and the *National Review* clique that inspired the Draft Goldwater movement and Youth for Goldwater in 1960. Goldwater's ideological manifesto of 1960, *The Conscience of a Conservative*, was ghostwritten by Brent Bozell, who wrote fiery articles in *National Review* attacking liberty even as an abstract principle, and upholding the function of the State in imposing and enforcing moral and religious creeds. Its foreign policy chapter, "The Soviet Menace," was a thinly disguised plea for all-out offensive war against the Soviet Union and other Communist nations. The Goldwater movement of 1960 was a warm-up for the future; and when Nixon was defeated in the 1960 election, Rusher and *National Review* launched a well-coordinated campaign to capture the Republican Party for Barry Goldwater in 1964.

It was this drastic shift to all-out and pervasive war-mongering that I found hardest to swallow. For years I had thought of myself politically as an "extreme right-winger," but this emotional identification with the right was becoming increasingly difficult. To be a political ally of Senator Taft was one thing; to be an ally of statists who thirsted for all-out war against Russia was quite another. For the first five years of its existence I moved in *National Review* circles. I had known Frank Meyer as a fellow analyst for the William Volker Fund, and through Meyer had met Buckley and the rest of the editorial staff. I attended *National Review* luncheons, rallies, and cocktail parties, and wrote a fair number of articles and book reviews for the magazine. But the more I circulated among these people, the greater my horror because I realized with growing certainty that what they wanted above all was total war against the Soviet Union; their fanatical warmongering would settle for no less.

Of course the New Rightists of *National Review* would never quite dare to admit this crazed goal in public, but the objective would always be slyly implied. At right-wing rallies no one cheered a single iota for the free market, if this minor item were ever so much as mentioned; what really stirred up the animals were demagogic appeals by *National Review* leaders for total victory, total destruction of the Communist world. It was that which brought the right-wing masses out of their seats. It was *National Review* editor Brent Bozell who trumpeted, at a right-wing rally: "I would favor destroying not only the whole world, but the entire universe out to the furthermost star, rather than suffer Communism to live." It was *National Review* editor Frank Meyer who once told me: "I have a vision, a great vision of the future: a totally devastated Soviet Union." I knew that this was the vision that really animated the new Conservatism. Frank Meyer, for example, had the following argument with his wife, Elsie, over foreign-policy strategy: Should we drop the H-Bomb on Moscow and destroy the Soviet Union *immediately* and without warning (Frank), or should we give the Soviet regime 24 hours with which to comply with an ultimatum to resign (Elsie)?

In the meanwhile, isolationist or antiwar sentiment disappeared totally from right-wing publications or organizations, as rightists hastened to follow the lead of *National Review* and its burgeoning political and activist organizations. The death of Colonel McCormick of the *Chicago Tribune* and the ouster of Felix Morley from *Human Events* meant that these crucial mass periodicals would swing behind the new pro-war line. Harry Elmer Barnes, the leader and promoter of World War II revisionism, was somehow able to publish an excellent article on Hiroshima in *National Review*, but apart from that, found that conservative interest in revisionism, prominent after World War II, had dried up and become hostile.[17] For as William Henry Chamberlin had discovered, the Munich analogy was a powerful one to use against opponents of the new war drive; besides, any questioning of American intervention in the previous war crusade inevitably cast doubts on its current role, let alone on New Right agitation for an even hotter war. Right-wing publishers like Henry Regnery and Devin-Adair lost interest in isolationist or revisionist works. Once in a while, a few libertarians who had not fallen silent about the war drive or even joined it expressed their opposition and concern; but they could only do so in private correspondence. There was no other outlet available.[18]

Particularly disgraceful was *National Review*'s refusal to give the great John T. Flynn an outlet for his opposition to the Cold War. The doughty veteran Flynn, who had, interestingly enough, championed Joe McCarthy, bitterly opposed the New Right emphasis

---

[17]Harry Elmer Barnes, "Hiroshima: Assault on a Beaten Foe," *National Review* 5, no. 19 (May 10, 1958): 441–43. See Murray N. Rothbard, "Harry Elmer Barnes as Revisionist of the Cold War," in *Harry Elmer Barnes: Learned Crusader*, A. Goddard, ed. (Colorado Springs, Colo.: Ralph Myles, 1968), pp. 314–38.

[18]Thus, see the letters in the late 1950s of Roland W. ("Rollie") Holmes, and of Dr. Paul Poirot of the FEE staff, in Toy, "Ideology and Conflict," pp. 206–07.

on a global military crusade. In the fall of 1956, Flynn submitted an article to *National Review* attacking the Cold War crusade, and charging, as he had in the 1940s, that militarism was a "job-making boondoggle," whose purpose was not to defend but to bolster "the economic system with jobs for soldiers and jobs and profits in the munitions plants." Presenting figures for swollen military spending between the start of Roosevelt's war buildup in 1939 and 1954, Flynn argued that the economy no longer consisted of a "socialist sector" and a "capitalist sector." Instead, Flynn warned, there was only the "racket" of military spending, "with the soldier-politician in the middle—unaware of the hell-broth of war, taxes and debt." The Eisenhower administration, Flynn charged, was no better than its Democratic predecessors; the administration is spending $66 billion a year, most going for "so-called 'national security'" and only a "small fraction" spent on "the legitimate functions of government."

A fascinating interchange followed between Buckley and Flynn. Rejecting Flynn's article in a letter on October 22, 1956, Buckley had the unmitigated chutzpah to tell this veteran anti-Communist that he didn't understand the nature of the Soviet military threat, and condescendingly advised him to read William Henry Chamberlin's latest pot-boiler in *National Review* describing "the difference in the nature of the threat posed by the Commies and the Nazis." Trying to sugar-coat the pill, Buckley sent Flynn $100 along with the rejection note. The next day, Flynn returned the $100, sarcastically adding that he was "greatly obliged" to Buckley for "the little lecture."

In this way, Buckley used the same argument for depriving Flynn of a publishing outlet that Bruce Bliven and the war liberals had employed when ousting Flynn from the *New Republic* in the 1940s. In both cases Flynn was accused of overlooking the alleged foreign threat to the United States, and in both cases Flynn's attempted answer was to stress that the real menace to American liberties was militarism, socialism, and fascism at home, imposed in the name of combating an alleged foreign threat. Flynn denied the existence of a Soviet military threat, and warned prophetically that the executive branch of the government was about to involve us in a futile war in Indo-China.[19]

Virtually the only published echo of the Old Right was a book by the redoubtable Felix Morley who, in the course of decrying the modern New Deal and post-New Deal destruction of federalism by strong central government, roundly attacked the developing and existing American Empire and militarism.[20]

Meanwhile, *National Review*'s image of me was that of a lovable though Utopian libertarian purist who, however, must be kept strictly confined to propounding *laissez-faire* economics, to which *National Review* had a kind of residual rhetorical attachment. There was even talk at one time of my becoming an economic columnist for *National Review*. But above all I was supposed to stay out of political matters and leave to the warmongering ideologues of *National Review* the gutsy real-world task of defending me from the depredations of world Communism, and allowing me the luxury of spinning Utopias about private fire-fighting services. I was increasingly unwilling to play that kind of a castrate role.

---

[19]On Buckley's rejection of the Flynn article, see Ronald Radosh, *Prophets on the Right: Profiles of Conservative Critics of American Globalism* (New York: Simon and Schuster, 1975), pp. 272–73; and Radosh, "Preface," in John T. Flynn, *As We Go Marching* (New York: Free Life Editions, 1973), pp. xiv–xv.

[20]Felix Morley, *Freedom and Federalism* (Chicago: Henry Regnery, 1959), especially the chapters "Democracy and Empire," "Nationalization through Foreign Policy," and "The Need for an Enemy."

13
The Early 1960s: From Right to Left

My total break with *National Review* and the right wing, my final emotional divorce from thinking of myself as a right winger or an ally of the Right, came around 1960. The break was precipitated by Khrushchev's visit to the United States in late 1959. During the torpid Eisenhower years of the late 1950s, when foreign affairs were in a frozen deadlock and when the American Left had all but disappeared, it was easy *not* to put the peace issue at the forefront of one's consciousness. But the Khrushchev visit was, for me, an exciting and welcome sign of a possible detente, of a break in the Cold War dike, of a significant move toward ending the Cold War and achieving peaceful coexistence. Hence I enthusiastically favored the visit; but at the same time *National Review* became hysterical at the very same possibility, and in conjunction with the still-secret John Birch Society, tried desperately to whip up public sentiment to disrupt the visit.

The New Rightist clamor continued in opposition to the summit conference of early 1960, which I had hoped would build on the good will of the preceding Khrushchev visit. I was particularly incensed at the demagogic argument used by *National Review* that we must not Shake the Hand of the Bloody Butcher of the Ukraine (Khrushchev); in a tart exchange of letters with Buckley, I pointed out that *National Review* had always revered Winston Churchill, and was proud to Shake His Hand, even though Churchill was responsible for far more slaughter (in World Wars I and II) than Khrushchev had ever been. It was not an argument calculated to endear me to *National Review*: libertarianism was threatening to expand from discussion of fire departments to war and peace!

By this time the New York libertarian movement had been virtually reduced to two: Leonard Liggio and myself; and I was even more isolated than when the decade had begun, for now the entire right wing had been captured from within by its former enemy: war and global intervention. The old Circle Bastiat had disappeared of attrition, as some members left town for graduate school and others surrendered to the blandishments of the New Right. And whatever libertarians remained in isolated pockets throughout the country were too benumbed to offer any resistance whatever to the New Right tide.

It was time to act; and politically, my total break with the Right came with the Stevenson movement of 1960. In 1956 I had been for Stevenson over Eisenhower, but only partly for his superior peace position; another reason was to try to depose the Republican "left" so as to allow the Old Right to recapture the party. Emotionally, I was then still a right-winger who yearned for a rightist third party. But now the third party lure was dead; the Right was massively Goldwaterite. And besides, Stevenson's courageous stand on the U-2 incident—his outrage that Eisenhower had wrecked the summit conference by refusing to make not only a routine, but a morally required apology for the U-2 spy incursion over Russia—made me a Stevensonian. Politically, I had ceased being a right-winger. I had determined that the crucial issue was peace or war; and that on that question the only viable political movement was the "left" wing of the Democratic Party. By consistently following an antiwar and isolationist star, I had shifted—or rather *been* shifted—from right-wing Republican to left-wing Democrat.

It was, of course, a mighty emotional wrench for "right-wing libertarians" to make; and as far as I know, there were only three of us who leaped over the wall to emotional left-wing Democracy: myself, Leonard Liggio, and former Circle member Ronald Hamowy, who had gone on to graduate school at the University of Chicago.

I was not politically active in the drive for the Stevenson nomination, but a strange concatenation of events was to thrust me into a prominent role among Stevensonians in New York. After Kennedy was able to scotch the Stevenson drive for the nomination at the Democratic convention, I saw a tiny ad in the *New York Post* for a Stevenson Pledge movement: an attempt by particularly embittered Stevensonians to try to force Kennedy to pledge that he would make Adlai Secretary of State. On going to the meeting, which included the eventually famous campaign manager Dave Garth, I suddenly found myself a leader in a new political organization: the League of Stevensonian Democrats (LSD), headed by the charismatic John R. Kuesell, who was soon to become prominent in the Reform Democratic movement in New York.[1] We held out for a Stevenson pledge as long as we could; and then, when not forthcoming, we took our stand firmly for Kennedy against Richard Nixon, a political figure whom I had always reviled as (a) a Republican "leftist," (b) an opportunist, and (c) a warmonger, if not, however, as consistent and dedicated a warmonger as the New Right.[2]

An amusing incident symbolized my political shift from Right to Left, while continuing to advance libertarianism. Wearing my extreme right-wing hat, I published a letter in the *Wall Street Journal* urging genuine conservatives not to vote for Richard Nixon, so as to allow conservatives to regain control of the Republican Party. When Kuesell saw the letter, he reasonably concluded that I was some sort of right-wing spy in the LSD, and was set to expel me from the organization. Coming in to see him, I was prepared to give him an hour lecture on libertarianism, on my hegira from right to left, and so on. As it happened, I was only able to get a few

---

[1]Coincidentally, one of the leaders of the League, economist Art Carol, has in recent years become a *laissez-faire* libertarian, and now leads the libertarian movement at the University of Hawaii.

[2]On Nixon, there was a division in *National Review*; the more pragmatic and opportunistic types, such as Buckley, Rusher, and Burnham, were ardently for Nixon once the nomination was secured; but the more principled types, such as Meyer and Bozell, were always reluctant.

words out of my mouth. "You see," I began, "I'm a . . . 'libertarian'." Kuesell, always quick on the mark, immediately cut in. "Say no more," he said, "I'm a libertarian, too." He immediately showed me a pamphlet he had written in high school, *Quo Warranto?*, challenging government on their right to interfere with people's lives and property. Since the word and concept of libertarian were scarcely household words, especially in that era, I was utterly astonished. From then on, Kuesell and I worked in happy tandem in the LSD until it withered away after the start of the Kennedy administration. This experience confirmed my view that left-wing Democracy rather than right-wing Republicanism was now the natural field for libertarian allies.

As one of the theoreticians of the League of Stevensonian Democrats, I became head of its National and International Affairs Committee, and as such managed to write and push through a platform for the League that was totally libertarian, since I concentrated on civil liberties and opposition to war and conscription.

Meanwhile, libertarianism itself was essentially isolated and "underground." Harry Elmer Barnes could publish his call for revisionism of all world wars, including the Cold War, only in the pages of the obscure left-pacifist magazine *Liberation* during 1958 and 1959; on the basis of this I struck up a correspondence and friendship with Barnes that lasted to the end of his life. In Chicago, former Circle Bastiat members Ron Hamowy and Ralph Raico helped found a new student quarterly, *New Individualist Review*, in early 1961, which quickly became the outstanding theoretical journal in the student conservative moment; however, its whole *modus operandi* was a commitment to the now-outmoded conservative-libertarian alliance. Hence it could not serve as a libertarian organ, especially in the crucial realm of foreign policy.

Ron Hamowy, however, managed to publish in *NIR* a blistering critique of the New Right, of *National Review*, its conservatism and its warmongering, in a debate with Bill Buckley. Hamowy, for the first time in print, pinpointed the betrayal of the Old Right at the hands of Buckley and *National Review*. Hamowy summed up his critique of *National Review* doctrines:

> They may be summed up as: (1) a belligerent foreign policy likely to result in war; (2) a suppression of civil liberties at home; (3) a devotion to imperialism and to a polite form of white supremacy; (4) a tendency towards the union of Church and State; (5) the conviction that the community is superior to the individual and that historic tradition is a far better guide than reason; and (6) a rather lukewarm support of the free economy. They wish, in gist, to substitute one group of masters (themselves) for another. They do not desire so much to limit the State as to control it. One would tend to describe this devotion to a hierarchical, warlike statism and this fundamental opposition to human reason and individual liberty as a species of corporativism suggestive of Mussolini or Franco, but let us be content with calling it "old-time conservatism," the conservatism not of the heroic band of libertarians who founded the anti-New Deal Right, but the traditional conservatism that has always been the enemy of true liberalism, the conservatism of Pharonic Egypt, of Medieval Europe, of Metternich and the Tsar, of James II, and the Inquisition; and Louis XVI, of the rack, the thumbscrew, the whip, and the firing squad. I, for one, do not very much mind that a philosophy which has for centuries dedicated itself to trampling upon the rights of the individual and glorifying the State should have its old name back.[3]

Buckley, in characteristic fashion, replied by stressing the primacy of the alleged Soviet threat, and sneered at the libertarian "tablet-keepers": "There is room in any society," Buckley wrote,

> for those whose only concern is tablet-keeping; but let them realize that it is only because of the conservatives' disposition to sacrifice in order to withstand the enemy, that they are able to enjoy their monasticism, and pursue their busy little seminars on whether or not to demunicipalize the garbage collectors.[4]

---

[3]Ronald Hamowy, "'*National Review*': Criticism and Reply," *New Individualist Review* 1, no. 3 (November 1961): 6–7.

[4]William F. Buckley, Jr., "Three Drafts of an Answer to Mr. Hamowy," ibid., p. 9.

Equally characteristically, Buckley concluded by accusing Hamowy (incorrectly, if that matters) of being a member of the Committee for a Sane Nuclear Policy (SANE). (One Buckleyite wag wrote at the time: "I hear that Ron Hamowy is in-SANE.")[5] In his sparkling rebuttal, Hamowy declared:

> It might appear ungrateful of me, but I must decline to thank Mr. Buckley for saving my life. It is, further, my belief that if his viewpoint prevails and that if he persists in his unsolicited aid the result will almost certainly be my death (and that of tens of millions of others) in nuclear war or my imminent imprisonment as an "un-American."[6]

Because of the libertarian-conservative foreign policy split on *New Individualist Review*, however, the editors agreed among themselves, as a result of the furor surrounding the Hamowy-Buckley debate, that nevermore would *any* statement whatever on foreign policy be published in the magazine. There was thus still no publishing outlet for an isolationist-libertarian position.

In early 1962, my last ties were cut with anything that might be construed as the organized right wing. The William Volker Fund, with which I had been associated for over a decade, and which had quietly but effectively served as the preeminent encourager and promoter of conservative and libertarian scholarship, suddenly and literally collapsed, and moved toward virtual dissolution. One of

---

[5]Actually, I attended one meeting of SANE around this time, in my search for a left-peace movement, and refused to join, rejecting it for its moderation, its concentration on such important but superficial issues as nuclear testing, and its egregious red-baiting. It was clear to me that SANE was not really opposed to the Cold War and certainly not to American imperialism. By this time, of course, I had given up even voluntary red-baiting; for if the Communists are opposed to nuclear weapons and atomic war, then why not join with them and anyone else in opposing these evils? Since the New Right favored these measures, wasn't it more of an Enemy than the Communists?)

[6]Hamowy, "'*National Review*': Criticism and Reply."

the formerly libertarian members of the Volker Fund staff (Dr. Ivan R. Bierly) had become a fundamentalist Calvinist convinced of the need for an elite Calvinist dictatorship, which would run the country, stamp out pornography, and prepare America for the (literal) Armageddon, which was supposedly due to arrive in a generation. Bierly managed to convince Harold Luhnow, the head of the Fund, that he was surrounded on his staff by a nefarious atheist-anarchist-pacifist conspiracy. As a result, the president dissolved the Fund one day in a fit of pique.[7]

The collapse of the William Volker Fund had even more fateful and grievous consequences than appeared on the surface. According to the terms of its charter, the Fund was supposed to be eventually self-liquidating, and so in the winter of 1961–62, the Volker Fund decided to take its $17 million of assets and to liquidate by transferring them to a new organization, the Institute for Humane Studies (IHS), a scholarly libertarian think-tank to be headed by Baldy Harper. For the first time, then, a libertarian research organization would be endowed, and would not have to expend its energies scrambling for funds. When Mr. Luhnow had his sudden change of heart before the decision was made final, and closed the fund down, IHS, with Harper at the helm, was suddenly out on the street as a pure and lovable libertarian research organization devoid of funding. For the rest of his life, Baldy Harper struggled on as head of IHS.

Isolated as we were in New York, and having broken with the Right, Leonard Liggio and myself had plenty of time to re-examine our basic premises, especially in relation to where we really fit on the ideological spectrum. The lead was taken by Liggio, a brilliant young historian with a remarkably encyclopedic knowledge of history, European and American. Actually, Leonard had always been

---

[7]There was a fitful attempt to revive the Volker Fund on the new ideological basis, but apparently the president began to be repelled or frightened by the new tendency, and the Fund ceased all activity. Because of publishing commitments, the splendid Volker Fund book series at Van Nostrand continued to be published into 1964.

more astute than I *vis-à-vis National Review*. When the first issue of *NR* appeared, featuring an article by the notorious "Senator from Formosa," William F. Knowland, Liggio resolved to have nothing to do with the magazine.[8]

In the first place, we began to rethink the origins of the Cold War that we had opposed for so long; we read the monumental work of D.F. Fleming, *The Cold War and its Origins*, and the seminal books of the founder of New Left historiography, William Appleman Williams, *The Tragedy of American Diplomacy* (1959) and *The Contours of American History* (1961). And we concluded that our older isolationism had suffered from a fatal weakness: the implicit acceptance of the basic Cold War premise that there *was* a Russian "threat," that Stalin had been partly responsible for the Cold War by engaging in aggressive expansion in Europe and Asia, and that Roosevelt had engaged in an evil "sellout" at Yalta. We concluded that all this was a tissue of myth; that on the contrary Russia had not expanded aggressively at all, its only "expansion" having been the inevitable and desirable result of rolling back the German invasion. That, indeed, the United States (with the aid of Britain) was solely responsible for the Cold War, in a continuing harassment and aggression against a Soviet Union whose foreign policy had been almost pathetic in its yearning for peace with the West at virtually any price. We began to realize that, even in Eastern Europe, Stalin had not imposed Communist regimes until the United States had been pressing it there and had launched the Cold War for several years. We also began to see that, far from Roosevelt "selling out" to Stalin at Yalta and the other wartime conferences,[9] that the "sellout" was the other way around: as

---

[8]The Knowland tie-in presumably reflected the pervasive influence of Alfred Kohlberg, China Lobbyist and a close friend of the magazine.

[9]The situation at Yalta involved East European territory that was not ours to control; we of course did not condone the monstrous agreement to ship anti-Communist POWs held by the Germans back to the Soviet bloc against their will, or endorse the mass expulsion of Germans from Poland or Czechoslovakia.

Stalin, in the vain hope of seeking peace with an implacably aggressive and imperialistic United States, repeatedly sold out the world Communist movement: scuttling the Communists of Greece in a sellout deal with Churchill; preventing the Communist partisans of Italy and France from taking power at the end of the war; and trying his mightiest to scuttle the Communist movements of Yugoslavia and China. In the latter cases, Stalin tried to force Tito and Mao into coalition regimes under their enemies; and it was only the fact that they had come to power by their own arms and not in the wake of the Soviet Army that permitted them to take over by telling Stalin to go to hell.

In short, we had come to the conclusion that the most astute analysis of the events of World War II and of the Communist movement was that of the Trotskyites; far from expanding vigorously in Europe and Asia, Stalin, devoted only to the national security of the Soviet Union, had tried his best to scuttle the world Communist movements in a vain attempt to appease the *American* aggressor. That Stalin had wanted only national security and the absence of anti-Soviet regimes on his borders was shown by the contrasting developments in Poland and Finland; in Poland, aggressive anti-Sovietism had forced Stalin to take full control; in Finland, in contrast, there had emerged the great statesman Paasikivi, who pushed a policy of conservative agrarianism at home and peace and friendship with the Soviet Union in foreign affairs; at which point Stalin was perfectly content to leave Finland at peace and to withdraw the Soviet army.

In contrast to the uniformly peaceful and victimized policies of the Soviet Union, we saw the United States using World War II to replace and go beyond Great Britain as the world's great imperial power; stationing its troops everywhere, presuming to control and dominate nations and governments throughout the world. For years, the U.S. tried also to roll back Soviet power in Eastern Europe; and its foreign policy was particularly devoted to suppressing revolutionary and pro-Communist movements in every country in the underdeveloped world. We saw too that the Soviet Union had always pushed for disarmament, and that it was the U.S. that resisted it, particularly in the menacing mass-slaughter weapons of the nuclear age. There was *no* Russian "threat"; the threat to the peace of the world, in Europe, in Asia, and throughout the globe was the United States Leviathan. For years, conservatives and libertarians had argued about the "external" (Russian) and the "internal" (Washington) threats to individual liberty, with libertarians and isolationists focusing on the latter and conservatives on the former. But now we—Leonard and I—were truly liberated; the scales had fallen from our eyes; and we saw that the "external threat," too, emanated from Washington, D.C.

Leonard and I were now "left-wing Democrats" indeed on foreign policy. But still more: we were chafing at the bit. Why was SANE ever so careful *not* to discuss imperialism? Why did it clearly favor the U.S. over the Soviet Union? We were now not only looking for an isolationist movement; we were looking for an anti-imperialist movement, a movement that zeroed in on the American Empire as the great threat to the peace, and therefore to the liberty, of the world. That movement did not yet exist.

In addition to our re-evaluation of the origins and nature of the Cold War, we engaged in a thorough reassessment of the whole "left-right" ideological spectrum in historical perspective. For it was clear to us that the European Throne-and-Altar Conservatism that had captured the right wing was statism in a virulent and despotic form; and yet only an imbecile could possibly call these people "leftists." But this meant that our old simple paradigm of the "left Communist/total government . . . right/no government" continuum, with liberals on the left of center and conservatives on the right of center, had been totally incorrect. We had therefore been misled in our basic view of the spectrum and in our whole conception of ourselves as natural "extreme rightists." There must have been a fatal flaw in the analysis. Plunging back into history, we concentrated on the reality that in the eighteenth and nineteenth centuries, *laissez-faire* liberals, radicals, and revolutionaries constituted the "extreme left" while our ancient foes, the conservatives, the Throne-and-Altar worshippers, constituted the right-wing Enemy.

Leonard Liggio then came up with the following profound analysis of the historical process, which I adopted.

First, and dominant in history, was the Old Order, the *ancien régime*, the regime of caste and frozen status, of exploitation by a war-making, feudal or despotic ruling class, using the church and the priesthood to dupe the masses into accepting its rule. This was pure statism; and this was the "right wing." Then, in seventeenth- and eighteenth-century Western Europe, a liberal and radical opposition movement arose, our old heroes, who championed a popular revolutionary movement on behalf of rationalism, individual liberty, minimal government, free markets and free trade, international peace, and separation of Church and State—and in opposition to Throne and Altar, to monarchy, the ruling class, theocracy, and war. These—"our people"—were the Left, and the purer their libertarian vision the more "extreme" a Left they were.

So far, so good, and our analysis was not yet so different from before; but what of socialism, that movement born in the nineteenth century which we had always reviled as the "extreme left"? Where did that fit in? Liggio analyzed socialism as a confused middle-of-the road movement, influenced historically by *both* the libertarian and individualist Left and by the conservative-statist Right. From the individualist Left the socialists took the *goals* of freedom: the withering away of the State, the replacement of the governing of men by the administration of things (a concept coined by the early nineteenth-century French *laissez-faire* libertarians Charles Comte and Charles Dunoyer), opposition to the ruling class and the search for its overthrow, the desire to establish international peace, an advanced industrial economy and a high standard of living for the mass of the people. From the conservative Right the socialists adopted the *means* to attempt to achieve these goals: collectivism, state planning, community control of the individual. But this put socialism in the *middle* of the ideological spectrum. It also meant that socialism was an unstable, self-contradictory doctrine bound to fly apart rapidly in the inner contradiction between its means and its ends. And in this belief we were bolstered by the old demonstration of my mentor Ludwig von Mises that socialist central planning simply cannot operate an advanced industrial economy.

The Socialist movement had, historically, also suffered ideologically and organizationally from a similar inner contradiction: with Social Democrats, from Engels to Kautsky to Sidney Hook, shifting inexorably *rightward* into accepting and strengthening the State apparatus and becoming "left" apologists for the Corporate State, while other socialists, such as Bakunin and Kropotkin, shifted *leftward* toward the individualist, libertarian pole. It was clear, too, that the Communist Party in America had taken, in domestic affairs, the same "rightward" path—hence the similarity which the "extreme" red-baiters had long discerned between Communists and liberals. In fact, the shift of so many ex-Communists from left to the conservative Right now seemed to be not very much of a shift at all; for they had been pro-Big Government in the 1930s and "Twentieth Century American" patriots in the 1940s, and now they were *still* patriots and statists.

From our new analysis of the spectrum we derived several important corollaries. One was the fact that alliance between libertarians and conservatism appeared, at the very least, to be no more "natural" than the older alliance during the 1900s and 1920s between libertarians and socialists. Alliances now seemed to depend on the given historical context.[10] Second, the older intense fear of Marxian socialism seemed inordinate; for conservatives had long ignored Mises's demonstration of the inevitable breakup of socialist planning, and had acted as if once a country had gone socialist, then that was the end, that the country was doomed and the process irreversible. But if ours—and Mises's—analysis was right, then socialism should fall apart before too many years had elapsed, and much more rapidly than the Old Order, which had had the capacity to last unchanged for centuries. Sure enough, by

---

[10]The relevant spectrum will, of course, differ in accordance with the critical issues that may be at stake in different historical situations. Thus, while near each other on the ideological spectrum on the issue of statism and centralized government, the individualist is at opposite poles from the left-wing Bakunin-Kropotkin anarchist on such an issue as egalitarianism and private property.

the early 1960s we already had seen the inspiring development of Yugoslavia, which after its break from Stalin had evolved rapidly away from socialism and central planning and in the direction of the free market, a course which the rest of Eastern Europe and even Soviet Russia were already beginning to emulate. And yet in contrast, we saw to our chagrin that even the most economic-minded of the New Right were so caught up in their hysterical anti-Communism that they refused to greet or even acknowledge the breakup of socialism in Eastern Europe. This blind spot was obviously connected with the conservatives' long-time refusal to acknowledge the corollary breakup of the international Stalinist monolith within the Communist movement; for both of these insights would have weakened greatly the Right's characteristic campaign of hysteria against the supposedly invincible and ever-expanding Communist world—an expansion that could, in its eyes, be checked only by nuclear war.

Our analysis was greatly bolstered, moreover, by our becoming familiar with the work of domestic revisionism of an exciting group of historians who had studied under William Appleman Williams at the University of Wisconsin. Williams himself, in *The Contours of American History*, Williams's students who founded *Studies on the Left* in 1959, and particularly the work of Williams's student Gabriel Kolko in his monumental *Triumph of Conservatism* (1963), changed our view of the twentieth-century American past, and hence of the genesis and nature of the current American system. From them we learned that all of us believers in the free market had erred in believing that somehow, down deep, Big Businessmen were really in favor of *laissez-faire*, and that their deviations from it, obviously clear and notorious in recent years, were either "sell-outs" of principle to expedience or the result of brainwashing and infusing of guilt into these businessmen by liberal intellectuals.

This is the general view on the Right; in the remarkable phrase of Ayn Rand, Big Business is "America's most persecuted minority." Persecuted minority, indeed! To be sure, there were charges aplenty against Big Business and its intimate connections with Big Government in the old McCormick *Chicago Tribune* and especially in the writings of Albert Jay Nock; but it took the Williams-Kolko analysis, and particularly the detailed investigation by Kolko, to portray the true anatomy and physiology of the America scene. As Kolko pointed out, all the various measures of federal regulation and welfare statism, beginning in the Progressive period, that Left and Right alike have always believed to be a mass movement *against* Big Business, are not only backed to the hilt by Big Business at the present time, but were originated by it for the very purpose of shifting from a free market to a cartelized economy. Under the guise of regulations "against monopoly" and "for the public welfare," Big Business has succeeded in granting itself cartels and privileges through the use of government.

As for the liberal intellectuals, their role has been to serve as "corporate liberals," as weavers of sophisticated apologies to inform the masses that the rulers of the American corporate state are ruling on behalf of the "common good" and the "general welfare." The role of the corporate liberal intellectual in justifying the ways of the modern State to man is precisely equivalent to the function of the priest in the Oriental despotisms who convinced the masses that their Emperor was all-wise and divine.

Liggio and I also focused anew on the crucial problem of the underdeveloped countries. We came to realize that the revolutions in the Third World were not only in behalf of national independence against imperialism but also, and conjointly, against feudal land monopolists in behalf of the just ownership of their land by the long-oppressed peasantry. Genuine believers in justice and in private property, we concluded, should favor the expropriation of the stolen and conquered lands of Asia and Latin America by the peasants who, on any sort of libertarian theory, were and still are their proper and just owners. And yet, tragically, only the Communists have supported peasant movements; American or native "free enterprisers," when they did not ignore the crucial land problem altogether, invariably and tragically came down on the side of the oppressive landlords in the name of "private property." But the "private" property of these monopoly landlords is "private" only by virtue of State conquest, theft, and land grants; and any genuine believer in the rights of private property must then side with the drive of the peasants to get their land back. The peasants of the world are not socialists or communists; instinctively, they are individualists and libertarians, consumed with a perfectly understandable passion to reclaim the right to own their own lands. The Zapata revolution in Mexico and the Reies Tijerina movement in the Southwest, are only the most clear-cut examples of the profoundly libertarian struggle of peasants to defend or reclaim their just property titles from loot and conquest at the hands of the central government.[11]

Isolated and alone, Leonard Liggio and I nevertheless set out on what seemed to be a superhuman threefold task: to advance the minuscule and scattered libertarian, anarcho-capitalist movement; to convert these libertarians at least to a solidly isolationist position; and finally, to try also to convert them to our newfound anti-imperialist and "left" or "left-right" perspective. On the libertarian front, there was one bright ray of hope: pacifist-individualist anarchist (who calls himself an "autarchist") Robert LeFevre had established a Freedom School in the Colorado Rockies in 1956, to supply intensive two-week summer courses on the freedom philosophy. LeFevre had previously worked in New York for Merwin K. Hart's National Economic Council, rising to vice-president, and then, in 1954, had moved out to Colorado Springs to be editorial page editor for R.C. Hoiles's anarcho-capitalist daily Colorado Springs *Gazette-Telegraph*. Over the years, since 1956, LeFevre had built a remarkable record of converting a great many people, and especially young people, to the libertarian creed. And so, slowly, throughout the country, a growing libertarian cadre, graduates of the Freedom School, were emerging. As a dedicated pacifist, LeFevre was of course opposed to the war drive of the New Right, and said so in a 1964 leaflet, *Those Who Protest*.

With the help of a base of Freedom School graduates, we were able to rebuild a small circle in New York, this time dedicated to the "left-right" analysis. There was Edward C. Facey, Robert J.

[11]For a definitive history of the Zapata revolution, incidentally making clear its libertarian goals, see John Womack, Jr., *Zapata and the Mexican Revolution* (New York: Knopf, 1969).

Smith, who had been influenced by the Volker Fund and the Freedom School, and Alan Milchman, whom we had managed to convert from his post as head of Brooklyn College YAF. And then there was the "first generation" of the libertarian youth movement at the University of Kansas, headed by Bob Gaskins and David Jackman. Gaskins and Jackman had been anarchists, but politically they had been "right-wing" *laissez-fairists* and they edited a magazine called *The Standard*. When Gaskins and Jackman moved to New York in late 1962 we were able to convert them to our perspective, and the result was an all-peace issue of *The Standard*, April 1963, which included antiwar reprints from Chodorov, Mises, and others, and an article of my own, "War, Peace, and the State," which greatly expanded and more firmly grounded my old *Faith and Freedom* derivation of isolationism and anti-imperialism from libertarian theory.

In the winter of 1963–64, LeFevre organized a winter-and-spring long "Phrontistery" at Colorado to pave the way for transforming Freedom School into a Rampart College. To the Phrontistery flocked some of the nation's leading young libertarians, including Smith, Gaskins, Jackman, Peter Blake, and Mike Helm, many of whom formed for the first time in public an aggressive "Rothbardian" block that stunned the visiting conservative and *laissez-faire* dignitaries who had been invited to teach there. For the first time in public some of the group also unfurled the "black-and-gold flag," the colors of which we had all decided best represented anarcho-capitalism: black as the classic color of anarchism and gold as the color of capitalism and hard money.

Meanwhile, on the larger political scene, things grew more dismal as the *National Review* game plan finally succeeded, and Barry Goldwater won the Republican nomination. I personally grew frantic; at long last, the fingers of my old *National Review* associates were getting close to the nuclear button, and I *knew*, I knew to my very marrow that they were aching to push it. I felt that I had to do *something* to warn the public about the menace of nuclear war that Goldwaterism presented; I felt like a Paul Revere come to warn everyone about the threat of global war that these people were about to loose upon the world.

Second, I tried to hive off some conservative and libertarian votes from Goldwater by recalling to them their long-forgotten libertarian heritage. In contrast to many "fair-play minded" liberals, I was not at all horrified at the famous Democratic TV spot showing a little girl picking flowers while a Goldwaterite nuclear explosion loomed to annihilate her. On the contrary, I rejoiced at what I believed to be, at last, a zeroing in on the true dimensions of the Goldwaterite menace.

I could, however, play only a very small direct role in the stop-Goldwater crusade. *The Standard* was now defunct, and so the most I could do was to write in the Southern California anarcho-Randian newsletter, *The Innovator*, warning the readers of Goldwaterite war and fascism (which can be defined, after all, as global war, anti-Communist crusading, suppression of civil liberties, and corporate statism disguised in free-market rhetoric—which delineated the New Right). I succeeded, however, only in alienating the stunned readership.[12] I also addressed a group of veteran disciples of Frank Chodorov—the "Fragments" group—just before the election, denouncing Goldwaterism, and unaccountably found myself engaged in a lengthy defense of the foreign policies of Communist China as being pacific and nonaggressive—for wasn't there at least a "Chinese menace"? The only result of my endeavors was to have half the audience brandishing their canes in my direction and shouting, "We haven't voted in thirty years, but by God we're going out next Tuesday and voting for Barry Goldwater." My only success was in greatly weakening the Goldwaterite enthusiasm of the Queens College libertarian movement, headed by Larry Moss and Dave Glauberman. Looking around also for some periodical, any periodical, in which to publish a critique of

---

[12]Among the Rightists, again it was doughty Felix Morley who, virtually alone and unheeded, denounced the Goldwater movement in no uncertain terms as akin to the early days of the Nazi movement, as he had observed it in Germany.

the transformation of the American Right from Old to New, from isolation to global war, I could find only the obscure Catholic quarterly *Continuum*.[13] For the Left was still defunct in America.

---

[13]Murray N. Rothbard, "The Transformation of the American Right," *Continuum* 2 (Summer 1964): 220–31.

14
The Later 1960s: The New Left

For years now, Leonard Liggio and I had been looking for a "left," for an antiwar movement, with which we could ally ourselves. Then suddenly, as if by magic, the New Left emerged in American life, particularly in two great events: the Berkeley Free Speech Movement (FSM) of the fall of 1964, which inaugurated the campus movement of the 1960s; and the March on Washington of April 17, 1965, organized by the Students for a Democratic Society to protest the dramatic escalation of our war in Vietnam in February. The SDS march inaugurated the great anti-Vietnam War movement, which undoubtedly constituted the deepest and most widespread opposition in the midst of war since the conflict with Mexico in the 1840s. The opposition during World War I was strong, but isolated and brutally suppressed by the government; the isolationist movement of World War II collapsed completely as soon as we entered the war; and the Korean War never generated a powerful mass opposition. But here at last was an exciting, massive opposition to the war proceeding during the war itself! Another point that cheered Leonard and myself was that here at last was not a namby-pamby "peace" group like SANE, which always carefully balanced its criticism of the U.S. and of Russia, and which also took pains to exclude "undesirables" from antiwar activity; here was a truly antiwar movement which zeroed in on the evils of American war-making; and here was a movement that excluded no one, that baited neither reds nor rightists, that welcomed all Americans willing to join in struggle against the immoral and aggressive war that we were waging in Vietnam. Here at last was an antiwar Left that we could be happy about!

It is true that SDS, the unquestioned leader of this new antiwar movement, had been born in unfortunate circumstances; for it was originally and was then still officially the student arm of the social democratic League for Industrial Democracy, an old-line socialist and red-baiting organization that represented the worst of Old Left liberalism. But SDS was clearly in the process of breaking with its parentage. Not only was it militant on the war, but it was also no longer doctrinaire socialist—a pleasant change indeed from the Old Left. On the contrary, its ideology was vague enough to encompass even "right-wing libertarians." In fact, there was a good deal of instinctive libertarian sentiment in that early SDS which was to intensify for the next several years. There was a new hunger for individual freedom, for self-development, and a new concern about bureaucracy and technocratic statism that boded well for SDS's future.

Thus, SDS was shaping up as instinctively quasi-libertarian even on "domestic" issues. This libertarianism was reinforced by the campus movement generated by the Berkeley Free Speech Movement. For hadn't conservatives and libertarians for decades been bitterly critical of our state-ridden educational system—its public schools, compulsory attendance laws, and giant, impersonal bureaucratic training factories replacing genuine education? Hadn't we long been critical of the influence of John Dewey, the emphasis on vocational training, the giant tie-ins of education with government and the military-industrial complex? And here was the New Left which, while admittedly inchoate and lacking a constructive theory, was at least arising to zero in on many of the educational evils that we had been denouncing unheeded for over a generation. If, for example, we take a New Left hero such as Paul Goodman and compare him with Albert Jay Nock on education, we see that from very different philosophical and cultural perspectives they were making very similar critiques of the mass training public school-compulsory attendance system. Without making light of the philosophical differences—particularly individualistic versus egalitarian underpinnings—both Goodman and Nock clearly attacked the problem from a libertarian perspective.

It was therefore not an accident that a newly developing "right-wing libertarian" group at Berkeley, headed by the young graduate math student Danny Rosenthal, should have helped lead the Free Speech and allied movements. Rosenthal and his group, who founded the Alliance of Libertarian Activists in the Berkeley-San Francisco area and were also ardent Goldwaterites, fought alongside the New Left on behalf of freedom of speech and assembly, and in opposition to censorship and to the swollen bureaucratic establishment at Berkeley. Rosenthal also exerted considerable influence on the views of Mario Savio, the famous FSM leader, though Savio was of course also subject to socialistic influences and pressures.

The emergence of the New Left persuaded Leonard and me that the time had come to act, to break out of our ideological and political isolation. Hence we founded, in the spring of 1965, the three-times-a-year journal *Left and Right*. The purpose of founding *L&R* was twofold: to influence libertarians throughout the country to break with the right wing and to ally themselves with the emerging New Left and try to push that left further in a libertarian direction; and second, to "find" the New Left ourselves as a group to ally with and possibly influence. The first issue of *Left and Right* had three lengthy articles which managed to touch all of the important bases of our new libertarian "line": my own article, "Left and Right: The Prospects for Liberty," which set forth the Liggio analysis of the Left/Right historical spectrum; Liggio's own "Why the Futile Crusade?" which brought back and portrayed the isolationist and anti-imperialist views of Senator Taft and the Taftite wing of the Republican Party; and Alan Milchman's review of Fleming's *Origins of the Cold War* which, for the first time, brought Cold War revisionism to a libertarian audience.

In the second issue, in autumn 1965, I wrote an article hailing the substantial libertarian elements of the New Left ("Liberty and the New Left"). I praised the New Left for taking up important libertarian and Old Right causes: opposition to bureaucracy and centralized government; enthusiasm for Thoreau and the idea of civil disobedience to unjust laws; a shift from Old Left compulsory racial integration to opposition to police brutality and what would soon be termed "black power" in black communities; opposition to urban renewal and to restrictive and monopolistic labor unionism; opposition to the Clark Kerr-type of modern educational bureaucracy; and of course the total opposition to the American War in Vietnam. In addition to comparing the educational views of Goodman and Nock, I also pointed to the hopeful sign of Goodman (in his *People or Personnel*)[1] favorably treating a free-market economy.

The impact of *Left and Right* was remarkable, considering our paucity of subscribers and the total absence of funds. For one thing, we immediately had considerable impact on conservative and libertarian youth. Danny Rosenthal was converted to an isolationist position by Liggio's article in the first issue; Wilson A. Clark, Jr., head of the Conservative Club of the University of North Carolina, abandoned conservatism for our position; and the entire YAF unit at the University of Kansas (the "second generation" of libertarians there), headed by Becky Glaser, left YAF to form an SDS chapter on that campus. And Ronald Hamowy, by then a professor of history at Stanford, expounded our new "Left-Right" position in the *New Republic*, recalling the free market, civil libertarian, isolationist and anti-imperialist position of Old Rightists Spencer, Bastiat, Sumner, and Nock, contrasting them to the New Right and the current partnership of government and big business, and lauding Paul Goodman and other aspects of libertarianism on the New Left.[2]

We were also interested in the new experiments which some of the New Left were conducting in alternative and "parallel institutions" in education, in particular the "Free University" movement which for a short while held promise as establishing "communities

---

[1]See Paul Goodman, *People or Personnel* (New York: Random House, 1965).

[2]Ronald Hamowy, "Left and Right Meet," *The New Republic* 154, no. 11 (March 12, 1966), reprinted in *Thoughts of the Young Radicals* (New York: New Republic, 1966), pp. 81–88.

of scholars" free from the bureaucratic and Establishment trappings of the American educational system. Through *Left and Right* and through Leonard Liggio's teaching courses at the Free University of New York on imperialism, we had the opportunity of meeting the bright young William Appleman Williams students in the New York area, in particular Jim Weinstein, Ronald Radosh, and Marty Sklar. This also launched Liggio's role for several years as a leading New Left scholar-activist, as Leonard's expertise in the history of foreign policy and of Vietnam led him to play a considerable part in the Vietnam Teach-In movement, in editing *Leviathan*, and *Viet-Report*, in becoming managing editor of the *Guardian* (from which he was purged for "taking the capitalist road" in trying to cut costs), and eventually in becoming head of the American branch of the Bertrand Russell Peace Foundation and aiding its great work in the War Crimes Tribunal. In those days, too, SDS, while totally opposed morally to the war in Vietnam, was not yet anti-imperialist; and Leonard played a major role in advising the May 2nd Movement, which pioneered on the New Left in advancing an anti-American-imperialist perspective, one which SDS soon came to adopt. He also led in opposing what turned out to be the domination of M-2-M by the Maoist Progressive Labor Movement, a domination which soon brought about the dissolution of the organization.

Meanwhile, *Left and Right* continued to present our "left-right" perspective, concentrating on foreign policy and militarism but also covering other libertarian areas, and presenting a left-right spectrum of authors: libertarians (the editors, philosophy professor "Eric Dalton," Larry Moss, reprints of Lysander Spooner and Herbert Spencer), Old Rightists and isolationists (Harry Elmer Barnes, Garet Garrett, William L. Neumann), leftists (Marvin Gettleman, Ronald Radosh, Janet McCloud, Russell Stetler, and Conrad Lynn), and free-market conservatives (Yale Brozen, Gordon Tullock). In particular, I hailed the decisive turn during 1966 of SDS toward an anti-imperialist and militantly antidraft position, and the final repudiation of its social Democratic Old Guard. During 1966 and 1967, the libertarian elements of SDS grew in influence; there was a growth of the "Texas anarchists" in the organization, and a proliferation of buttons proclaiming "I Hate the State."[3]

The high point of SDS and New Left interest in the "left-right" libertarian position came in the work of former SDS President Carl Oglesby. In 1967, Oglesby published *Containment and Change*, a critique of the Vietnam War and the American Empire. In his concluding pages on strategy, Oglesby called for an alliance with the Old Right. He called upon the libertarian, *laissez-faire* wing of the Right to abandon the conservative movement which held the libertarians in thrall by convincing them of the existence of a "foreign threat." Oglesby cited my article in *Continuum*, and quoted from the Old Right view on war and peace of General MacArthur, Buffett, Garrett, Chodorov, and Dean Russell. In particular, Oglesby cited Garrett at length, stating that his "analysis of the totalitarian impulse of imperialism" had been verified repeatedly over the intervening years.

Oglesby concluded that libertarian right-wing thought, along with the black power movement and the anti-imperialist student movement, were all "rootedly American" and were

> of the grain of American humanist individualism and voluntaristic associational action; and it is only through them that the libertarian tradition is activated and kept alive. In a strong sense, the Old Right and the New Left are morally and politically coordinate.[4]

But Oglesby prophetically warned that both the libertarian Right and the New Left could miss out on this alliance and conjunction, for the former could remain in thrall to the militarism and imperialism of the right-wing, while the latter could revert to a form of Stalinism.

---

[3]See "'SDS': The New Turn," *Left and Right* (Winter, 1967).

[4]Carl Oglesby and Richard Shaull, *Containment and Change* (New York: Macmillan, 1967), pp. 166–67.

The peak of my political activity on the New Left came during the 1968 campaign. In the spring of 1968, my old enthusiasm for third party politics was rekindled, albeit in a different direction. The Peace and Freedom Party (PFP) which had become (and still is) established in California, decided to go national, and opened up shop in New York. I found that the preliminary platform and the only requirement for membership contained only two planks: the first was immediate U.S. withdrawal from Vietnam, and the second was some plank so vague about being nice to everyone that almost anyone, left, right, center could have endorsed it. Great: here was a coalition party dedicated only to immediate withdrawal from Vietnam and requiring no commitment whatever to statism! As a result, our entire libertarian group in New York poured happily into the new party.

The PFP was structured around clubs, most of them regional—such as the powerful West Side (of Manhattan) club, the hippie Greenwich Village Club, etc. One was occupational—a Faculty Club. Since there were very few actual faculty members in this very youthful party, the PFP generously widened the definition of "faculty" to include graduate students. Lo and behold! On that basis, of approximately 24 members in the Faculty Club, almost exactly one-half were our people: libertarians, including myself, Leonard Liggio, Joe Peden, Walter Block and his wife, Sherryl, and Larry Moss. The legislative arm of the PFP was to be the Delegate Assembly, consisting of delegates from the various clubs. The Faculty Club was entitled to two delegates, and so we naturally divvied it up: one going to the socialists, and one to us, who turned out to be me.

At the first meeting of the Delegate Assembly, then, here I was, only in the Party for about a week, but suddenly vaulted to top rank in the power elite. Then, early in the meeting, some people got up and advocated abolishing the Delegate Assembly as somehow "undemocratic." Jeez! I was just about to get a taste of juicy political power, when some SOBs were trying to take it away from me! As I listened further, I realized that something even more sinister and of broader concern was taking place. Apparently, the New York party was being run by a self-perpetuating oligarchical executive committee, who, in the name of "democracy," were trying to eliminate all intermediate social institutions, and to operate upon the party mass unimpeded, all in the name of "democracy." To me it smacked of rotten Jacobinism, and I got up and delivered an impassioned speech to that effect. After the session ended, a few people came up to me and said that some like-minded thinkers, who constituted the West Side Club, were having a gathering to discuss these matters. So began our nefarious alliance with the Progressive Labor faction within Peace and Freedom.

It later turned out that the PFP and its executive committee were being run, both in California and in New York, by the Leninist-Trotskyite Draperites, International Socialists run by Berkeley librarian Hal Draper. The Draperites were the original Schachtmanites, Trotskyites who had rebelled against Trotsky as Third Camp opponents of both the U.S. and the Soviet Union. The New York party was being run by the Draperites, including as their allies a motley collection of assorted socialists, pacifists, countercultural druggies, and Left Libertarians.

The opposition within PFP was indeed being run by the Maoist Progressive Labor Party (PL), who the Draperites feared were plotting a takeover. Actually, it soon became clear that PL had no such intention, but were only keeping their hand in, and were using the West Side Club to recruit candidate-members into PL. Both PL and the Draperites were keeping the structure loose while waiting for an expected flood of Gene McCarthy followers after Humphrey's expected Democratic nomination victory—a flood that, of course, never materialized. Hence the loose ideological requirement, and the fact that the platform was up for grabs. The alliance between PL and us libertarians was highly useful to both sides, in addition to cooperating in fending off Draperite dictatorship in the name of democracy. What PL got out of it was a cover for their recruiting, since no one could of course call *us* vehement antisocialists tools of Progressive Labor. What *we* got out of it was PL's firm support for an ideological platform—adopted by our joint caucus—that was probably the most libertarian of any party since the days of Cleveland Democracy. The PL people were pleasantly "straight" and nondruggie, although quite robotic, resembling left-wing Randians.

The great exception was the delightful Jake Rosen, the absolute head of PL's fraction in the PFP. Rosen, bright, joyous, witty, and decidedly nonrobotic, knew the score. One of my fondest memories of life in the PFP was of Jake Rosen trying to justify our *laissez-faire* platform to his Maoist dunderheads. "Hey, Jake, what does this mean: absolute freedom of trade and opposition to all government restrictions?" "Er, that's the 'antimonopoly coalition'." "Oh, yeah." Jake, with more sincerity, joined us in opposing guaranteed annual income plans; he considered them bourgeois and "reactionary." About the only thing Jake balked at was our proposal that our caucus come out for immediate abolition of rent control. "Hey, fellas, look, I'd love to do it, but we have commitments to tenant groups." Graciously, we let him off the hook.

With his personality, I didn't think Jake would last in PL. In addition he had already implicitly rebelled against party discipline. An obviously bright guy, Jake had accepted PL's orders to be "working class" and became a construction worker; but he stubbornly failed to obey orders and move from the hip, cosmopolitan West Side of Manhattan to Queens. ("Jake, no construction worker lives on the West Side.") Indeed, a year or so after the breakup of the PFP, Jake left or was expelled from PL, and immediately went upwardly mobile, moving to Chicago and becoming a successful commodity broker.

As the McCarthy people failed to come in, conflicts within the party became ever greater, and the New York PFP began having almost weekly conventions. In addition to the PL Draperite conflict, the Communist Party set up its competing front in New York, the "Freedom and Peace Party" (FPP), the existence of which began to confuse everyone, including the Left. Trying to put down the schisms, the California Draperites sent to run the New York party the supposedly legendary organizer Comrade Carlos, a Chicano whom the Draperite wing found to be charismatic, and to whom the rest of us took a strong dislike.[5]

---

[5]One memorable moment at one of the PFP conventions was the usually phlegmatic Leonard Liggio leaping on a chair, and beginning the provocative chant: "Carlos Out! Carlos Out!"

Although the PFP was clearly fizzling, the time finally came in late summer for nominations. The Draperites had decided on the ex-rapist Eldridge Cleaver for president, then head of the Black Panther Party. Cleaver displayed his contempt for the PFP by not showing up, and sending Black Panther sidekick Bobby Seale to sneer openly at his honkie admirers, who masochistically welcomed every sign of Panther derision. No one opposed Cleaver for the nomination; and since the PL bloc abstained, and since my libertarian colleagues did not make the early morning hour, it turned out that mine was the only vote cast against Eldridge Cleaver for president—not a bad legacy of my time on the New Left. For the U.S. Senate nomination, the veteran socialist-pacifist David McReynolds was the Draperite candidate, and I was persuaded to run against him to represent the PL-libertarian opposition. I agreed to run only because I knew darn well that there was no chance at all to defeat McReynolds.

I did not envy McReynolds's day in the sun. The Freedom and Peace Party was running a black candidate for Senate, and the Black Panthers did not wish to oppose a fellow Afro-American with the white McReynolds. The Black Panthers apparently pulled a gun on McReynolds, ordering him to withdraw his candidacy. What happened after that is hazy; I don't believe that McReynolds withdrew, but on the other hand I don't believe that either of these people made it to the ballot—and the 1968 election turned out to be the end of the PFP (except in California) and the FPP. And, oh yes, I heard later that Comrade Carlos had turned out to be a police agent.

A coda: years later, I happened to run into McReynolds, at a meeting trying vainly to bring some people into libertarianism. He kept telling me mournfully: "You gave us a lot of trouble in '68. A lot of trouble." I was trying to be polite at this little gathering, so I didn't tell him how delighted I was at his tribute.

By the end of the 1960s, the New Left had unfortunately vindicated Carl Oglesby's warning, and had abandoned its high libertarian promise of the mid-'60s. Unstable and lacking a coherent ideology, SDS, in response to the Leninism and Stalinism of its Progressive Labor faction, itself reverted to these Old Left creeds, albeit in a still more radical and hopped-up form. Increasingly lured by the "counter-culture" and by anti-intellectualism generally, the New Left increasingly ignored scholarship in favor of unthinking "action," and the Free Universities faded away into scattered centers of *avant-garde* eurythmics and instruction in radio repair.[6] And educational reform increasingly turned into an attempt to destroy all intellectual and educational standards, and to replace content in courses by rap sessions about the students' "feelings." Finally, shorn of scholarship, of intellectuality, and of strategic perspective, the remnants of the New Left were to burn themselves out in and disappear after the breakup of SDS in 1969 into an orgy of senseless and indiscriminate violence. Despairing of the entire American population as hopelessly bourgeois, the SDS remnants had disastrously concluded that all America—working class, middle class, or whatever—was The Enemy and had to be destroyed. By 1970 the New Left was effectively dead, and put out of its misery by Mr. Nixon's masterstroke of repealing the draft that year. Deprived of worry about being drafted, the student idealists effectively ended their protest—though the war in Vietnam was to continue for several years.

Looking back over the experiment of alliance with the New Left, it also became clear that the result had in many cases been disastrous for libertarians; for, isolated and scattered as these

---

[6]Another complete bust was the New Left ideal of "participatory democracy." It *sounded* good: in an attractive contrast to the "coercive" system of majority rule, participatory democracy could agree on decisions only by means of persuasion and unanimous consensus. Voting was believed to violate minority rights. I still remember vividly the "board meetings" of the Free University of New York, where equal votes were cast by staff, unpaid faculty, and students alike. Since every decision, no matter how trivial, had to be attained by unanimous consent, the result was that the board meeting stretched on, indecisively and interminably, to *become* life itself. Those of us who left the meeting in the evening to go home were accused of "betraying the meeting." It is not surprising that the Free University collapsed after a few years.

young libertarians were, the Clarks and the Milchmans and some of the Glaser-Kansas group were soon to *become* leftists in fact, and in particular to abandon the very devotion to individualism, private property rights, and the free-market economy that had brought them to libertarianism, and then to the New Left alliance, in the first place. We came to realize that, as Marxian groups had discovered in the past, a cadre with no organization and with no continuing program of "internal education" and reinforcement is bound to defect and melt away in the course of working with far stronger allies. The libertarian groupings would have to be rebuilt as a self-conscious movement, and its major emphasis would have to be on nourishing, maintaining, and extending the libertarian cadre itself. Only operating *from* such a cadre could we make strong and fruitful alliances with no danger to the libertarian movement itself.

In the meanwhile, the Buckleyite right wing was progressively abandoning even its rhetorical devotion to libertarian ideals. For *National Review* and its associates had learned what they believed to be the lesson of the Goldwater rout; from that point on, the conservative movement would shed itself of any and all "extremist" elements, whether in domestic or foreign affairs, and move in a "responsible" and "respectable" manner toward the seats of Power for which it had yearned for so many years. As the Pope, as well as the insult-comic of the movement, Bill Buckley presided over the excommunicating and purging from Conservatism of any and all elements that might prove embarrassing in its quest for respectability and Power: libertarians, Birchers, atheists, ultra-Catholics, Randians, *anyone* who might disturb Conservatism in its cozy sharing of political rule. Hence by 1968, with the exception of Frank Meyer who still adhered to Ronald Reagan, all conservative doubts about the greatness and wisdom of Richard Milhous Nixon had been effectively stilled; and Bill Buckley was suitably rewarded by the Nixon administration with a post as member of the Advisory Commission of the U.S. Information Agency (USIA), our Ministry of Propaganda overseas. Buckley induced Frank Shakespeare, the conservative head of USIA, to hire *National Review* editor James Burnham to compile a list of deserving books to be placed in USIA libraries in foreign countries. Prominent on

Burnham's list were—surprise! surprise!—the works of both Burnham and Buckley who, wrote Burnham, is "one of the best-known writers of his generation."

In a perceptive review of one of Buckley's later books, left-liberal Margot Hentoff noted and lamented the drift of Conservatism into joining the Establishment, the very Establishment which even *National Review*, in its early years, used to attack. As Mrs. Hentoff stated:

> What happened to Mr. Buckley, along with the rest of us, was the breaking down of traditional ideological compartments, the blurring of traditional alliances and enmities. Not only did the old New Deal and New Frontier politics lose credence with the left, but the left then walked off with the conservative banners of nonintervention, freedom from governmental coercion, rugged individualism, decentralization, and, in some cases, racial separatism. . . .
>
> It appears that Mr. Buckley is beginning to take on the weight of middle-aged responsibility, sounding more often like a resilient prince of the Church than like a purifying spirit.

Mrs. Hentoff concluded that Buckley had been moving "toward a rather awful kind of moderation. . . . He is now more aware of consequence, as he moves away from the absence of power, that condition which was his abiding charm."[7]

Thus, apart from its abiding thirst for war, the existing (1971) right wing is scarcely distinguishable from old-style, conservative Liberalism. (And even on war the difference is really one of degree.) Apart from style, there is very little to distinguish, say, Bill Buckley from Sidney Hook, or Senator Tower from former Senator Dodd, despite the latter's more New Dealish voting record. On hawkish foreign policy, on aggrandizing militarism and the military-industrial complex, on crushing civil liberties and granting

[7]Margot Hentoff, "Unbuckled," *New York Review of Books*, December 3, 1970, p. 19.

unchecked powers to the police, on aggrandizing Executive power and privilege—in short, on the major problems of our time, the Conservatives and Liberals are in broad agreement. And even their seeming disagreement on free-market versus liberal economics has virtually disappeared in the implicit acceptance by both conservatives and liberals of the New Deal-Great Society Corporate State neo-Mercantilist Consensus. With his adoption of the Milton Friedman-Robert Theobald guaranteed income proposal, with his fight to bail out the SST (supersonic transport) program and Lockheed, with his nationalization of the passenger-car industry to the hosannas of conservatives, liberals and the industry itself, Richard Nixon has completed the process of integrating the right wing into the post-New Deal consensus. As the Marxist historian Eugene D. Genovese has perceptively put it: "President Nixon's right-wing liberalism is the counterpart of the Communist Party's left-wing liberalism—that is, each advances solutions within the established consensus of liberal social policy."[8]

And so we now face an America ruled alternately by scarcely differentiated conservative and liberal wings of the same state-corporatist system. Within the ranks of liberalism there is a growing number of disaffected people who are increasingly facing the fact that their own credo, liberalism, has been in power for forty years, and what has it wrought? Executive dictation, unending war in Vietnam, imperialism abroad and militarism and conscription at home, intimate partnership between Big Business and Leviathan Government. An increasing number of liberals are facing this critical failure and are recognizing that liberalism itself is to blame. They are beginning to see that Lyndon Johnson was absolutely correct in habitually referring to Franklin Roosevelt as his "Big Daddy." The paternity is clear, and the whole crew stands or falls together.

Where, then, can disaffected liberals turn? Not to the current Right, which offers them only more of the same, spiced with a

---

[8]Eugene D. Genovese, "The Fortunes of the Left," *National Review* 22, no. 47 (December 1, 1970): 1269.

more jingoistic and theocratic flavor. Not to the New Left, which destroyed itself in despair and random violence. Libertarianism, to many liberals, offers itself as the place to turn.

And so libertarianism itself grows apace, fueled by split-offs from conservatism and liberalism alike. Just as conservatives and liberals have effectively blended into a consensus to uphold the Establishment, so what America needs now—and *can* have—is a counter-coalition in opposition to the Welfare-Warfare State. A coalition that would favor the short-term libertarian goals of militant opposition to the Vietnam War and the Cold War generally, and to conscription, the military-industrial complex, and the high taxes and accelerated inflation that the state has needed to finance these statist measures. It would be a coalition to advance the cause of both civil liberty and economic freedom from government dictation. It would be, in many ways, a renaissance of a coalition between the best of the Old Right and the old New Left, a return to the glorious days when elements of *Left and Right* stood shoulder to shoulder to oppose the conquest of the Philippines and America's entry into World Wars I and II. Here would be a coalition that could appeal to all groups throughout America, to the middle class, workers, students, liberals, and conservatives alike. But Middle America, for the sake of gaining freedom from high taxes, inflation, and monopoly, would have to accept the idea of personal liberty and a loss of national face abroad. And liberals and leftists, for the sake of dismantling the war machine and the American Empire, would have to give up the cherished Old Left-liberal dream of high taxes and Federal expenditures for every goody on the face of the earth. The difficulties are great, but the signs are excellent that such an anti-Establishment and antistatist coalition can and might come into being. Big government and corporate liberalism are showing themselves to be increasingly incapable of coping with the problems that they have brought into being. And so objective reality is on our side.

But more than that: the passion for justice and moral principle that is infusing more and more people can only move them in the same direction; morality and practical utility are fusing ever more clearly to greater numbers of people in one great call: for the liberty of people, of individuals and voluntary groups, to work out their own destiny, to take control over their own lives. We have it in our power to reclaim the American Dream.

Bibliography

Articles

"'SDS': The New Turn." *Left and Right* (Winter, 1967).

"Hoover's Folly." *Nation* 171, no. 27 (December 30, 1950).

"Korea: Will China Fight the UN?" *New Republic* 123 (November 20, 1950).

"The Hoover Line Grows." *New Republic* 124 (January 15, 1951). Quoted in Liggio, "Why the Futile Crusade?"

Barnes, Harry Elmer. "Hiroshima: Assault on a Beaten Foe." *National Review* 5, no. 19 (May 10, 1958).

Buckley, Jr., William F. "A Young Republican's View." *Commonweal* 55, no. 16 (January 25, 1952).

——. "Three Drafts of an Answer to Mr. Hamowy." *New Individualist Review* 1, no. 3 (November 1961).

Bundy, McGeorge. "Appeasement, Provocation, and Policy." *The Reporter*, January 9, 1951. See Leonard Liggio, "Why the Futile Crusade?"

——. "The Private World of Robert Taft." *The Reporter* (December 11, 1951).

Chamberlin, William Henry. "Appeasement on the Right." *New Leader* (May 17, 1954).

——. Reply to letter by Aubrey Herbert. *New Leader* (June 21, 1954).

Chodorov, Frank. "A War to Communize America." *Freeman* 5 (November, 1954).

——. "How to Curb the Commies." *analysis* 5, no. 7 (May 1949).

——. "The Return of 1940?" *Freeman* (September 1954).

——. "The Spy-Hunt." *analysis* 4, no. 11 (September 1948). Reprinted in Chodorov, *Out of Step*. New York: Devin-Adair, 1962.

——. "Trailing the Trend." *analysis* 6, no. 6 (April 1950). Quoted in *Fugitive Writings: Selected Writings of Frank Chodorov*, Charles Hamilton, ed. Indianapolis, Ind.: Liberty Press, 1980.

Francis, Samuel. "Beautiful Losers: the Failure of American Conservatism." *Chronicles* (May 1991).

Garrett, Garet. "The Suicidal Impulse." *Faith and Freedom* 5, no. 8 (April 1954).

Genovese, Eugene D. "The Fortunes of the Left." *National Review* 22, no. 47 (December 1, 1970).

Hamowy, Ronald. "'*National Review*': Criticism and Reply." *New Individualist Review* 1, no. 3 (November 1961).

——. "Left and Right Meet." *The New Republic* 154, no. 11 (March 12, 1966). Reprinted in *Thoughts of the Young Radicals*. New York: New Republic, 1966.

Hentoff, Margot. "Unbuckled." *New York Review of Books*, December 3, 1970.

Hoover, Herbert. "Our National Policies in This Crisis." *Vital Speeches* 17, no. 6 (January 1, 1951).

Kennedy, Joseph P. "Present Policy is Politically and Morally Bankrupt." *Vital Speeches* 17, no. 6 (January 1, 1951).

Letter to *National Review* 2, no. 20 (October 6, 1956). Cited in "Introduction," *Fugitive Writings: Selected Writings of Frank Chodorov*, Charles Hamilton, ed. Indianapolis, Ind.: Liberty Press, 1980.

Liggio, Leonard P. "Why the Futile Crusade?" *Left and Right* 1, no. 1 (Spring, 1965).

Mencken, H.L. "Babbitt as Philosopher" (review of Henry Ford, *Today and Tomorrow*, and Ernest J.P. Benn, *The Confessions of a Capitalist*), *American Mercury* 9 (September 1926).

——. "Breathing Space." *Baltimore Evening Sun*, August 4, 1924; reprinted in H.L. Mencken, *A Carnival of Buncombe*. Baltimore: Johns Hopkins Press, 1956.

——. "Capitalism." *Baltimore Evening Sun*, January 14, 1935; reprinted in Mencken, *Chrestomathy*. New York: Knopf, 1949.

——. "Next Year's Struggle." *Baltimore Evening Sun*, June 11, 1923; reprinted in Mencken, *A Carnival of Buncombe*.

——. "What I Believe." *The Forum* 84 (September 1930).

Milchman, Alan. "D.F. Fleming on 'The Origins of the Cold War.'" *Left and Right* 1, no. 1 (Spring 1965).

Morgenstern, George. "The Past Marches On." *Human Events* (April 22, 1953).

Rothbard, Murray N. "The Real Aggressor." *Faith and Freedom* (April 1954); under *nom de plume* Aubrey Herbert.

——. "Confessions of a Right-Wing Liberal." *Ramparts* 6, no. 11 (June 15, 1968).

——. "H.L. Mencken: The Joyous Libertarian." *New Individualist Review* 2, no. 2 (Summer, 1962).

——. "Left and Right: The Prospects for Liberty." *Left and Right* 1, no. 1 (Spring, 1965).

——. "Liberty and the New Left." *Left and Right* 1, no. 2 (Autumn, 1965).

——. "The Foreign Policy of the Old Right." *Journal of Libertarian Studies* 2 (Winter, 1978).

——. "The Transformation of the American Right." *Continuum* 2 (Summer, 1964).

Russell, Dean. "The Conscription Idea." *Ideas on Liberty* (May 1955).

Schlesinger, Jr., Arthur. "Can Willkie Save His Party?" *Nation* 153, no. 23 (December 6, 1941).

Taft, Robert A. "'Hang On' To Formosa: Hold Until Peace Treaty with Japan Is Signed." *Vital Speeches* 16, no. 8 (February 1, 1950). Quoted in Liggio, "Why the Futile Crusade?"

——. "United States Foreign Policy: Forget United Nations in Korea and Far East." *Vital Speeches* 19, no. 17 (June 15, 1953).

Villard, Oswald Garrison. "Valedictory." *Nation* (June 22, 1940).

Weir, Ernest T. "Leaving Emotions Out of Our Foreign Policy." *Faith and Freedom* 5, no. 8 (April 1954).

Books

Bell, Daniel, ed., *The New American Right*. New York: Criterion Books, 1955.

——, *The New American Right: Expanded and Updated.* Garden City, N.Y.: Doubleday Anchor, 1963.

Bourne, Randolph. *Untimely Papers*. New York: B.W. Huebach, 1919.

Branden, Nathaniel. *Who Is Ayn Rand?* New York: Paperback Library, 1964.

Bromfield, Louis. *A New Pattern for a Tired World.* New York: Harper and Bros., 1954.

Buckley, Jr., William F. *God and Man at Yale: The Superstitions of Academic Freedom*. Chicago: Regnery, 1951.

Buckley, Jr., William F., and L. Brent Bozell. *McCarthy and His Enemies.* Washington, D.C.: Regnery Publishing, [1954] 1995.

Carlson, John Roy. *Under Cover.* New York: E.P. Dutton, 1943.

Chamberlain, John. *Farewell to Reform: The Rise, Life and Decay of the Progressive Mind in America.* Chicago: Quadrangle Books, 1965.

Chamberlin, William Henry. *America's Second Crusade.* Chicago: Henry Regnery, 1950.

Chodorov, Frank. *One is a Crowd.* New York: Devin-Adair, 1952.

——. *The Economics of Society, Government, and State.* New York: Analysis Associates, 1946.

Cole, Wayne S. *America First: The Battle Against Intervention, 1940–1941.* Madison: University of Wisconsin Press, 1953.

Cornuelle, Herbert C. *"Mr. Anonymous": The Story of William Volker.* Caldwell, Id.: Caxton Printers, 1951.

Crunden, Robert M. *The Mind and Art of Albert Jay Nock.* Chicago: Henry Regnery, 1964.

Dawson, William H. *Richard Cobden and Foreign Policy.* London: George Allen and Unwin, 1926.

Dilling, Elizabeth. *The Roosevelt Red Record and Its Background.* Chicago: Elizabeth Dilling, 1936.

Doenecke, Justus D. *Not to the Swift: The Old Isolationists in the Cold War Era.* Lewisburg, Penn.: Bucknell University Press, 1979.

Domhoff, G. William. *The Higher Circles: The Governing Class in America.* New York: Random House, 1970.

Dutt, R. Palme. *Fascism and Social Revolution.* New York: International Publishers, 1934.

Engelbrecht, H.C., and F.C. Hanighen. *Merchants of Death.* New York: Dodd Mead, 1934.

Fall, Bernard B. *The Two Viet-Nams.* New York: Frederick A. Praeger, 1963.

Finer, Hermann. *Road to Reaction.* Westport, Conn.: Greenwood Press, 1977.

Fleming, D.F. *The Cold War and its Origins, 1917–1960.* Garden City, N.Y.: Doubleday, 1961.

Flynn, John T. *As We Go Marching.* Garden City, N.Y.: Doubleday, Doran and Co., 1944.

Forgue, Guy, ed. *Letters of H.L. Mencken.* New York: Knopf, 1961.

Garrett, Garet. *The People's Pottage.* Caldwell, Id.: Caxton Printers, 1953.

Garrison, F.W., ed. *Letters from Albert Jay Nock.* Caldwell, Id.: Caxton Printers, 1949.

Goldwater, Barry M. *The Conscience of a Conservative*. Shepherdsville, Ky.: Victor Publishers, 1960.

Goodman, Paul. *People or Personnel.* New York: Random House, 1965.

Halevy, Elie. *The Era of Tyrannies*. Garden City, N.Y.: Doubleday, 1965.

Hayek, Friedrich A. *The Road to Serfdom.* Chicago: University of Chicago Press, 1944.

Hobbs, Albert H. *Social Problems and Scientism.* Pittsburgh: Stackpole, 1953.

Holman, Frank E. *Story of the "Bricker" Amendment (The First Phase).* New York: Committee for Constitutional Government, 1954.

Hoover, Herbert. *The Challenge to Liberty*. New York: C. Scribner's Sons, 1934.

Hughes, Frank. *Prejudice and the Press.* New York: Devin-Adair, 1950.

Kolko, Gabriel. *The Triumph of Conservatism.* Glencoe, Ill.: The Free Press, 1963.

LaMonte, Robert R., and H.L. Mencken. *Men versus the Man.* New York: Henry Holt, 1910.

Lindbergh, Charles A. *The Wartime Journals of Charles A. Lindbergh.* New York: Harcourt Brace Jovanovich, 1970.

Manly, Chesly. *The Twenty-Year Revolution: From Roosevelt to Eisenhower.* Chicago: Henry Regnery Company, 1954.

Martin, James J. *American Liberalism and World Politics*, 2 vols. New York: Devin-Adair, 1964.

Mencken, H.L. *A Carnival of Buncombe.* Baltimore: Johns Hopkins Press, 1956.

——. *A Mencken Chrestomathy*. New York: Knopf, 1949.

Mises, Ludwig von. *Bureaucracy.* New Haven, Conn.: Yale University Press, 1944.

——. *Human Action*. Irvington-on-Hudson, N.Y.: Foundation for Economic Education, 1996.

——. *Omnipotent Government.* New Haven, Conn.: Yale University Press, 1944.

Morgenstern, George. *Pearl Harbor: Story of a Secret War.* New York: Devin-Adair, 1947.

Morley, Felix. *For the Record.* South Bend, Ind.: Regnery Gateway, 1979.

——. *Freedom and Federalism.* Chicago: Henry Regnery, 1959.

Morse, Arthur D. *While Six Million Died.* New York: Random House, 1968.

Nash, George H. *The Conservative Intellectual Movement in America Since 1945.* New York: Basic Books, 1976.

Neilson, Francis. *How Diplomats Make War*. New York: B.W. Huebsch, 1915.

Nock, Albert Jay. *Journal of Forgotten Days*. Hinsdale, Ill.: Henry Regnery, 1948.

——. *Memoirs of a Superfluous Man*. New York: Harper and Bros., 1943.

——. *On Doing the Right Thing, and Other Essays*. New York: Harper and Row, 1928.

——. *Our Enemy, the State*. New York: William Morrow, [1922] 1935.

——. *The Myth of a Guilty Nation*. New York: B.W. Huebsch, 1922.

——. *Theory of Education in the United States*. New York: Harcourt Brace, 1932.

Nock, F. J., ed. *Selected Letters of Albert Jay Nock*. Caldwell, Id.: Caxton Printers, 1962.

Oglesby, Carl, and Richard Schaull. *Containment and Change*. New York: Macmillan, 1967.

Oppenheimer, Franz. *The State: Its History and Development Viewed Sociologically*. Translated by John M. Gitterman. New York: B.W. Huebsch, 1922.

Parks, Mercer H. "In Support of Limited Government." Unpublished ms., March 5, 1955.

Passos, John Dos. *The Grand Design*. Boston: Houghton Mifflin, 1949.

Paterson, Isabel. *The God of the Machine*. New York: G.P. Putnam's Sons, 1943.

Preis, Art. *Labor's Giant Step*. New York: Pioneer Publishers, 1964.

Radosh, Ronald. *Prophets on the Right: Profiles of Conservative Critics of American Globalism*. New York: Simon and Schuster, 1975.

Lane, Rose Wilder. *The Discovery of Freedom*. New York: John Day, 1943.

Rand, Ayn. *The Fountainhead*. New York: Plume Books, [1943] 1994.

Read, Leonard E. *Government—An Ideal Concept*. Irvington-on-Hudson, N.Y: Foundation for Economic Education, 1997.

Rothbard, Murray N. *America's Great Depression*. Princeton, N.J.: D. Van Nostrand, 1963.

——. *Egalitarianism as a Revolt Against Nature and Other Essays*. Auburn Ala.: Ludwig von Mises Institute, [1974] 2000.

——. *Man, Economy, and State with Power and Market*, Scholar's Edition. Auburn, Ala.: Ludwig von Mises Institute, 2001.

Roy, Ralph Lord. *Apostles of Discord: A Study of Organized Bigotry and Disruption on the Fringes of Protestantism*. Boston: Beacon Press, 1953.

Spooner, Lysander. *A Letter to Grover Cleveland, On His False Inaugural Address, the Usurpations and Crimes of Lawmakers and Judges, and the Consequent Poverty, Ignorance and Servitude of the People.* Boston: Benjamin R. Tucker, 1886.

——. *No Treason.* Larkspur, Colo.: Pine Tree Press, 1966.

St. George, Maximilian, and Lawrence Dennis. *A Trial on Trial.* National Civil Rights Committee, 1946.

Stromberg, Joseph R. "The Cold War and the Transformation of the American Right: The Decline of Right-Wing Liberalism." M.A. essay, Florida Atlantic University, 1971.

Taft, Robert A. *A Foreign Policy for Americans.* New York: Doubleday, 1951. Quoted in Liggio, "Why the Futile Crusade?"

Tolstoy, Leo. *The Law of Love and the Law of Violence.* University Press of the Pacific, 2001.

Toy, Jr., Eckard Vance. "Ideology and Conflict in American Ultra-Conservatism, 1945–1960." Ph.D. diss., University of Oregon, 1965.

Tsou, Tang. *America's Failure in China, 1941–50.* Chicago: University of Chicago Press, 1963. Quoted in Liggio, "Why the Futile Crusade?"

Williams, William Appleman. *The Contours of American History.* Chicago: Quadrangle Books, [1961] 1966.

——. *The Tragedy of American Diplomacy.* New York: Norton, [1959] 1988.

Womack, Jr., John. *Zapata and the Mexican Revolution.* New York: Knopf, 1969.

Wooten, Barbara. *Plan or No Plan.* London: V. Gollancz, 1934.

Wormser, René A. *Foundations: Their Power and Influence.* New York: Devin-Adair, 1958.

Wreszin, Michael. *Oswald Garrison Villard.* Bloomington: Indiana University Press, 1965.

Chapters in Books

Garrett, Garet. "The Revolution Was." In *The People's Pottage.* Caldwell, Id.: Caxwell Printers, 1953.

Hamilton, Charles H. "Introduction." In *Fugitive Writings: Selected Writings of Frank Chodorov*, Hamilton, ed. Indianapolis, Ind.: Liberty Press, 1980.

Liggio, Leonard, and Ronald Radosh. "Henry A. Wallace and the Open Door." In *Cold War Critics*, Thomas Paterson, ed. Chicago: Quadrangle, 1971.

Miller, Clyde R. "Harry Elmer Barnes' Experience in Journalism." In *Harry Elmer Barnes: Learned Crusader*, A. Goddard, ed. Colorado Springs, Colo.: Ralph Myles, 1968.

Radosh, Ronald. "Preface." In John T. Flynn, *As We Go Marching*. New York: Free Life Editions, 1973.

Rothbard, Murray N. "Harry Elmer Barnes as Revisionist of the Cold War." In *Harry Elmer Barnes: Learned Crusader*, A. Goddard, ed. Colorado Springs, Colo.: Ralph Myles, 1968.

Steinke, John, and James Weinstein. "McCarthy and the Liberals." In *For a New America: Essays in History and Politics from Studies on the Left, 1959–1967*, James Weinstein and David Eakins, eds. New York: Random House, 1970.

Viereck, Peter. "Revolt Against the Elite." In *New American Right*, Daniel Bell, ed. New York: Criterion Books, 1955.

Miscellaneous

Parmentel, Noel E. "Folk Songs for Conservatives."

Point of Order. Film. Directed by Emile de Antonio (Point Films, 1964).

Pamphlets and Leaflets

Chodorov, Frank. *Taxation Is Robbery*. Chicago: Human Events Associates, 1947; reprinted in Chodorov, *Out of Step*. New York: Devin-Adair, 1962.

Flynn, John T. *The Smear Terror*. New York: privately published, 1947.

Garrett, Garet. *The Revolution Was*. Caldwell, Id.: The Caxton Printers, Ltd., 1944.

Garrett, Garet. *The Rise of Empire*. Caldwell, Id.: Caxton Press, [1952] 1961.

Harper, F.A. *In Search of Peace*. Irvington-on-Hudson, N.Y.: Foundation for Economic Education, 1951; reprinted by the Institute for Humane Studies, 1971.

——. *The Crisis of the Free Market*. New York: National Industrial Conference Board, 1945.

Kuesell, John R. *Quo Warranto?* Unpublished.

LeFevre, Robert. *Those Who Protest*. Undated.

Read, Leonard E. "On That Day Began Lies." *Essays on Liberty*. Irvington-on-Hudson, N.Y.: Foundation for Economic Education, 1952. Vol. 1.

——. *Conscience on the Battlefield*. Irvington-on-Hudson, N.Y: Foundation for Economic Education, 1951.

——. *Students of Liberty*. Irvington-on-Hudson, N.Y: Foundation for Economic Education, 1950.

Stigler, George, and Milton Friedman. "Roofs or Ceilings? The Current Housing Problem." Irvington-on-Hudson, N.Y.: Foundation for Economic Education, 1946.

Periodicals

American Affairs
American Mercury
analysis
Atlantic Monthly
Chicago Tribune
Christian Economics (*CE*)
Colorado Springs *Gazette-Telegraph*
Commercial and Financial Chronicle
Communist New Masses
Continuum
Daily Worker
Die Rote Fahne
Economic Council Review of Books
Essays on Liberty
Faith and Freedom
Freeman
Human Events
Harper's
Harvard *Lampoon*
Herald-Tribune Review of Books
Journal of Libertarian Studies
Leviathan
Liberation
Libertarian Forum
Libertarian Republican
Libertarian Review
Liberty [Benjamin Tucker's]
Liberty
Left and Right
Masses and Mainstream

Nation
National Review
National Guardian
New Individualist Review
New Leader
New Republic
New York Compass
New York Herald-Tribune
New York Journal-American
New York Mirror
New York Times
New York World-Telegram
New York World-Telegram and Sun
Plain Talk
Politics
Ramparts
RIGHT
Santa Ana Register
Saturday Evening Post
Scribner's Commentator
The Innovator
The Standard
Time
Studies on the Left
Viet-Report
Warsaw *Trybuna Ludu*

Public Documents

Congressional Record, 80th Cong., 1st sess. (June 6, 1947).

Congressional Record, 80th Cong., 1st sess. (March 18, 1947).

Congressional Record, 80th Cong., 1st sess. (March 28, 1947).

Congressional Record, 82nd Cong., 1st sess. (January 5, 1951).

U.S. Congress. House. Special Committee to Investigate Tax Exempt Foundations and Comparable Organizations. *Hearings Before the Special Committee to Investigate Tax Exempt Foundations and Comparable Organizations.* 83rd Cong., 2nd sess., Parts 1 and 2 (Washington, D.C.: U.S. Government Printing Office, 1954).

INDEX